BENEATH A WIDE SKY: H

AND ITS ENVIRO

Adam Yamey is a London-based retired dental surgeon, who was brought up in and around Hampstead. He is the author of several books including *"Albania on my Mind"*, *"Rediscovering Albania"*, *"Charlie Chaplin waved to me"*, *"Exodus to Africa"*, *"Indian Freedom Fighters in London (1905-1910)"*, *"Soap to Senate: A German Jew at the dawn of apartheid"*, and *"Scrabble with Slivovitz - 'Once upon a time in Yugoslavia"*.

1

Published by Adam Yamey

with

AMAZON

ISBN 9798407539520

www.adamyamey.co.uk

BENEATH A WIDE SKY:

HAMPSTEAD

AND

ITS ENVIRONS

By Adam Yamey

"Hampstead, that, towering in superior sky,

Now with Parnassus does in honour vie."

From *The Kit-Cats*, by Richard Blackmore (1654-1729)

"A steeple issuing from a leafy rise,

With farmy fields in front, and sloping green,

Dear Hampstead, is thy southern face serene,

Silently smiling on approaching eyes.

Within, thine ever-shifting looks surprise,

Streets, hills, and dells, trees overhead now seen,

Now down below, with smoking roofs between,-

A village, revelling in varieties..."

From *Description of Hampstead*, a sonnet by Leigh Hunt (1784-1859)

TABLE OF CONTENTS

PREFACE ... 7

INTRODUCTION: OH NO, NOT IN HAMPSTEAD ... 7

SOME GEOGRAPHY AND HISTORY ... 13

HEATH AND HIGH STREETS WITH SOME MEMORIES ... 25

SATURDAY STROLLS ... 25

PERRINS LANE, THE EVERYMAN, AND LOUIS ... 34

DISCOVERING HAMPSTEAD ... 41

A HOUSE ON HEATH STREET AND THE KIT CAT CLUB ... 41

A CHURCH ON HEATH STREET ... 45

FLASK WALK AND THE HAMPSTEAD SPA ... 46

MORE ABOUT THE SPA ... 56

THE VALE OF HEALTH ... 60

POETS AND THE VALE OF HEALTH ... 70

FRENCH CONNECTIONS AND ST MARYS ON HOLLY WALK ... 76

ARTISTS IN HAMPSTEAD: ROMNEY, CONSTABLE, AND OTHERS 84

MODERN ARTISTS AND THE ISOKON ... 95

BOLSHEVISM AND HEATH STREET ... 109

A SINGER AND A PHILOSOPHER ON BRANCH HILL ... 114

JUDGES WALK ... 118

WHITESTONE POND ... 122

EAST HEATH ROAD AND SOUTH END GREEN ... 126

SIR HARRY AND ROSSLYN HILL ... 137

PILGRIMS LANE AND MORE ON ROSSLYN HILL … 143

NEW END, CHOLERA, AND GROVE PLACE … 150

FITZJOHNS AVENUE AND SWISS COTTAGE … 155

SHEPHERDS WELL … 171

CHURCH ROW … 174

GRACIE FIELDS, FROGNAL WAY, AND FROGNAL … 179

WEST HEATH ROAD AND PLATTS LANE … 187

WEST HAMPSTEAD … 193

SHOOT UP HILL … 198

PRIMROSE HILL … 201

NORTH END AND GOLDERS GREEN … 211

NORTH END AND GOLDERS HILL PARK … 211

POETS AND GOLDERS GREEN … 228

LIFE AND DEATH ON HOOP LANE … 232

HIGHGATE … 241

CODA … 273

SOME BOOKS CONSULTED … 275

ACKNOWLEDGEMENTS … 278

INDEX … 279

PREFACE

Hampstead is one of the highest places in London. There, the heavens are vast and wide. Beneath this expanse of sky is an area with an eventful past and a vibrant present. This book takes a fresh look at the locality and shows that Hampstead is richly imbued with historical memories and has been home to a multitude of fascinating and noteworthy people. Many books have been written about Hampstead. Doubtless, there will be more. This one is different. It looks at Hampstead from unusual as well as familiar viewpoints and gives the reader a richer appreciation of what makes the place both delightful and intriguing. This volume explores a wide variety of subjects, familiar and obscure, as well as some which have never been described in other books about the locality. Here is a fresh and at times quirky look at this place on a hill, one of London's treasures: a district, which is familiar to many people, yet full of surprises. Although the bulk of this book is about Hampstead, there are also sections describing some of its environs.

INTRODUCTION:
OH NO, *NOT* IN HAMPSTEAD

The international fast-food chain, McDonald's, had a branch on the High Street of Hampstead in north London until 2013. When the company first mooted the idea of opening one of their outlets in Hampstead in 1980, it met with opposition. Maybe, residents were concerned it might attract the 'wrong kind of crowd' to the area. For twelve years, Camden, the London borough which contains Hampstead, and many local people objected to the company opening their store. Some of Hampstead's inhabitants were so against the idea of having a branch of McDonald's in their neighbourhood that they mounted the 'Burger Off Campaign', which included amongst its supporters some famous residents including Melvyn Bragg, Michael Foot, and Peggy Jay. To put it bluntly, many of the residents of Hampstead seemed reluctant to have something that they considered to be so 'common' or 'downmarket' in the heart of their community, something that they believed would lower the tone of the area. Eventually in 1992, after agreeing to various demands to make their shop look less obvious than usual, McDonald's opened their branch a few yards downhill from Hampstead Underground Station. Richard Osley of *The Camden New Journal* noted in a blog dated 23rd of November 2011:

"The old cliche about Hampstead is that it is such a rarefied, picturesque place that even the local McDonald's has a chic black storefront. No garish red and yellow here."

Currently (2022), the site occupied by the former McDonald's outlet is occupied by a branch of the Pain Quotidien chain of cafés, which is rated by locals as being in better taste than the renowned purveyors of the Big Mac and related delicacies. McDonald's have been welcomed throughout the world, from Buenos Aires to Moscow and from Cape Town to Beijing, but not in Hampstead.

Amongst many other things, this book looks at what makes Hampstead a "rarefied, picturesque place".

Many decades before McDonald's fought their battle to serve fast-food to customers in Hampstead and before the First World War, Arthur Waugh, father of the novelist Evelyn Waugh, bought a house on North End Road, north of Hampstead and close to Golders Green. Although it was closer to the latter than the former, it fell into the Hampstead postal district, so that stamps on letters posted near the house would have been franked with a Hampstead postmark. Soon after the First World War, the Waugh's postal district was changed from Hampstead to Golders Green. Writing in his autobiographical *A Little Learning*, Evelyn noted that his father was appalled by the change because in his mind Hampstead had been associated with Keats, Blake, and Constable, but Golders Green was in his opinion merely a station on London's Underground railway. I think that this prejudice noted by Evelyn Waugh might explain the problem that people in Hampstead had with having a branch of McDonalds in their neighbourhood. They felt that while the burger outlet might not disturb the ambience of Golders Green and other similarly undistinguished localities, it would jar with Hampstead's cultural heritage and artistic reputation.

The Waugh's home on North End Road was close to the Hampstead Garden Suburb, whose construction began in 1904. The Suburb, bordering Golders Green, was north of Hampstead and separated from it by open fields, now the Hampstead Heath Extension. Evelyn Waugh wrote about it thus:

9

"The houses there were better designed and their tenants were under particular restrictions about the height of their garden fences."

He continued by saying that the Suburb was:

"… inhabited not exactly by cranks, nor by bohemians, but mainly by a community of unconventional bourgeois of artistic interests."

My parents bought a house in the Suburb in about 1950. I am not sure that they were particularly unconventional, but they were both bourgeois and artistic. I was born in 1952 and lived in the Suburb until 1982. During my early childhood, my parents used to take me to Hampstead almost every Saturday morning. In my teens and early twenties, I used to visit Hampstead often, usually walking there across the green meadows and wooded spaces between it and my home. The first date that I had with the girl, who is now my wife, was in Louis, a café in Hampstead. During the many years I worked as a dental surgeon, I visited the place regularly to spend time with friends and relatives. Since retiring in 2017, I have been visiting Hampstead for pleasure and to enjoy its fresh air several times a month. So, even if I cannot claim to have been born and bred in the place, Hampstead is very much a part of my DNA.

This book demonstrates that over the past few centuries Hampstead has been the site of much artistic endeavour and home to many who have enriched both the cultural and the political spheres of London and the rest of Great Britain. Although the area has changed dramatically since my childhood sixty years ago, it retains much of what has made it a unique part of Greater London.

This volume is an exploration of Hampstead: its many beautiful sights, as well as its intriguing past and current attractions. Its aim is to stimulate interest and enthusiasm for a part of London that has had a far greater influence on the city's story than many other of London's localities.

The book has several sections.

The first is a brief survey of Hampstead's general history and geography.

Next, there is an introduction to Hampstead's main thoroughfares with some reminiscences of the area as it was during my youth.

This is followed by the largest section of the book: a collection of chapters about various aspects of Hampstead's past and present. Recently, a friend of mine bemoaned the fact that Hampstead High Street and Heath Street are lined with branches of shops and cafés that can be found all over London. He is right. So, if you wish to capture the true character of Hampstead, you need to stray into the side streets and explore, which is what I hope this book will stimulate you to do.

The last few sections of the book deal with some places of interest near to Hampstead: Primrose Hill, North End, Golders Green, and Highgate.

While reading this volume, you might find it helpful to have a detailed street atlas, online or otherwise, close at hand.

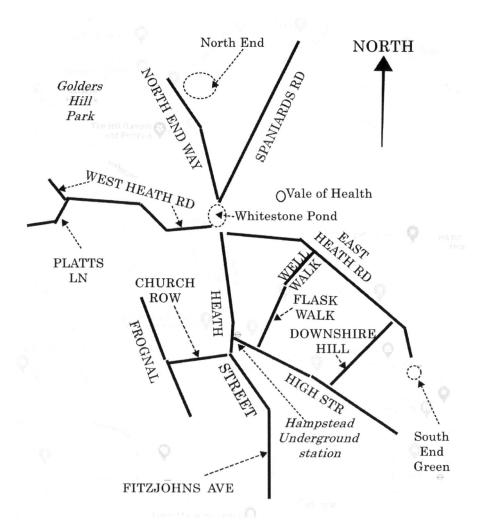

North End

NORTH

Golders
Hill
Park

NORTH END WAY

SPANIARDS RD

Vale of Health

WEST HEATH RD

Whitestone Pond

EAST HEATH RD

PLATTS
LN

WELL WALK

CHURCH
ROW

FLASK
WALK

HEATH

DOWNSHIRE
HILL

FROGNAL

STREET

HIGH STR

Hampstead
Underground
station

South
End
Green

FITZJOHNS AVE

SOME GEOGRAPHY AND HISTORY

The essayist and poet Leigh Hunt (1784-1859), a sometime resident of Hampstead, related in his book *The Town* (published in 1848):

"In Elizabeth's time, you might set out from the site of the present Pall-mall, and, leaving St. Giles in the Fields on the right hand, walk all the way to Hampstead without encountering perhaps a dwelling-place."

During the first few decades of the 19th century, the village (or town: call it what you wish; I will stick to 'village') of Hampstead was still as it was in Elizabethan times: separated from the rest of London by open countryside. It was linked to London by a single road, which followed the course of the present Haverstock Hill and its continuation, Hampstead High Street. However, by 1848, Hunt noted that:

"...every village which was in the immediate and even the remote neighbourhood of London, and was quite distinct from one another at the beginning of the reign of George the Third, is now almost, if not quite, joined with it, including Highgate and Hampstead ..."

George III reigned from 1760 until 1820. Only half a century after his death, a new road, the present Fitzjohn's Avenue, was constructed. It links the centre of

Hampstead village with Swiss Cottage. Although much of what was open countryside separating Hampstead from other urban areas has become built-up since the early 19th century, Hampstead remains separated from some neighbouring conurbations, such as Golders Green, Hampstead Garden Suburb, and Highgate, by uninhabited terrain (woods, heath, and parkland). Had it not been for protesters, like those who later tried to prevent McDonalds from opening in Hampstead village, these open spaces, some of London's so-called 'lungs', might well have been heavily built-up to become dreary suburbs.

Hampstead village with its many quaint, sharply inclined streets, narrow alleys, and steep staircases, lies mainly on the south facing slopes of a line of hills connecting Whitestone Pond to the top of Highgate Village. However, Hampstead's detailed topography is complex. The pond and Hampstead's observatory are at the highest point in Hampstead. If we imagine the pond as the centre of a compass rose, then the following applies. East of the pond, the land falls away abruptly, affording what could be a wonderful view of London if it were not for the dense vegetation that, except in winter, obscures the panorama. This slope, which faces roughly southeast and whose gradient decreases gradually contains features including East Heath Road, the Vale of Health, the Hampstead Ponds, and reaches South End Green, which is almost level. South of the pond, the hill drops steeply to Hampstead Underground station and from there, the High Street, and then its continuation Rosslyn Hill, runs further downhill in a south easterly direction towards Belsize Park. A few yards south of the station, there is a further steep incline along which Fitzjohns Avenue, a continuation of Heath Street, descends straight as an arrow southward to Swiss Cottage. West of the pond, the predominantly west facing slope of the hill on which it is located falls at first steeply and then more gradually towards West Hampstead. The pond is connected by a straight ridge running northeast from it to the Spaniards Inn. It carries Spaniards Road and separates a mainly northwest facing slope from a mostly southeast facing one. Beyond the Spaniards Inn, the land slopes downwards and mostly east towards Kenwood House and its lake. North of the pond and the ridge, the terrain slopes down to the hamlet of North End, an isolated part of Hampstead, and beyond that to Golders Green and the Hampstead Garden Suburb. In summary, most of old (pre-1850s) Hampstead village lies sheltered from the north wind on an uneven, undulating south and east facing slope.

The ticket hall of Hampstead Underground Station, which is in the centre of Hampstead village, is about 350 feet above sea level. The highest point in the locality is the observatory, a few feet higher than its close neighbour Whitestone Pond, is at about 440 feet above sea level. Long ago, the views from Whitestone Pond must have been amazing. Writing between 1724 to 1727 in his *A Tour Through the Whole Island of Great Britain*, Daniel Defoe, author of many books including *Robinson Crusoe*, described the view from Hampstead as follows:

"The Heath extends about a mile each way and affords a most beautiful Prospect; for we see Hanslip steeple one way, which is within about eight Miles of Northampton. N.W. to Landsdown hill in Essex, another way East, at least 66 miles from one another. The prospect to London and beyond it to Banstead downs, South; Shooters hill, South east; Red hill southwest, and Windsor-castle is also uninterrupted. Indeed, due North, we see no further than to Barnet, which is not above six miles from it."

Well, with today's richly polluted air, you would be lucky to see but a few of the places mentioned by Defoe. From various points in Hampstead one can get great views of the forest of tall buildings that has sprouted up in central London, particularly in the City of London and the developments east of it.

Hampstead village slopes down from its highest point to South End Green, which is down at about 270 feet. All of Hampstead village is well above the altitude of what was London until the early 19th century. Compared with what was old London, Hampstead village, high above the city, had much cleaner air. Within easy reach of the metropolis, it became a resort to which Londoners could gain rest and relief from the city's stressful life and foul air. Not only was Hampstead a popular destination for the 'common people', but it was also favoured by artists, writers, musicians, and politicians. The discovery of curative iron-containing spring water added to its attractiveness especially during the 18th century. Defoe, notes, somewhat exaggeratedly, in his *Tour*:

"Hampstead indeed is risen from a little country village to a city…"

He wrote that this occurred:

"… not upon the credit only of the waters, though 'tis apparent, its growing greatness began there; but company increasing gradually, and the people liking both the place and the diversions together; it grew populous, and the concourse of people was incredible. This consequently raised the rate of lodgings …"

Well, little has changed since then. Hampstead has become a place with some of London's highest value properties. It appears from what Defoe described that Hampstead was already expanding in the 1720s and that it was becoming a popular visiting place for many people, some of whom are still remembered today and are mentioned in this book.

Next, here is a concise general history of Hampstead. I will keep it brief because some details will be related later. According to Eilert Ekwall's *The Concise Oxford Dictionary of English Place-Names*, the name Hampstead has its origin in the Old English *hamstede* meaning 'homestead' or, more likely, 'manor'.

I have sourced the early history of Hampstead mainly from the *Handbook to The Environs of London* by James Thorne, published in 1876, and another, *The Annals of Hampstead Volume I* by Thomas Barratt, published in 1912 as part of a set of three volumes. These older books tend to give more detail than later ones about the area's history. Archaeological finds indicate that there was some human activity in the area that is now Hampstead during both the Stone and Iron Ages. In 1774, some Roman remains including urns containing burnt bones, vases, lamps, and other objects, were found near the former mineral water wells (close to Well Walk). These finds and those from earlier times are either indicative of settlements in the area or simply early examples of man's tendency to leave unwanted litter lying around. In connection with the Romans, Hampstead was not on any of the great roads these invaders built. The nearest one was Watling Street, which followed the course of the current Edgware Road.

At its nearest point, the road is at least 1.4 miles from both Whitestone Pond and Hampstead Underground station. I have seen it suggested that the Romans might have used a track passing through the high ground of Hampstead when the low-lying Watling Street became flooded or waterlogged, but this idea is unsubstantiated.

Barratt suggested that the wooded high ground in the area made it less easily accessible to invaders, such as the Romans and later arrivals, and this might have made it a satisfactory refuge for Britons trying to avoid the invaders. Hampstead might have begun as a clearing in these woods, but this is only conjecture. After the Norman invasion, the Manor of Hampstead is mentioned in the 1086 *Domesday Book*, which means it was in existence by then. Earlier than that, a charter dated 986 AD, the original of which had been lost by 1912, mentioned that King Ethelred the Unready had granted the manor to the Monastery of St Peter in Westminster, whose church was Westminster Abbey. The nature of the settlement(s), if any, before that date is unknown.

The *Domesday Book* gives some impression of Hampstead as it was at the end of the 11th century. The online version of the document reveals that Hampstead had 1 villager, 5 smallholders, and 1 slave. As for the settlement's resources: 3 ploughlands, 1 lord's plough team, and 1 men's plough team, as well as: 3.5 lord's lands, woodland, and 100 pigs. So, by 1086 Hampstead was a small farming settlement. In those far off days, we can imagine seeing a few houses or huts amid a patchwork of fields, surrounded by dense woods and untamed heathland, with pigs scurrying around whilst the locals tilled their land. It was a very far cry from what Hampstead was to become many centuries later. The lord at the time when the Domesday Book was compiled was Ranulf Peverel, who was born in Normandy and died in about 1090 in England. In addition to Hampstead, Peverel was Lord of another 42 settlements. The historian Christopher Wade wrote in his book *For the poor of Hampstead, for ever. 300 years of the Hampstead Wells Trust* that the settlement of Hampstead was valuable to the monks of Westminster not only as a source of fresh produce but also of good water from the area's many springs and streams. He also noted that when plague struck Westminster in 1349, Abbott Simon de Barchester (aka Simon de Bircheston) and others from the abbey fled to Hampstead to escape illness. Unfortunately, they brought the plague with them and the abbot and 26 of his monks died of it in Hampstead. In the 16th century, the main streams supplying water to London had deteriorated so much that, according to John Stow (c1524-1605) in his *Survey of London*, a large grant was provided in 1589 to try:

"… by drawing divers springs about Hampstead heath into one head and course, both the city should be served of fresh water in all places of want; and also, by such a follower, as men call it, the channel of this brook should be scowered into the river of Thames …"

Despite much money having been spent on the project, the scheme failed because the banks of the new channel collapsed, and it became clogged with refuse.

Hampstead became a place of refuge from disease-ridden London and during the times of flood and fire. For example, during the Great Plague of 1665, Barratt noted:

"When the Great Plague was raging the residents clung closely to the hill; but the refugees from the city brought the epidemic with them, the Hampstead deaths from plague in 1665 amounting to no fewer than 180, nearly a fourth of the population. The parish clerk, Thomas Rippon or Rippin, was among the victims; indeed, nearly all who died at Hampstead at this time were inhabitants of the village, less than a dozen Londoners being mentioned in the burial register. The disease did not appear in a very fatal form in other villages round the metropolis; whereas the Hampstead death record was seven times the average number."

The historian George William Potter in his *Hampstead Wells* (1904) imagined Hampstead as it might have been at the end of the 17th century:

"There was the main thoroughfare from London, running through Hampstead, with extensive strips of waste land on either side of it. On the north and north-east the Heath extended nearly up to High Street. The six acres of land, now known as the Wells Charity Estate, were open heath, chiefly swamp, and therefore not of much value. It was useless for grazing or cultivation. A little to the north-west was a very deep bog. On this portion of boggy land there were probably numerous springs…"

These springs became important for Hampstead's development.

The Manor of Hampstead remained the property of the Monastery of St Peter until it was dissolved by King Henry VIII in 1539. While it was a monastic possession, two windmills and a chapel, which later became a parish church, were constructed in Hampstead. The existence of these during the Middle Ages indicates that by then the village and its surroundings had a substantial enough populace to need them. Although the mills are no longer standing, there is still a road named Windmill Hill near Whitestone Pond. In 1551, King Edward VI granted the Manor of Hampstead (as well as several other manors) to Sir Thomas Wroth (c1518-1573), a politician and supporter of the Protestant Reformation. It is said that this king died in his arms. Hampstead remained in the Wroth family until 1620, when it was sold by Sir Thomas's grandson, John Wroth, to Sir Baptist Hick(e)s (1551-1629), a lawyer who became Lord Campden.

Lord Campden, whose name is now celebrated in the names of streets in Kensington where he had a large mansion (now demolished), was a generous man. The *Middlesex County Records (Volume 4)* noted that he gave money to the parish of Hampstead to help support an "able preacher." Also, he paid for repairs to the chapel in that place. His widow continued his generosity by bequeathing money to the poor of Hampstead. This, in addition to land in Hampstead donated in the name of her great grandson, the first Earl of Gainsborough (1641-1689), formed the basis of The Wells and Campden Charity founded in 1642. This entity still exists today under the name of The Hampstead Wells and Campden Trust. Incidentally, one should not confuse the

Campden family with the borough of Camden in which Hampstead lies. Camden is named after Charles Pratt, 1st Earl Camden (1714-1794).

During the 17th century, Hampstead not only became a place of refuge because of the plague of 1665 but also during the Great Fire of London that followed it in 1666, as Barratt related:

"The Great Fire, next year, was another memorable event that sent terror-stricken Londoners to the Hampstead and Highgate heights. There were 200,000 people rendered homeless, and the open spaces near the town were soon filled to overflowing. From Hampstead Heath what an impressive spectacle the fire would be, as from day to day and night to night it swept on its fierce course…"

By the end of the century, Hampstead had become a destination for artists, writers, and politicians, seeking to gain, often temporary, relief from the stresses of city life. These people and other factors, such as the discovery of mineral waters, helped put Hampstead 'on the map' of places worth visiting from the metropolis.

The land donated in the name of the Earl of Gainsborough, whilst he was still an infant, was in Hampstead and was six acres in extent. It included some of Hampstead's chalybeate (ferruginous) wells, whose waters attracted many visitors to Hampstead. The wells providing it were at one stage in competition with those still providing health-promoting waters at Tunbridge Wells in Kent. The popularity of taking the waters in Hampstead began at the end of the 17th century but had declined gradually by late in the 18th. It was from the end of the

17th century onwards that Hampstead began attracting many people who made their names in cultural activities and politics. Some of them visited the area and others chose to live there. Too many to list, they include notable names such as John Constable, John Keats, George Romney, Leigh Hunt, William Pitt the Elder, Percy Bysshe Shelley, and Lord Byron. More recently, people associated with Hampstead included Sigmund Freud, DH Lawrence, Harold Pinter, Barbara Hepworth, Ernő Goldfinger, Michael Foot, Jacqueline du Pré, Charles de Gaulle, and Hugh Gaitskell. It is worth emphasising that these examples are only a tiny sample taken from a huge population of Hampstead's noteworthy people.

In 1707, Baptist, the 3rd Earl of Gainsborough (1684-1714) sold Hampstead to a wealthy East India merchant, Sir William Langhorne (c1631-1715), who was the East India Company's Agent in Madras (now Chennai) from 1670 to 1678. The fortune he made in India, some of which is said to have been obtained illegally, paid for his purchase of the manors of Hampstead and Charlton (in Kent). After his death, Hampstead passed into the possession of his nephew William Langhorne Games, and then later to a distant relative, Mrs Margaret Wilson. Later, the manor passed into the hands of the Maryon-Wilson family. In 1829, a member of the family, Sir Thomas Maryon-Wilson (1800-1869) petitioned Parliament to allow him to build houses on Hampstead Heath, but his plans, which would have wrecked the area, met with local opposition, and were never realised. His younger brother, John Maryon-Wilson (1802-1876), who inherited the manor, sold his rights to the manor of Hampstead to the

Metropolitan Board of Works (the first metropolitan-wide local authority for London) in 1871. Writing in 1984 in his *The Streets of Hampstead*, Christopher Wade noted that although the manor was no longer in the possession of the Maryon-Wilson family, much of its land was then owned by a great-great-nephew of Sir Thomas.

By the 1870s, the space between Hampstead and the rest of London was already becoming intensively developed, urbanised. This is evident on a detailed map surveyed in 1871. In 1900, the Borough of Hampstead was established under the aegis of London County Council. Its boundaries were like that of its predecessor, the Parish of Hampstead, but included areas including Primrose Hill, Hampstead, Belsize Park, West Hampstead, South Hampstead, much of Hampstead Heath and a small part of Kilburn and Cricklewood.

Seven years after the borough's birth, Hampstead Underground station was opened to passengers using the Charing Cross, Euston, and Hampstead Railway, now the Edgware Branch of the Northern Line. Its platforms, 192 feet below ground level, are the deepest on the Underground network. For a while, its high-speed lifts were some of the fastest in London. However, this was not the first railway station in Hampstead. In 1860, the present Hampstead Heath station was opened near to South End Green. In 1965, the Borough of Hampstead was incorporated into the newly formed Borough of Camden. Regarding this, Wade wrote:

"Hampstead has now lost its autonomy but is not without a mind of its own."

Although much has changed in Hampstead since he wrote these words in 1984, they still ring true.

The Borough of Hampstead and its successor, Camden, include a former manor to the west of the Manor of Hampstead. The other manor was called Shuttop or Shot-up Hill and is remembered by Shoot Up Hill, the stretch of the former Watling Street, now Edgware Road, which ran through the manor. It belonged to the Knights Templars until that order was suppressed in 1309. Then, it was given to the Priory of St John of Jerusalem, which held it until the establishment was dissolved by King Henry VIII. In 1547, the manor was granted to Sir Roger Cholmeley (1485-1565), who founded Highgate School in the last year of his life. I was a pupil at that venerable institution between 1965 and 1970. After Cholmeley, the ownership of the manor passed through many other hands.

My outline of the history of Hampstead ends here. Many of the locality's long-established inhabitants might bemoan the changes that have occurred there during the last few decades, but Hampstead remains one of the most distinctive parts of London.

HEATH AND HIGH STREETS WITH SOME MEMORIES

SATURDAY STROLLS

Almost every Saturday morning during the late 1950s and early 1960s, my parents took my sister and me on a trip to Hampstead village. Although it was not far from our home in the Hampstead Garden Suburb, we always travelled there in our car. We used to park in the gravelly, potholed, circular car park next to Jack Straws Castle. The building, which still stands, was a large pub whose walls were lined with clapboard. It was designed by Raymond Erith and constructed in 1964 on the site of an earlier building. A pub was already in existence on the site in the early 18th century. It was visited by authors including Charles Dickens, William Makepeace Thackeray and Wilkie Collins. Bram Stoker makes mention of this pub in his novel *Dracula*, published in 1897:

"We dined at "Jack Straw's Castle" along with a little crowd of bicyclists and others who were genially noisy. About ten o'clock we started from the inn. It was then very dark, and the scattered lamps made the darkness greater when we were once outside their individual radius."

This entry in the book refers to the investigation of murky incidents on Hampstead Heath in Stoker's novel. According to Asa Briggs in his *Marx in London*, Jack Straws Castle was a favourite drinking place for Karl Marx and his friends. This was oddly appropriate because Jack Straw (died 1381) was a leader of the 1381 Peasants Revolt. It is said that he stood on a wagon filled with hay (Jack Straw's 'castle') and gave a speech near where the pub was later built. In 2002, the pub closed, and the building was converted to flats. The car park is still in use and its surface has little improved since my childhood.

From the carpark, we used to walk up a short slope to a flat area of grass that still contains a tall flagpole. Back in the 1960s, there used to be several donkeys and their owners near the pole. The creatures were available for hire to carry children on short rides. The flagpole overlooks Whitestone Pond, about which more later. This body of water, upon which children sailed toy boats and through which occasional horses walked, is at the top end of Heath Street down which we used to continue our weekly perambulation.

During the summer months, the top end of Heath Street, with its extremely wide pavement, became the site of a temporary open-air art exhibition. Most of the exhibits were paintings or drawings, many of them by local artists, both amateur and professional, and there were also some sculptures. Some exhibits were hung on the wall beside the pavement but most of them were hung on the walls of temporary shelters constructed with scaffolding poles and corrugated iron roofs. I remember that every year there was a man who exhibited and sold his highly polished wood carvings, made from tree branches. My mother, who was an accomplished sculptor, and my father, who was an enthusiastic amateur historian of art, used to look at what was on display, but little if anything met with their approval. Sadly, many years have passed since the last time, about 1985, that one of these exhibitions was held.

Further downhill, we passed a place that intrigued me when I was a youngster. It was the Hampstead Quaker Meeting House, which has a lovely front garden. The latter is overlooked by its neighbour, the late 18th century Mansfield

Cottage, which in the 1960s housed a tearoom or restaurant. The Meeting House with art nouveau (Arts and Crafts) features was built in about 1907 to the designs of Fred Rowntree (1860-1927). According to James D Hunt in his book *Gandhi in London*, Mohandas K Gandhi (1869-1948), the future Mahatma, spoke in this meeting house on the 13th of October 1909:

"… perhaps travelling there by the recently opened underground line … The Society of Friends (Quakers) were not at this time much interested in Indian affairs … The 1909 meeting was sponsored by the Hampstead Peace and Arbitration Society"

Robert Payne reported in his *The Life and Death of Mahatma Gandhi* that Gandhi's speech was entitled "East and West". It outlined the evils of the British occupation of India and the sufferings of Indians in South Africa.

La Gaffe, an Italian restaurant, stands on the west side of Heath Street almost opposite the Meeting House. Although it was established in 1962, I have never entered it. Across Heath Street and almost opposite it, there is a gap between the houses. It leads into an alley lined on one side by a wall covered with overlapping planks of timber, i.e., clapboard. Steps lead down from the alleyway to a small sunken paved square surrounded by houses, some of which are 18th century. This almost hidden nook is called Stamford Close. The name derives from the now-demolished Stamford Lodge, where the painter John Constable and his family were briefly lodgers in 1823 after they had left their rented accommodation on Hampstead's Lower Terrace, where they had lived between 1821 and 1823. According to Christopher Wade, in the 1930s, six old cottages were condemned and the close was considered to have been: "…a miserable dark square – a black spot." Today, the square is far from miserable, and many would kill to own a house there.

Elm Row meets Heath Street a few yards downhill from the Meeting House. From an early age, I was aware of a commemorative sign on this narrow road. It records that Sir Henry Cole (1808-1882) lived at number 3 from 1879 to 1880. Founder of what is now The Victoria and Albert Museum, he is believed to be the originator of the habit of sending Christmas cards. Apart from this, I was always aware of the single storey building with a rounded corner (with a built-in post box), occupying the northern corner where Elm Row meets Heath Street. Opposite this low building, across Elm Row, there is another single-storey building, which is wedge-shaped in plan. In the 1960s, this housed an Italian restaurant called The Pimpernel. Its entrance on the street corner led to a short bar, beyond which tables and chairs were set out. We always stopped at the Pimpernel and stood at the bar whilst my parents enjoyed cups of espresso coffee prepared by the Italian owner or one of his staff. My parents, who were Italophiles and spoke a little Italian, enjoyed conversing with the staff at the bar whilst they sipped their coffees. My sister and were given thick Italian fruit juice from small bottles and the staff always gifted us colourful boxes, the size of a small matchbox. These contained *torrone* (Italian nougat with nuts). I remember that the pieces of confectionery were coated on two sides with rice paper and the idea of a kind of paper that was edible amazed me. The Pimpernel closed many decades ago. Over the years, its building has housed several different, usually short-lived, restaurant businesses. It is located across the road from a double-front shop that once contained a wonderful gramophone records shop, Hampstead High Fidelity, and now houses a dental practice.

A little way down from the restaurant was the top end of the former New End Hospital. In 1969, during my last year at school, I did voluntary work once a week in the hospital. I worked in a cellar that contained the department where patients were given radioactive iodine to diagnose and treat their thyroid disorders. I found it very interesting and believe that working there was one of the factors that led me to choose to study physiology at university. Thinking back on it, the department would never have begun to get close to fulfilling even the most basic health and safety requirements of today, but the people and the work there were fun. The hospital closed in the late 1980s and has since been converted into private flats. The hospital, formerly a workhouse for the impoverished, had a central circular building that contained circular wards. The nursing staff used to sit in the centre of each ward, keeping an eye on the patients in the beds that radiated out from the centre. The small Victorian gothic mortuary building opposite the hospital on the steeply inclined thoroughfare, New End, is now used as a synagogue, The Village Shul.

The Horse and Groom pub stood a little further down Heath Street, between the former hospital and the Underground Station. This pub was already in existence in 1723. The gabled building, whose façade has alternating layers of brickwork and white stone facing and bears its name, dates from more recent times. When

I was a teenager, I used to walk over Hampstead Heath with my friends, and then we would have a drink in this pub, to which we gave the nickname "The Whores and Gloom". The pub is no longer in business, but since its closure the building has been used as a restaurant from time to time. One reason that my friends and I used to walk to Hampstead from our homes in Hampstead Garden Suburb was that there was little for us to do in the Suburb. We could have walked to Highgate, but back in the 1960s, Hampstead had a much livelier 'vibe' than the more genteel and less cosmopolitan Highgate; it still has. The pub is closed but its building is still obvious. This is not the case with the once popular American style diner, Maxwell's, which closed many years ago. Like the still working Hard Rock Café, Maxwell's was one of the first examples of this kind of eatery in London.

Just before reaching the Underground station, we used to leave Heath Street and descend the steep Back Lane, which still has a cobbled surface (more accurately, its surface is made of setts). The Flask Pub on Flask Walk is opposite the lower end of Back Lane. We never entered it and, as I will relate later, I first stepped inside it in 2021. In my childhood, the short section of Flask Walk between Back Lane and Hampstead High Street had some shops where we stopped. In one of them almost opposite the pub, there was a lady, probably South African, with whom my parents always stopped to have a brief chat. I do not remember her name, but I feel sure that she was involved in creating and/or works of art or craft, maybe ceramics. The only person I could find recently, who might have known the lady's name was Keith Fawkes. He has been running his second-hand bookshop in Flask Walk since 1964 but could not recall her. Oddly, I cannot recall his bookshop from my childhood visits to Hampstead. Maybe, that is because most of them were made before 1964 when I became 12 and started doing things independently of my parents. However, I do remember that on the same side of Flask Walk as the pub, there used to be another bookshop, which sold a few used books and many remaindered volumes. There was also a butcher's shop.

From Flask Walk we used to walk downhill along the north side of Hampstead High Street, always stopping to look at the window of an antique shop that exists no longer. It always had an object that fascinated me. It was a model of a dog that contained a mechanism that made its small red tongue move in and out of its mouth. Opposite this shop, across the High Street, the Coffee Cup is still in business. First opened in 1954 and looking unchanged since then, this was a place that we never visited on our weekly visits to Hampstead. During the 1960s, when I was at school, many of my school friends frequented this coffee bar, but I did not. In those days, I was under the impression that it had a dubious reputation, possibly something to do with drug-taking, and therefore not the place for me. Recently, I learnt that a friend's daughter used to gather there with friends while playing truant. From a review by Michael Darvell (uk.locale.online), I learned:

"Hampstead is awash with celebrities of all hues – artists, actors, politicians, philosophers – and at some time or other they all end up at The Coffee Cup, from

Peter Cook and Dudley Moore to Paul McCartney and Sting, from Betty Grable to Emma Thompson and from Michael Foot to Tom Conti."

It was not until the 21st century that I first entered it and found it to be a delightful place with old-fashioned décor including wood panelling. It is a perfect place for enjoying a hot beverage and/or a tasty lunch.

Further down the High Street and occupying three neighbouring shopfronts, each on a different level because of the slope of the hill, was the High Hill Bookshop. Inside the bookshop, the three constituent shops were interconnected. This marvellous, well-stocked, bookshop was the highlight of our Saturday morning strolls. My parents always encouraged us to read. So, each week, my sister and I were allowed to choose one book each. The choice was bewildering. Visiting this bookshop in my early childhood instilled in me a habit that I would find very difficult to contemplate abandoning: book buying. Between 1957 and 1988, the bookshop was run by its creator Ian Norrie (1927-2009). High Hill Bookshop went out of business in the late 1980s, following the opening of a branch of the Waterstones bookstore chain in the High Street. I do not hold anything against Waterstones but feel saddened that its arrival was able to threaten, and then end, the existence of Norrie's bookshop. High Hill Bookshop was the furthest we reached on our Saturday morning excursions. After purchasing books, we retraced our steps to Jack Straw's car park and returned home. I accompanied my parents on these outings until about 1963. Then, as a teenager and in my early twenties, I used to visit Hampstead for several purposes to be revealed in the next chapter.

PERRINS LANE, THE EVERYMAN, AND LOUIS

Today, apart from an Oxfam charity shop dedicated to selling used (or 'preloved') books, there is only one second-hand (or antiquarian) bookshop in Hampstead village. It is owned by Keith Fawkes in Flask Walk. During my teens and early twenties, in the 1960s and early 1970s, there were several other second-hand bookshops in Hampstead village and one near to South End Green at the corner of Fleet Road and Cressy Road. At most of these, there were great bargains to be found. In those days, one could pick up real treasures for less than £1, which was my self-imposed spending limit. Only one of the shops was not a good place for bargains; it was on the High Street. Once, I picked up a very cheap first edition of a book by Mervyn Peake at a jumble sale. It was not in great condition but out of interest I offered it for sale at the costlier shop on the High Street. The owner examined the unprepossessing-looking book and immediately offered me £5, which I refused, deciding that if he was prepared to offer me what was then so much for such a tatty item, the book must have been worth a great deal more. I have not yet sold it.

My favourite bookshop in Hampstead had no name. My friends and I called it 'the Old Man's Bookshop'. It was in an early 19th century terraced house, number 25 Perrins Lane, near what was for many years the Photocraft photographic shop on Heath Street (currently, The Pharm-Hampstead Village salon). The house was the home and shop of an aged second-hand book seller, whose name we never knew. In about 2017, I visited Keith Hawkes at his bookshop and asked him if he remembered the old man. He told me that he was Mr Francis Norman.

One of Mr Norman's customers was the famous John Fowles (1926-2005), author of novels including *The Collector* and *The French Lieutenant's Woman*. Fowles wrote in his *The Journals (Volume 1)* that Norman was:

"… a bluff, awkward, friendly second-hand bookseller with a mind like a jackdaw's nest and a shop which must rank as one of the dirtiest, most disorganised and lovable in North London. … Prices vary according to Norman's mood."

That was in 1956. Ten years later, Norman's bookshop had become a regular haunt for me and my friends, the Jacobs brothers, Francis and Michael, both of whom went on to publish successful books. By then, Mr Norman seemed to us to be a very old man. His shop was just as Fowles described. In *Old Books, Rare Friends: Two Literary Sleuths and Their Shared Passion*, M Stern and L Rostenberg wrote of Mr Norman:

"When he moved from his Gower Street basement to Hampstead Heath, he had moved not only his books but all the dust and grime and debris …"

Mr Norman did not mind us spending hours rummaging through his totally disorganised heaps of books. He seemed to enjoy our company. Every now and then, he would read aloud something out of a book, often in Latin or Ancient Greek, and then began to guffaw. We had no idea what he had found so humorous. I found all kinds of wonderful books in his shop, including several beautiful world atlases dating from between the two World Wars. Mr Norman never charged us much for whatever we managed to dig up in his ground floor shop. He kept the truly valuable old books on an upper floor in his personal quarters. Occasionally, on Sunday mornings, we would visit Mr Norman's shop when it was closed. We used to knock on his front door, and uncomplainingly he would open the shop for us, still dressed in his pyjamas. During my years as a student at University College London (from 1970 onwards), I would occasionally to see him on the Underground train, carrying bundles of antiquarian books. Sadly, he has long since died, as has one of my book-buying friends, the art historian and author of many books about Spanish and South American culture, Michael Jacobs (1952-2014).

By the time I knew Mr Norman, he was a very sad man, although we did not notice his sadness. Fowles writes in his *The Journals (Volume 2)* that in November 1968, he visited the shop and learnt that not only had Mr Norman recently lost his fifteen-year-old daughter, Janey, when she slipped off the roof of his shop whilst trying to rescue her cat. Also, his second wife had been seriously schizophrenic, and he had not seen her for years. Mr Norman had had to be both father and mother to Janey. In addition to all these misfortunes, Mr Norman had lost his first wife and family when they were all killed by a V ('flying') bomb in WW2. It is no wonder that Norman told Fowles:

"Money does not mean anything to me now … The shop keeps me alive, that's all I keep it on for."

Today, both Mr Norman and his shop remain only as memories. About 100 yards north of the site of his bookshop, you will reach Louis Patisserie at number 32 Heath Street. Now under new management, this used to bear the words "Hungarian Confectionery" on the sign above its window. This 'continental' café opened in 1963, and, from its appearance, it looks as if not much has been done to its wood-panelled interior décor since then. When it opened, it was one of the few places in Hampstead offering high quality central European style patisserie. It was a welcome newcomer, contrasting favourably with the then mostly old-fashioned places offering teas and coffees. When it was opened in 1963 by a Hungarian ex-patriot Louis Permayer (1932-2017), it was London's only Hungarian patisserie. Many of its clientele were Central European émigrés drawn to it from their homes in Hampstead and surrounding areas. These were probably some of the same people who frequented the long-since closed Cosmo, which had opened by 1939 in nearby Swiss Cottage, a restaurant specialising in Central European dishes.

After the 1956 uprising in Hungary, many of those who fled their country, settled in and around Hampstead. One of these was Louis Permayer. An article in the London *Times* of 5th of April 1999 noted:

"Louis Permayer, 67. the owner and manager of Louis Patisserie in Hampstead, North London, was plucked from an Austrian camp. "A British man came saying he wanted 300 strong Hungarians to become miners in Alfreton. Derbyshire. We went to a camp, where we were taught English, and were trained for the mines. But the English people went on strike because they wanted their own sons to go into the mines. I had trained as a chef in Hungary, so I went to work for Egon Ronay (who then had a restaurant)." After a couple of years he took a job in the patisserie that he now runs, having bought out the owner in 1963."

In 1971, after commencing my first degree at London's University College, I invited one of my fellow students to join me for afternoon tea at Louis. It was the first time I had ever asked a girl out for a date. This lady is now my wife. She remembers that in those now distant days when coffee was served at Louis, it was accompanied by a little bowl of whipped cream, which one could spoon into the drink. Today, although the café still looks as it did long ago and is popular, the place has lost its Austro-Hungarian quaintness and the cakes are not the same high quality as they used to be. As Ian Norrie wrote in his contribution to *Hampstead Memories*, an anthology published in 2000:

"Hampstead, bless it, never is, what it was"

This is true of Louis and, also, of one of its near neighbours, the Everyman cinema in Holly Bush Vale, a cul-de-sac leading off Heath Street.

It was at the Everyman that I went to the cinema for the first time in my life. My parents, who were not regular cinemagoers, decided that the rather sad French film, *The Red Balloon* (first released in the UK in late 1956), was a suitable production to introduce me, a four-and-a-half-year-old, to the joys of cinema. My parents, who tended to avoid popular culture, probably selected the *Red Balloon*, an arty French film, because it was a little more recherché than the much more popular Disney films that appeared in the late 1950s. The cinema,

38

which still exists, was, according to Christopher Wade, built in 1888 as a drill hall for The Hampstead Rifle Volunteers. Then, in 1919 its windows were bricked-in, and it became MacDermott's Everyman Theatre. In 1933, it became a cinema. I saw many more films there in my childhood and adolescence. Every year, there used to be a festival of Marx Brothers films in the summer months. I loved these films and used to visit the Everyman on hot sunny afternoons when I was often the only person in the auditorium. In those days, the cinema's auditorium had a strange smell that strongly resembled household gas. Indeed, there were gas lamps attached to the walls of the auditorium, but I am certain that I never saw them working. They might have there for use as emergency lighting in case there was an electricity supply failure. These were quite frequent during my childhood but never happened when I was at the Everyman.

The cinema is, I have been told, now a very luxurious place. The seats are comfortable and have tables beside them, at which waiting staff serve food and drinks. This is a far cry from what I can remember of the rather basic cinema in the 1960s. Back in those days, the Everyman, like the now long-gone Academy cinemas in Oxford Street, favoured screenings of 'arty' films rather than the more popular films that most cinemas showed. Now, the Everyman, formerly an art-house cinema, thrives by screening films that are most likely to attract full houses. That this is the case is yet more evidence to support the idea that Hampstead is not what it was. Many of the sort of people who might enjoy arty films that attract often small niche audiences, who used to live in Hampstead, can no longer afford to reside in the area.

I have been recalling Hampstead as I knew it during the first 25 years of my life. Between 1982 and 1993, I worked and lived in Gillingham, Kent. During that time, I used to visit my widowed father at our family home in Hampstead Garden Suburb most weekends. Often, we had Sunday lunch in Hampstead. There, we patronised two places, both still in business. One was a small French style restaurant at the bottom of the steep Back Lane, La Cage Imaginaire, which opened soon after the film *Cage aux Folles* (1978) was released. Dad's favourite restaurant in Hampstead was the Villa Bianca, an upmarket Italian 'trattoria' in Perrins Walk. He was always given a warm welcome there. After lunch, we used to walk to Waterstones on Hampstead High Street to browse and often buy. By the time that Mom died, High Hill Bookshop was no longer. Waterstones was next door to a branch of Our Price, now closed, which sold cassettes and CDs. Often, I used to buy my unmusical father a classical music CD to add to his small collection in the vain hope that he might learn to enjoy it.

Since I retired in 2017, my wife and I have been visiting Hampstead often, always for pleasure. It is these visits that have greatly stimulated my interest in Hampstead's history and its curiosities. Much of what follows in the chapters of the next section of this book was inspired by things noticed during these trips, which we continue making, always discovering something new.

DISCOVERING HAMPSTEAD

The chapters in this section will immerse you in the story of Hampstead, both past and present. I am starting with a small, seemingly insignificant detail I noticed whilst walking along Heath Street because it exemplifies what makes Hampstead so intriguing for me: that is, the area is full of sights, often picturesque, which on investigation reveal fascinating aspects of history.

A HOUSE ON HEATH STREET AND THE KIT CAT CLUB

Chocolate covered Kit Kat confectionery bars are familiar to many people. The "Kit Kat" and "Kit Cat" tradenames were registered by the Rowntree's confectionery company in 1911, but the first chocolates bearing this name only appeared in 1920. Had you wanted to eat a Kit Kat in early 18th century London, you would have been served a type of mutton pie, but not a chocolate biscuit. The Kit Kat mutton pie was the creation of Christopher Catling (aka 'Katt' and 'Cat'), who had a pie house in Shire Lane near Temple Bar, an archway that used to stand near the present-day Royal Courts of Justice on the Strand.

When walking in Hampstead village recently (2020), I saw some wording above the doorway of a house on the corner of Heath Street and the much narrower Holly Bush Steps. The words are: "Kit Cat House" and (below them) "A.D. 1745". Above one of the ground-floor windows on the wall facing the steps, there are some painted letters, to which I will return.

41

The Kit Cat Club (also sometimes spelled as 'Kit Kat') was an early 18th century club whose members were of the Whig political persuasion. Members included literary men such as William Congreve, John Locke, Sir John Vanbrugh, and Joseph Addison; and politicians including Duke of Somerset, the Earl of Burlington, Duke of Newcastle-upon-Tyne, The Earl of Stanhope, Viscount Cobham, Abraham Stanyan and Sir Robert Walpole, who was Prime Minister between 1721 and 1742. The painter Sir Godfrey Kneller (1646-1723) was yet another member. He painted portraits of 48 members of the club, which are now kept in the National Portrait Gallery. Ophelia Field, author of a detailed book about the club, *The Kit-Cat Club*, noted that:

"… the Kit-Cats were first and foremost a remarkable group of friends, several of whom had known each other since childhood."

The club is believed to be named after Christopher Catling and his mutton pies. The club's meetings were held at first in Catling's tavern in Shire Lane (which no longer exists). Then, they were held at the Fountain Tavern on the Strand, which stood where Simpsons on the Strand stands today, and then later at purpose-built premises at Barn Elms. Ophelia Field wrote that:

"… for summer gatherings the Kit-Cat Club planned to build some sort of clubhouse … in the fresher air of Hampstead."

This happened in about 1702 when, according to Ms Field:

"The village of Hampstead was then visited mainly for its proximity to the Bellsise (now Belsize) Gardens – pleasure gardens like those in Kilburn,

Vauxhall, and St Pancras where Londoners could enjoy music, dancing, gambling, and sex in the shrubbery."

The clubhouse was never built. Instead, the club held some meetings in the Upper Flask pub. Demolished long ago, this was a pub located on the corner of East Heath Road and Heath Mount. That is near the south corner of East Heath Road and Heath Street, about 190 yards north of the present Kit Cat House on Holly Bush Steps. The pub was, to quote Ms Field:

"…known for its 'races, raffles and private marriages'"

Edward Walford, writing in his encyclopaedic *Old and New London* (published in 1878), noted:

"The 'Upper Flask' was at one time called 'Upper Bowling-green House,' from its possessing a very good bowling green … when the Kit-Kat Club was in its glory, its members were accustomed to transfer their meetings in summer time to this tavern, whose walls – if walls have ears – must have listened to some rare and racy conversations … Mr Howitt in his 'Northern Heights of London' gives a view of the house as it appeared when that work was published (1869). The author states that the members of the Kit-Kat Club used 'to sip their ale under the old mulberry tree, which still flourishes, though now bound together by iron bands, and showing signs of great age…'"

During the later years of the Club's existence, in the first quarter of the 18th century, some of those members who sipped ale under this tree included poets who lived in Hampstead. One of these was the poet and physician Richard Blackmore (1654-1729), who penned these lines in his poem *The Kit-Kats* (published in 1708):

"Or when, Apollo-like, thou'st pleased to lead

Thy sons to feast on Hampstead's airy head:

Hampstead, that, towering in superior sky,

Now with Parnassus does in honour vie."

The Upper Flask closed in 1750. It was on the site later occupied by the former Queen Mary's Maternity Home, which received patients between 1919 and 1975. The site now contains a residential facility run by the NHS, Queen Mary's Residence.

So, the Kit Cat Club did have an association with Hampstead, but was there any connection between the Club and the house next to Holly Bush Steps, which bears the date 1745? The house was built in about 1800, which is after the period between 1696 and 1720, when the Club was active. It was built after the date above the door, '1745'. An old postcard, published sometime between 1903 and 1930, reveals that the house was once a shop belonging to 'Francis'. This was J Francis of number 1 Holly Bush Steps. What J Francis sold is not certain but above the whitewash that covers the wall of the ground floor, the remains of an old painted sign can be seen on the brickwork. It reads "Libraries" and also "S ?? D" (the two question marks represent letters that have disappeared). Other letters below the word 'libraries' have also gone. I wonder whether it once read 'Libraries bought and sold'. Interesting as this is, it does not explain to me why the house is so named or the significance of the date 1745. So far, and this might be purely coincidental, the only connection I have found is that Robert Walpole, a member of the Kit Cat Club, died in 1745.

A CHURCH ON HEATH STREET

The typical Victorian gothic façade of Hampstead's Heath Street Baptist Church looks unremarkable. Only by entering the building can one discover why the church is remarkable. It was designed by the architect and surveyor Charles Gray Searle (1816-81) and completed 1860-61. Searle was himself a Baptist. He had been apprenticed to the renowned master builder Thomas Cubitt (1788-1855), who bought stone from his father, John Searle, who owned a quarry near Wapping. Charles set up his own practice in about 1846. According to CW Ikin, in his *A Revised Guide to Heath Street Chapel*:

"An early print of the proposed chapel shows buttresses but in its method of construction it was more modern, cast iron being used not only for the pillars and probably for the whole interior framework, but also for the gallery fronts and the mouldings of the pew-ends. The strength of the building is based upon this framework formed by the cast-iron pillars in church and hall below and their linking beams. The brick walls cling to the framework and have tiebars linking the hammer beam roof."

Cast iron, which has high compressive strength, began being used to create buildings at the end of the 18th century. Pillars made of this material can be made much leaner than masonry columns required to support the same load. The slender nature of the columns in the Heath Street Chapel is immediately evident when you enter the building. What is less obvious is that the decorative fronts of the gallery that overlooks the nave are also made from cast-iron. The material has hardly been used for structural elements of buildings since modern steel and concrete became available at the start of the 20th century. Although the Heath Street Chapel was certainly not the first church to be built using cast-iron structural elements, it must have been one of the first buildings of its kind to have been built in Hampstead. When you visit this church, do not miss the fine art-nouveau stained glass window at its western end. Lunchtime music concerts are held in the church weekly on Tuesdays. These provide a nice way of seeing the church.

FLASK WALK AND THE HAMPSTEAD SPA

Once upon a time, Hampstead had two pubs or taverns whose names contained the word 'Flask'. This is not surprising because the word 'flask' used to be common in the naming of pubs. One of them, the erstwhile Upper Flask, has already been described. The other, the once named 'Lower Flask', now renamed, is on Flask Walk, not far from Hampstead high Street. The Upper Flask was a remarkable establishment, as already described. It figures several times in *Clarissa*, a lengthy novel by Samuel Richardson (1689-1761), first published in 1747. The Lower Flask pub (in Flask Walk) is also mentioned in the novel, but unflatteringly, as:

"… a place where second-rate persons are to be found often in a swinish condition …"

46

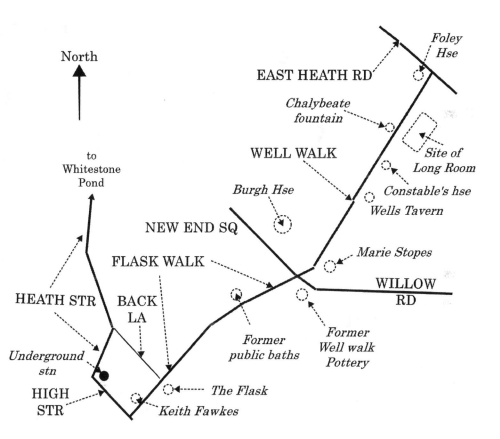

North

to
Whitestone
Pond

*Foley
Hse*

EAST HEATH RD

*Chalybeate
fountain*

WELL WALK

*Site of
Long Room*

Burgh Hse

Constable's hse

Wells Tavern

NEW END SQ

Marie Stopes

FLASK WALK

WILLOW
RD

HEATH STR

BACK
LA

*Former
public baths*

*Former
Well walk
Pottery*

*Underground
stn*

HIGH
STR

The Flask

Keith Fawkes

Unlike the Upper Flask, the Lower Flask is still in business, but much, including its name and clientele, has changed since Richardson published his novel. Located at the eastern end of the pedestrianised stretch of Flask Walk, the Lower Flask, now The Flask, was rebuilt in 1874. Formerly, it had been a thatched building and was a place where mineral water from Hampstead's chalybeate springs was sold. Oddly, despite visiting Hampstead literally innumerable times during the last more than 65 years, it was only on Halloween 2021 that I first set foot in the Flask pub, and I am pleased that I did. The front rooms of the pub retain much of their Victorian charm and the rear rooms, one of them with a glass roof, are spacious. Although we only stopped for a drink, I could see that the Sunday lunches being served to customers around us looked delicious. Since that first visit, I have eaten at The Flask and can confirm that good food is served there.

Heading north-east along the rest of Flask Walk, which slopes downhill away from The Flask, this street is lined by beautiful old houses interspersed with a few contemporary buildings. The road dates to the beginning of the 18th century, if not before. A few 'workers' cottages, dating back to about 1811, stand a few yards away from Rose Mount House, which was built in 1812. This is where Emily Tennyson Jesse (1811-1887), the sister of the poet Alfred Lord Tennyson (1809-1892), lived. She was married to the naval officer Captain Richard Jesse. In a letter dated 25th October 1858, the poet wrote:

"My mother and my sister Matilda have made their home with the Jesses at Rose Mount, Hampstead…"

Before reaching Rose Mount House, Flask walk widens to become a lozenge shaped open space with a grassy area enclosed within it. It was here that a fair used to be held for a few days every August. Nearby, on Flask Walk, miscreants could be found languishing in the parish stocks. Both the stocks and the fair are now but distant memories recorded only in books published many decades ago. On the north side of this open area, there stands a red brick building with the date 1888, which proclaims itself to be: 'The Wells and Camden Baths and Wash Houses'. Its existence reflects the fact that when it was built, many of the workers' homes in 19th century Hampstead had no running water. D Bohm and I Lorrie (owner of the former High Hill Bookshop) wrote in their excellent *Hampstead: London Hill Town* that:

"…it was built for the use of the natives as an encouragement to them to wash themselves and their garments."

For many years during the 19th and 20th centuries, Hampstead was home to numerous poor people and these baths must have been a godsend. Parts of Hampstead were then slums, as Christopher Wade noted in his *For the poor of Hampstead, for ever. 300 years of the Hampstead Wells Trust*. He wrote that in the 1870s:

"The trustees speedily set about finding a suitable site for 'more convenient dwellings for the Poor'. This they found in Crockett's Court, a notorious slum area to the west of the upper part of Hampstead High Street,"

Tenement buildings, which still stand today, were built on the site. An acquaintance, who lived in Hampstead in the 1960s, remembers that even then

49

it was far from being as affluent as it is today; many parts looked poor. The bathhouse building was converted for upmarket residential use in about 1985.

On the south side of the grassy space, facing the former bathhouse, stands Gardnor House. Entered through an unusual double set of wrought iron gates, this fine mansion was constructed in 1736. It was built for the successful upholsterer Thomas Gardnor (c1685-1775) opposite the stocks that were used for punishment until 1831. He and his family were responsible for the development of several streets and buildings in Hampstead. Thomas was responsible for building terraces of houses in Flask Walk and homes in what is now Gardnor's Place. His family also acquired land in other parts of Hampstead: Streatley Place, Heath Street, the High Street, New End, and Church Row. In addition to his property interests, Thomas was a trustee of the Hampstead Wells Charity, which aided the local poor, in 1761. Gardnor is believed to have died of smallpox and was buried in the graveyard of Hampstead Parish Church, where his tomb may be found.

During the mid-19th century, Gardnor House was owned by a dealer in chinaware. Later that century, by which time most of the area around Flask Walk was inhabited by poor people, the grand Gardnor House was the home of an architect. George William Potter (1831-1919), a builder, local historian, and author of *Hampstead Wells* (1904) and *Random Recollections of Hampstead* (1907), also once lived in Gardnor House. Later, Gardnor House was the home of the author Kingsley Amis (1922-1995) and his wife Elizabeth Jane Howard (1923-2014). By the time they moved in, their marriage was crumbling. When they separated, the house was sold in 1981. On the 14th of October 2020, the house, which contains five bedrooms, five reception rooms, and four bathrooms, was sold for £11,000,000.

The house that Thomas Gardnor built for himself is one of the larger residences within the bounds of old Hampstead. It is evidence of his success as an upholsterer and a property developer. Luckily, the house seems to be well-maintained. Many of us, who spent our childhood in or near Hampstead, bemoan it having become a more upmarket area than it used to be, but with property values rising, the condition of many its historic buildings is being well-maintained.

Flask Walk ends just beyond Rose Mount and continues as Well Walk. Burgh House stands high above the southwest end of Well Walk and is entered from a steep side street called New End Square. The house, built in 1704, is close to the Hampstead Well Spa (see below). According to Bohm and Norrie, the House is named after its 10th owner, The Reverend Allatson Burgh (1769-1856), who was the vicar of St Lawrence Jewry in the City of London. Burgh, who was keener on music than looking after his parishioners, neglected both them and his house. Thomas Barratt wrote:

"Mr. Burgh was a rector in the city, and the composer of a work on church music, published by Longmans. Burgh House is depicted on five pieces of the Wedgwood service, made in 1774, for Catherine II., Empress of Russia."

Between 1858 and 1884, Burgh House became the headquarters of the Royal East Middlesex Militia. After having been put to a variety of uses, the house became used as a cultural centre in 1979. It now contains a small art gallery, a café, a shop, and a Hampstead Museum. The Reverend Burgh would have been pleased to know that today his former home also hosts many fine concerts of classical music.

From the bottom of the garden of Burgh House, the 'Wells Tavern' pub can be seen dominating the view along the gently inclined Well Walk. Known as 'The Green Man' until 1850, when it was rebuilt and renamed the 'Wells Tavern', a pub has stood on his spot since at least 1762. The pub's name reflects one of the reasons that Hampstead became popular in the 17th century. Apart from enjoying clean air, people were attracted to the mineral water springs issuing chalybeate (iron-rich) water that were beginning to be exploited in Hampstead at that time. The historian Potter noted:

"The search for a larger and purer supply of water made by the Corporation of London in the reign of Henry VIII … must have led to the discovery of the chalybeate waters near what is now known as Well Walk, if, as is improbable, they were not known before. Well Walk, as we have seen, was then part of the Heath. The older conduits, viz., that by Gayton Road and that in the Conduit Fields, were, of course, in existence, and were the chief sources for the supply of drinking water. The water from the chalybeate spring was so unpleasant to the taste that it never could have been ordinarily used for drinking."

In 1698, the Wells Charity was formed, and soon after this the waters were commercially exploited. The website of a restaurant on Heath Street, La Gaffe, noted:

"A Long Room was erected on the south side of Well Walk. This comprised a Pump Room where the chalybeate water could be drunk and an Assembly Room for dancing, concerts and other forms of entertainment. Nearby was a tavern and various raffling shops."

Daniel Defoe (1660-1731), writing in his *Tour*, first published 1724-1727, observed:

"Besides the Long Room at Hamstead, in which the Company meet publicly on a Monday Evening to play at Cards, &c. the Master of that built an Assembly-room 60 Feet long, and 30 wide, elegantly decorated. Every one who does not inscribe pays half a Crown for Admittance. Every Gentleman who subscribes a Guinea for the Season, has a Ticket for himself, and for two Ladies. Gentlemen and Ladies, who lodge in the Town, are entertained every Sunday for 6d, each, with Tea and Coffee; but with no other Amusements, but what they find out for one another, and from one another."

In 1725, the Long Room was converted for use as a chapel and was used as such until about 1860, when the congregation shifted to the newly built Presbyterian Chapel on the High Street. In 1862, the Long Room became a drill hall for the local Rifle Volunteers. Potter noted:

"In order to fit the interior of the building for its new purpose it became necessary to remove pulpit, pews, galleries, etc. When this was done there was left a clear space of 90 feet by 36 feet. It was while this work was being carried out, and also during some decorative works to the inside walls a few years later, that some interesting discoveries were made. In the wall at the north end, on removing some wainscot, there was revealed a large niche or recess with traces of basin and pipes having been fixed in it. This was beyond all doubt the spot where the basin and fountains which supplied the visitors to the Spa with the chalybeate water, used to stand."

These extensive premises were demolished in 1882 to make way for an estate of residential buildings. The former Pump Room and Assembly Room occupied a plot that is bounded by Well Walk, East Heath Road, and Gainsborough Gardens. Present day Gainsborough Gardens runs around an oval open space, which is shown as a pond in the gardens of the former Pump Rooms on an 1866 map. The pond was later filled in.

At the corner of Gainsborough Gardens and Well Walk, there is a tall building with attractive neo gothic windows. This was built in about 1704. Next to this house, but separated from it by Gainsborough Gardens, stands Wellside, a house built in 1892 on the site of the Pump Room. Opposite the 1704 house, a small ornate drinking fountain stands on Well Walk. Labelled 'Chalybeate Well', this elegantly designed public well was donated to the people of Hampstead by the mother of the third Earl of Gainsborough in 1698. Nowadays, the 'Chalybeate Well' is dried up. This was already the case when Potter was writing in 1904: "The handsome new fountain in Well Walk, a fountain without water, is now only a monument - a monument to commemorate the memory of the departed glories of the once famous Hampstead Spa."

Apart from one relatively modern building, all the buildings between Gainsborough Gardens and The Wells Tavern are pre-20th century. One of them was once the home of the painter John Constable (1770-1837), who made many paintings of Hampstead and Hampstead Heath (see below). Constable had rented various houses in Hampstead as summer retreats before moving into the house in Well Walk where he lived the last few years of his life. He was buried in Hampstead Parish Church. Other notable people who have lived in Well Walk include the socialist writer and politician Henry Hyndman (1842-1921), who promoted the works of Karl Marx, and the pioneer of birth-control Marie Stopes (1880-1958), whose mother also lived in Hampstead, in Kemplay Road.

At the west end of Well Walk and the uppermost section of Willow Road, there is a corner building with a Georgian shop front. This is now a small theatre but for many years it housed the Well Walk Pottery. The pottery was started by the potter Christopher Magarshack in 1959. According to Bohm and Norrie, writing in their *Hampstead: London Hill Town*, Elsie, the widow of the Russian Jewish translator and writer David Magarshack (1899-1977), lived there. In 1957, she bought this corner building, which had formerly been Sidney Spall's grocery shop, for Christopher to use as his pottery. His father, David, left his birthplace Riga, then in Russia in 1918, and also lived above the shop. Elsie died in 1999, aged 100. In addition to creating and selling pottery, the establishment also held classes for ceramicists, some of whom now have good reputations. David's daughter, Stella, a fine artist, was the Head Art Teacher at King Alfred's, a 'progressive' school situated between Hampstead and Golders Green. In 2016, aged 87, she was brutally attacked in the street close to her home. Now, the premises is home to a theatrical enterprise, The Wells Theatre. Its present owners have decorated one of its windows with a pictorial history of the premises.

Before returning uphill along Flask Walk towards the Flask, you will pass a pair of doors covered in metal studs arranged neatly in geometric patterns. According to an article in the January 2018 issue of *Heath and Hampstead Society Newsletter*, this pair of studded doors:

"…is supposed to have come from Newgate Prison,"

The prison closed in 1902. While walking back towards the High Street, stop to look at a set of cottages, numbers 3 to 7 Flask Walk. They have a pair of unusual crooked, brick-built chimney stacks.

MORE ABOUT THE SPA

On the corner of East Heath Road and Well Walk, there is a pair of wooden doors facing East Heath Road. They are framed by a substantial brick archway. These doors are the entrance to the grounds of Foley House, which stands on a plot at the corner of Well Walk and East Heath Road. Even though it is partially hidden by trees, the upper windows of this three-storey brick building can be seen. From its architectural style, I guessed that it was pre-Victorian, maybe 18th century. Just south of the main building, there is an outhouse with a white painted wooden weatherboard façade. The top of the façade has six small apertures each above one of two shelves. Presumably, these are parts of a dovecote. GW Potter, writing in 1904, noted:

"The old weather-boarded stable belonging to this house is the only building of this kind of construction left in Well Walk. At one time there were several other such structures there."

Potter believed that the present Foley House might have been built in 1706:

"It is stated in one of the records of the manor, dated 1706, "That John Duffield hath built himself a good bricke house at a cost of £1,000" From the description given of the plot I think it almost certain that this house, or a great part of it, is still standing, and is the house known as Foley House."

However, others, such as the authors of the website, britishlistedbuildings.co.uk, consider that the Foley House we see today was built between 1771 and 1773 by the Holborn glazier Edward Helling, who died in about 1781. This house or an earlier one on the same site was built for Mr John Duffield, who was the first manager of Hampstead's spa in Well Walk. Thomas Barratt wrote:

"John Duffield took a lease of the land and springs, except the upper (or flask) spring, from June 2, 1701, at a yearly rent of £50, for a term in 1701 of 21 years. There was a reservation providing that the inhabitants of Hampstead and their children and servants should be permitted to drink or carry away gratis every day " so much of the said purging waters " as they should have occasion for ; but the visits of the villagers were to be made "between the hours of five and twelve of the clock in the forenoon," leaving the afternoons and evenings for John Duffield and his visitors to make what they could of their opportunities."

The spa was across Well Walk, opposite Foley House.

In the late 17th century, when Hampstead became well-known for its curative chalybeate spring water, the spa was established on land that was leased in 1698 by Susannah Noel on behalf of her son Baptist, 3rd Earl of Gainsborough (1684-1714), who was lord of the manor, but a minor. According to the website www.british-history.ac.uk, the lease:

"…granted 6 a[cres]. of Hampstead Heath, including the well of mineral water, to 14 trustees, who were admitted as copyholders at a rent of 5s. a year to use the income for the poor of Hampstead. The trustees leased all the property except the pond or springhead north-west of the mineral spring to John Duffield in 1701 for 21 years at £50 a year, on condition he spent £300 over 3 years improving it, and agreed for a second term for improvements worth £200."

Thomas Barratt wrote that one of these fourteen men was one Thomas Foley. Duffield was quick to develop the mineral spring into a spa. Christopher Wade, author of *For the poor of Hampstead, forever. 300 years of the Hampstead Wells Trust*, quoted an advertisement for a concert that was to be held in the Hampstead Wells on the 18th of August 1701. By then, Duffield had built his Long Room, an edifice containing a 'Pump Room' and an 'Assembly Room', described by Daniel Defoe (see above). The Long Room (Defoe's 'Assembly Room'), which was demolished in 1882, as already mentioned. Wade wrote that Duffield:

"… had done well enough for himself to build 'a goode brick house' costing £1000. Some historians claim that that this became Foley House on East Heath Road, but the evidence is confused. (The house is not shown on a detailed map of 1762)"

Barratt noted:

"Mr GW Potter is of the opinion from the description given in the record that this house was, in all or in part, that now called Foley House…"

Well, if the house that we see today was only built in 1771, it is not surprising that it was not shown on the map created in 1762. I looked at that map and Wade is right. There is no building marked where Foley House should be found. However, in *The Buildings of England. London 4: North*, the architectural historians Nikolaus Pevsner with Bridget Cherry wrote that Foley House was:

"… built in 1698 for J Duffield, the first spa manager …, but with mid-c18 three-bay front … Early c18 stables, weatherboarded."

Pevsner and Cherry were describing the house that stands today, but its absence from the 1762 map is puzzling. I speculate the following. Maybe, Duffield did have a house built in about 1698 on the plot where the present Foley House stands and perhaps it had been demolished by 1762, when the map was drawn, and then later replaced by the house built by Edward Helling, mentioned above. Alternatively, the map was not 100% accurate.

Several Victorian buildings neighbouring Foley House on Well Walk (currently numbers 21-27) bear the name 'Foley Avenue'. Designed by Henry S Legg, these were built in 1881 on land that was once part of the grounds of Foley House.

One of the many people who lived in Foley House was the physiologist and surgeon Sir Benjamin Brodie (1783-1862). In an autobiographical note, *The works of Sir Benjamin Collins Brodie ... with an autobiography* (published 1865), he wrote:

"In the year 1828 I engaged a house on Hampstead Heath, which at that time was a comparatively rural retreat. My family resided there during the summer and part of the autumnal season, and I generally was able to go thither to dinner, returning to my occupation in London in the morning."

Brodie helped to acquire the building at the north end of Kinnerton Street in Belgravia, which became the first medical school for St Georges Hospital (while it was located at Hyde Park Corner in what is now The Lanesborough Hotel). One of the students, who was taught by Brodie in Kinnerton Street, was Henry Gray (1827-1861), author of one of the most famous medical textbooks, *Gray's Anatomy*. Gray dedicated his masterpiece to his teacher and colleague Brodie. The latter used Foley House between 1828 and 1837, and then bought a property in Surrey.

Across East Heath Road, there is a footpath that leads north by northwest from Well Walk to the Vale of Health.

THE VALE OF HEALTH

Whereas most of modern Hampstead is now connected to the rest of London by built-up thoroughfares, two small parts of it are still surrounded completely by land devoid of buildings. One of these is the hamlet of North End, which I will describe later, and the other, closer to the centre of Hampstead village, is the

Vale of Health. Had it not been for the vigorous efforts of local activists at the end of the 19th beginning of the 20th centuries, the heathland surrounding these two places, centuries-old small settlements, would have been cut down and replaced by extensive housing estates.

The land on which the Vale is situated is mentioned in the *Domesday Book* (1086 AD). It was then owned by the abbots and monks of Westminster. By the 18th century, this swampland in the middle of the part of the Heath, then known as part of 'Gangmoor', was inhabited by impoverished people and was malarial. In the 1770s, the area was known as 'Hatches' or 'Hatchett's' Bottom, because Samuel Hatch, a harness-maker, had owned a cottage there before 1770. This unsavoury hollow was described in about 1817 as a "stagnate bottom, a pit in the heath" by Mary, wife of the sculptor Joseph Nollekens (1737-1823). The artist John Thomas Smith (1766-1833), who had studied under Nollekens, wrote a book about the sculptor, *Nollekens and his Times* (edited by Edmund Gosse (1849-1928)), which was published in 1895. From it, we learn more about Mrs Nollekens (who died in 1817), the Vale, and Hampstead as a whole:

"Towards the later part of her life she expressed a wish to go once more to Hampstead, a spot considered by most physicians and landscape-painters as the most salubrious and beautiful of all the Montpeliers of England; but she could neither make up her mind as to the enormous expense of its accommodations, nor as to the peculiar fragrance of its seven sorts of air, which of them she ought then to prefer. The latter perplexity afforded her at times much conversation; and when she was requested to name the seven airs, she, in an elevated voice, stated them thus: "My dear sir, there are the four sides of the hill, each receiving freely the air from the four quarters. There is the hill itself, very clear, but certainly often bleak. Then there is the 'Vale of Health', as it is called, in a stagnant bottom; a pit in the heath ..."

It was a vale, but not a healthy one. It is interesting to note that even back in the early part of the 18th century, Mrs Nollekens considered accommodation in Hampstead to have been costly.

By 1801 (or '02), the name 'Vale of Health' began to be used to refer to this area. By then, the marshland had been drained, and property developers began building houses in the Vale. The new name was probably chosen to entice people to buy homes in the greatly improved, isolated hollow. According to one source (www.british-history.ac.uk):

"The middle-class element became increasingly important from the early 19th century. In 1801 the attractions of the area included 'unbounded prospects' of Kent and the river Thames, and screening, presumably by trees and the lie of the land, from north winds. By 1821 the inhabitants, petitioning for the removal of the poor houses, observed that the neighbourhood had 'greatly increased in respectability' through the 'improvement of property'."

The early 'respectable' residents of the Vale included: the law reformer Sir Samuel Romilly (1757-1818); the poet and essayist James Leigh Hunt (1784-1859), who entertained leading literary figures such as Hazlitt, Keats, Lord Byron and Shelley in his house in the Vale; the publisher Charles Knight (1791- 1873); and, also, a Prince Eszterhazy. Between 1815 and 1851, the number of houses built in the Vale grew from four to eighteen. These figures do not include other cottages that were already built there. The Vale also attracted many trippers. A weekly fair was established, as well as a tavern and tea gardens. Two hotels were built in the Vale, but neither of these nor other 'attractions' exist today. This 'vulgarisation' of the area did not deter 'elevated' people from settling there.

Over-expansion of the Vale was limited by law. The Hampstead Heath Act, 1871 stated that: "the board shall at all times preserve, as far as may be, the natural aspect and state of the Heath" (the 'board' being the Metropolitan Board of Works). This law effectively protected what was left of Hampstead Heath from becoming further urbanised. This far-sighted legislation is paying off dividends today by making the Heath a place where one can escape from London and almost imagine that one might be in the heart of the country. As one of my friends put it: who needs to live in rural Hampshire when countryside like this is within a few minutes journey from the city?

The only vehicular access to the Vale is a winding road leading downhill from East Heath Road. This lane is bordered by dense woodland and by luxuriant banks of stinging nettles in spring and summer. At the bottom of this thoroughfare, there are houses. Most of the expensive cars parked outside them suggest that the Vale is no longer a home for the impoverished. At the bottom end of the road, there two large Victorian buildings whose front doors are framed by gothic-style archways. They have the name 'Villas on the Heath'.

One of them bears a circular blue commemorative plaque, which has leafy creepers growing over it. It states:

"Rabindranath Tagore 1861-1941 Indian poet stayed here in 1912."

I have visited the palatial Jorasanko where Tagore was brought up in Calcutta. The large (by London standards) 'villa' in the Vale is tiny in comparison. An article published in a Calcutta newspaper, *The Telegraph*, on the 13th of September 2009 reported with some accuracy:

"In Hampstead, north London, regarded as a cultural "village" today for left-wing but arty champagne socialists, there is a plaque to Rabindranath Tagore at 3 Villas on Vale of Heath."

Tagore was one of India's geniuses: artist, poet, writer, dramatist, musician, educator, promoter of Indian independence, Nobel laureate, and much more. But what was he doing in the Vale of Health in 1912? An article published in the local newspaper, the *Ham & High*, on the 6th of April 2013 provides the answer. In February 1911, Tagore met the English artist William Rothenstein (1872-1945) in Calcutta, where he was visiting Rabindranath's brother, the artist Abanindranath Tagore (1871-1951), many of whose works I have seen at the lovely National Gallery of Modern Art in Bangalore (India) and at Jorasanko. According to Rothenstein in his *Men and Memories...* (publ. 1932):

"Before leaving Darjeeling a telegram came from Rabindranath Tagore, asking me to join him at Bolpur; but my passage was booked, and I must reluctantly refuse."

64

Rothenstein, who lived for a while in Hampstead, and Rabindranath became friends. They began a lively correspondence. In 1912, Tagore arrived in England. It was Rothenstein who found him lodgings at Number 3 Villas on the Heath, where he stayed for a few months in the summer. While living in the Vale, Tagore worked on translating several of his works from Bengali into English. Some of these were published later in 1912 in London as the English version of *Gitanjali* (meaning 'song offerings'). It was this work that, to a great extent, led to its author being awarded the Nobel Prize for literature in 1913.

After Tagore's London visit, Rothenstein wrote an extensive account of it:
"Promotto Loll Sen ... brought to our house Dr Brajendranath Seal, then on a visit to London, a philosopher with a brilliant mind ... They both wrote Tagore, urging him to come to London; he would meet, they said, at our house and elsewhere, men after his heart. Then news came that Rabindranath was on his way. I eagerly awaited his visit. At last he arrived, accompanied by two friends, and by his son... I sent word to Yeats, who failed to reply; but when I wrote again he asked me to send him the poems, and when he had read them his enthusiasm equalled mine... Tagore's dignity and handsome presence, the ease of his manners and his quiet wisdom made a marked impression on all who met him... BEFORE TAGORE LEFT for India, Yeats and I arranged a small dinner in his honour. After dinner we asked Tagore to sing Bande Mataram, the nationalist song. He hummed the tune but after the first words broke down; he could not remember the rest. Then Yeats began the Irish anthem—and his memory, again, was at fault; and Ernest Rhys could not for the life of him

recollect the words of the Welsh national anthem. 'What a crew!' I said, when I too stumbled over God save the King….."

After leaving Hampstead, Tagore wrote to Rothenstein in November 1912 (following the publication of *Gitanjali*). Here are some extracts from his letter: "I am so glad to learn from your letter that my book has been favourably criticised in The Times Literary Supplement. … I feel that the success of my book is your own success. But for your assurance I never could have dreamt that my translations were worth anything… Remember me kindly to Mrs Rothenstein and give our love to the children. Ever your affectionate friend, RABINDRANATH TAGORE"

On the 18th of August 2015, the *Ham and High* reported that an important Indian visitor wanted to acquire the house where Tagore lived in the Vale:

"On her recent visit to London, Bengal's chief minister Mamata Banerjee reportedly asked the Indian high commissioner if he would make an offer to the owners on Bengal's behalf – valued at an estimated £2.7 million. … Business tycoon Harsh Neotia accompanied Ms Banerjee on her official visit, and said: "It would be a lot of pride and interest for the people of India and Bengal if the state government could get the house and convert it into a museum or study and research centre.""

Tagore was not the only notable resident of the Vale in later times. The author Compton Mackenzie (1883-1972) lived in the Vale at Woodbine Cottage in the 1930s, writing the *Four Wings of Love* (publ. 1937-1945). Near his house, was the abode of the barrister Alfred Harmsworth (1837-1889) and his family between 1870 and 1873 when family fortunes declined temporarily. Part of the reason for this decline was drink and the size of his family. Amongst his fourteen children were the two who became 'press barons': Alfred Harmsworth, 1st Viscount Northcliffe (1865–1922) and Harold Harmsworth, 1st Viscount Rothermere (1868–1940).

A terrace of houses, Byron Villas, stands on a road, a cul-de-sac, that leads downwards towards a large pond. The author DH Lawrence (1885-1930) and his wife Frieda lived in the Vale briefly in 1915 at number 1 Byron Villas. The authoress Stella Gibbons (1902-1989) lived in the Vale from about 1926. According to Compton Mackenzie, the appeal of the Vale to writers was:

"… village life half an hour from Piccadilly Circus was a continuous refreshment and stimulus…"

Just before the short road ends abruptly, there is something that seems quite out of character with the smart residences in the Vale. It is a square lot on which several caravans are parked. It resembles a Romany encampment. This plot of land, where once there stood a pub, has been owned by the Abbotts family for over 160 years. Since the late 19th century, it has been fairground land. About ten members of the family live on the site in caravans, and other travelling-fair workers are allowed to camp there free of charge. In exchange, members of the Abbott family, who operate travelling fairs, are allowed camp for nothing on other fairground owners' sites when they travel around the country. The Abbotts do not regard themselves as 'Travellers' (Romany people), but as 'fairground people'. An article published in 2011 in the *Evening Standard* revealed:

"Residents in nearby Byron Villas all look as though they read the London Review of Books. 'No trouble at all, never bother us,' they say of the 20 or so residents of the caravan site. A father and son, both called Charlie Abbott, invite me to sit down outside their caravan, part of a tidy settlement about half the size of a football pitch. Again, the caravans are more like what you would find at a seaside holiday site, though some have traditional shiny Travellers' water pots with spouts on their front steps. Mr Abbott Jr looks and talks like any other North Londoner, while his father has the more wizened features and air of a man who has spent his whole life in a caravan, much of it travelling. 'We are not Travellers, we are fairground people, all members of the Showmen's Guild,' Mr Abbott Snr, 81, tells me firmly…"

An attempt was made to buy the land for development in 2008, but this has not happened (yet). Given the strict protection of the integrity of the Heath, it is highly improbable that planning permission to build on this site would ever be granted.

Beyond the caravan site, a path leads to the pond, a source of the River Fleet. This water feature was built as a reservoir as part of the waterworks of the New River Company. It was here, many years ago, that I attempted fishing with a friend's rod and other angling tackle. This was my first and, as yet, only experience of angling. Most of the pond is surrounded by the wild Heath, but the northwest side of it has well-manicured private gardens that run down to the water's edge.

Many years ago, there was a club in the Vale. It was named The Athenaeum. Of it, Dorothy Bohm and Ian Norrie wrote:

"It started as a hotel in the late 1870s, catering for invalids, then it became a factory, after that a lecture hall, and, in 1877, a club. This did not prosper ..."

Later, it was used by The Salvation Army, then in 1910 it became a club devoted to Anglo-German friendship. After becoming a factory once again, it was demolished. After the late 1950s, a block of flats, named The Athenaeum, was constructed on its site, which overlooks the pond.

There was another hotel and a popular resort by the pond. Lasting for longer than that which was housed in the former Athenaeum, it was the large Vale of Health Hotel (also called The Vale of Health Tavern). A tall Victorian gothic style building with turrets and crenellations, it was built in about 1863. William Howitt, author of *The Northern Heights of London*, published in 1869, was not keen on the hotel:

"The Vale of Health used, till of late years, to present a sight at once picturesque and pleasant. In front of a row of cottages, and under the shade of willows, were set out long tables for tea, where many hundreds, at a trifling cost, partook of a homely and exhilarating refreshment ... but then came this great tavern with its towers and battlements and cast them literally and practically into the shade. It was, however, really gratifying to see that the more imposing and dangerous

69

place of entertainment never could compete with the more primitive tea-tables, nor banish the homely and happy groups of families…"

Howitt did not reveal why he considered the hotel to have been dangerous. By the early 20th century, parts of the hotel contained workshops and some artists' studios, one of which was used by the artist Stanley Spencer (1891-1959), and about which more later. The studios were closed in 1939 and the hotel was demolished and replaced in 1964 by a block of flats called Spencer House.

POETS AND THE VALE OF HEALTH

One house in the Vale of Health intrigues me: Vale Lodge. It is a late Georgian (early 19th century, pre-1831) house modernised in the 20th century. It is difficult to see from the lane by which it stands because it is surrounded by a high wall. People, who have lived in Vale Lodge include the writer Edgar Wallace (1875-1932); the Russian-born industrialist Sir Leon Bagrit (1902-1979); and the banker Sir Paul Chambers (1904-1981). One source (historicengland.org.uk) mentions that Vale Lodge was:

"… probably also the residence of Leigh Hunt, poet."

That interested me because I had read that Leigh Hunt (1784-1859) lived in the Vale of Health from 1816 onwards for a few years. Hunt, a radical, was a critic, essayist, and poet. He was a co-founder and/or collaborator of several periodicals including *The Examiner*, *The Reflector*, *The Indicator*, and *The Companion*. In about 1812/13, Hunt and his two brothers, also involved with

70

The Examiner, were imprisoned for libelling the Prince Regent (the future King George IV). Whilst incarcerated in the Surrey County Jail, Hunt was visited by his eminent friends including Lord Byron, Thomas Moore, Lord Henry Brougham, Charles Lamb, and Jeremy Bentham. The painter Benjamin Robert Haydon (1786-1846) wrote in his *Autobiography and Memoirs* that Bentham:

"…came to see Hunt in Surrey Gaol, and played battledore and shuttlecock with him. Hunt told me after of the prodigious power of Bentham's mind…"

While in prison he wrote a poem *To Hampstead* in 1813, in which he looks forward to returning there:

"…Till I return, and find thee doubly fair.

Wait then my coming on that lightsome land,

Health, and the joy that out of nature springs,

And Freedom's air-blown locks; but stay with me,

Friendship, frank entering with the cordial hand,

And Honor, and the Muse with growing wings,

And Love Domestic, smiling equably."

On his release from prison in 1815, Leigh went to live in the Vale of Health until 1819, returning briefly between 1820 and the following year. Hunt's home in the Vale of Health not only inspired him to write some poetry extolling the virtues of Hampstead, including this verse, which depicted it as he knew it in the early 19th century:

"A STEEPLE issuing from a leafy rise

With farmy fields in front and sloping green.

Dear Hampstead, is thy southern face serene.

Silently smiling on approaching eyes.

Within, thine ever-shifting looks surprise.

Streets, hills, and dells, trees overhead now seen.

Now down below, with smoking roofs between,

— A village, revelling in varieties.

Then northward what a range,—with heath and pond. Nature's own ground;

woods that let mansions through.

And cottaged vales with pillowy fields beyond …"

Hunt attracted several of his contemporaries to the Vale. These were notable literary figures including the poets Percy Bysshe Shelley (1792-1822), Bryan Waller Procter (1787-1874) and John Keats (1795-1821) as well as the painter Haydon, and the essayist William Hazlitt (1778-1830). Haydon's book also reveals that his and Hunt's friend, the poet John Keats, did not entirely approve of Hunt's lifestyle in Hampstead:

"It is a great pity that people by associating themselves with the finest things spoil them. Hunt has damned Hampstead with masks and sonnets and Italian tales; Wordsworth has damned the Lakes…"

Keats, who had slept in Leigh Hunt's home in the Vale of Health, took a great liking to Hampstead and settled there in 1817. He lived in Wentworth House, which was later renamed 'Keats House'. The house in Keats Grove was built in about 1815 and divided in two separate dwellings. One half was occupied by Charles Armitage Brown (1787-1842), a poet and friend of Leigh Hunt and the other half by Charles Wentworth Dilke (1789–1864), a literary associate of Hunt and a visitor to his home in the Vale of Health. Keats became Brown's lodger. This was after Keats had visited his neighbour Dilke, with whom he became acquainted following an introduction by the poet and playwright John Hamilton Reynolds (1784-1852), who was part of Leigh Hunt's circle of friends.

While living in Hampstead, Keats wrote much poetry including *Ode to a Nightingale* (and other "Odes"), *Isabella, Hyperion, St Agnes, La Belle dame sans Merci*, and began working on *Endymion*. It has been suggested that Keat's poem *I Stood Tiptoe Upon a Little Hill* was inspired by his experience of Hampstead. Another of his works, *Dedication. To Leigh Hunt esq* relates directly to his friend Hunt. His poem *Sleep and Poetry*, according to Leigh Hunt:

"… originated in sleeping in a room adorned with busts and pictures … 'On Sleep and Poetry,' was occasioned by his sleeping in one of the cottages in the Vale of Health, the first one that fronts the valley, beginning from the same quarter."

The house was Leigh Hunt's. Another of Hunt's regular visitors in Hampstead was the poet Percy Bysshe Shelley (1792-1822). Hunt, writing in his autobiography, recalled that Shelley:

"… delighted in the natural broken ground, and the fresh air of the place … Here also he swam his paper boats on the ponds, and delighted to play with my children …"

This must have been after 1810, after which the first of Hunt's ten children was born. Hunt relates several anecdotes about Shelley in Hampstead, one of which I will repeat using Hunt's words from his *Autobiography*:

"I was returning home one night to Hampstead after the opera. As I approached the door, I heard strange and alarming shrieks, mixed with the voice of a man. The next day it was reported by gossips that Mr Shelley ... had brought home "some very strange female" into the house, no better, of course, than she ought to be ... Shelley, in coming to our house that night, had found a woman lying near the top of the hill, in fits. It was a fierce winter night ...and winter loses nothing of its fierceness in Hampstead. My friend, always the promptest as well as the most pitying on these occasions, knocked at the first houses he could reach, in order to have the woman taken in ... In vain ..."

Eventually, after Shelley's many unsuccessful attempts to elicit help:

"The woman was then brought into our house, which was at some distance down a bleak path (it was in the Vale of Health); and Shelley and her son were obliged to hold her till the doctor could arrive. It appeared she had been attending this son at a criminal charge made against him, the agitation of which had thrown her into fits ... The doctor said she would have perished, had she laid she laid there a short time longer..."

Many now famous literary and artistic people congregated around Leigh Hunt while he has living in the Vale of Health. However, there is some uncertainty about where exactly he resided. One suggestion, already mentioned, is Vale Lodge. However, William Howitt, wrote of Hunt's residence:

"The house, which he occupied ... was pulled down to make way for the great hotel ..."

The hotel has now gone but Vale Lodge still stands.

In 1900, Mrs Caroline A White published *Sweet Hampstead and its Associations*, in which she noted:

"Neither William Howitt, Baines, nor a writer in the Bookman ... appears to have known anything decided of the whereabouts of Leigh Hunt's cottage, otherwise than that it was situated in the Vale of Health ... The desire on all sides appears to have been to furnish the poet with a more important habitation than he himself tells us he occupied. In or about 1855-56, it was believed that Vale Lodge, then the hospitable home of the talented writers of 'The Wife's Secret' and 'Ingomar', was the veritable house in which the poet had resided, and in one of the rooms of which Keats had composed the first verses of 'Endymion'."

The Wife's Secret was written by the actor Charles Kean (1811-1868), son of the actor Edmund Kean, and *Ingomar* by Maria Lovell (1803-1877), who died in Hampstead. White continued:

"...I found, both from description and allusion, that Vale Lodge could not possibly be the 'little packing-case, by courtesy called a house,' which Leigh Hunt himself describes as his home at Hampstead, where he had gone for the sake of his 'health, and his old walks in the fields.'"

Mrs White also believed that Lord Byron had lived in the Vale:

"My informant told me that Lord Byron had at one time lodged in another of these cottages, and had written with a diamond on a pane of one of the windows two lines which afterwards appeared in 'Childe Harold.' The pane existed in his time, but had either been broken, or cut out and removed. This was before Leigh Hunt's residence there."

As there is uncertainty about where exactly Hunt resided in the Vale, then Vale Lodge can at least be remembered for at least three literary figures: Charles Kean, Maria Lovell, and Edgar Wallace.

The next chapter moves us away from The Vale and back to the heart of Hampstead village.

FRENCH CONNECTIONS AND ST MARY'S ON HOLLY WALK

General Charles de Gaulle (1890-1970), an eminent refugee from France, was dead against Britain joining what was the Common Market and is now the European Union, despite the country having generously hosted him during WW2, when his country was invaded by Germany. This is well known, but less known is that he lived in Hampstead. His home was at 99 Frognal in what is currently St Dorothy's Convent. The convent building, Frognal House, was built in about 1740 and later modified in various ways. It stands on the site of a 15th century tenement known as 'house called Frognal'. At the beginning of the 18th century, the land on which this stood was owned by the bricklayer Thomas Smith, who probably built the present building, which became known as 'Frognal House'. During the Crimean War (1853-1856), the house became The Sailors' Orphan Girls Home from 1862 until it shifted to Fitzjohns Avenue in 1869.

De Gaulle and his family lived in Frognal House between 1940 and 1942. Monique Riccardi-Cubitt, a writer and art-historian, stayed at there in about 2000 and described it as follows in her blog:

"The reception rooms on the ground floor have remained, but the General's Cabinet de travail is now the chapel ... The first floor panelled library is where I would feel his spirit most strongly hovering as I would work alone early in the morning ... In the garden roses grew, I drew and painted them in the late afternoon ... His spirit was there too, and I used to wonder how often he would have come back from his headquarters in Carlton Gardens worn and weary with cares, to wander off to the peace of the leafy bowers and refresh his tired mind and soul ... From the roof terrace overlooking the whole of London below, he would stand at night and watch the German bombings on the City of London during the Blitz ..."

While living in Hampstead, De Gaulle used to attend masses at St Mary's Catholic Church in Holly Walk. It was the first Catholic church to have been built in Hampstead since the Reformation in the 16th century. It opened its doors to worshippers in 1816. Its first pastor was a refugee, one of 500 clergy fleeing from the French Revolution, the Abbé Jean-Jacques Morel (1766-1852). Thomas Barratt noted:

"Towards the end of the eighteenth century another interesting religious association came into the life of Hampstead, in a very modest and unassertive way, as one of the minor overflows from the French Revolution. Among the priestly refugees from France was a certain Abbe Morel, who had been connected with the Grand Seminary at Bourg. He was attracted to Hampstead by the fact of there being several French families living there—Talleyrand among the rest, some say—exiles like himself, to whom the question of religious worship according to their own faith was becoming a matter of difficulty…"

Barrett believed that Talleyrand, Charles Maurice de Talleyrand-Périgord (1754-1838):

"… lived for a time at Tensleys, on Hampstead Green, during his service as French Ambassador from 1830 until 1834 … It was pulled down, and the site is now partly covered by the Hampstead General Hospital."

This is now the location of the Royal Free Hospital. Barrett quotes the following anecdote that reveals that the refugees included members of the French aristocracy:

"… A story is told of two handsomely dressed ladies visiting Hampstead in 1819. They drove in a carriage to the bottom of Holly Hill, and then got out and walked to the top; and sometime later the Abbe was seen walking down the road bareheaded, respectfully escorting them. As the elder of the two ladies got into the carriage she kissed the Abbe's hand and shed tears. This lady, it was said, was the Duchesse d'Angouleme."

After some years in Hampstead, Barratt wrote that Morel:

"… was put to a severe ordeal when, the Revolution having come to an end, it became possible for the refugees to go back to their native country. Most of the little congregation for which he had been officiating returned. He would fain have gone with them; but in Hampstead he had found a real haven of rest after the turbulence which had preceded his exile, and had formed many ties with the

78

people of the village. He decided to remain, and for many years after that Abbe Morel was a worthy and loved figure in Hampstead."

In 1941, Fr Joseph Geraerts became the parish priest. His notes, published on a website (www.parish.rcdow.org.uk), reveal that:

"… one of the more notable parishioners was General Charles de Gaulle who lived for about a year at 99 Frognal, now St. Dorothy's Convent. We are told that his tall and impressive figure was always to be seen in the front bench at the 11 o'clock Mass whenever he was home."

De Gaulle returned to France in June 1944. After initially declining to join the Common Market, Britain applied to join in 1963. De Gaulle was opposed to this. It was only after he resigned as President in 1969 that Britain was able to join the European community, which it has left recently.

Frognal House was converted into its present role, the home of St Dorothy's Convent, part of a religious community based in Malta, in 1968. The organisation's website explains that it:

"… caters for young ladies coming to study in London or for a short holiday from all over the world. It aims at providing not only a boarding house, but a homely environment where guidance and advice assure the wellbeing and comfort of all the students. Besides catering for the students, the sisters are very much involved in their Parish St Mary's."

On the 13th of October 2021, the *Ham & High* newspaper reported that Frognal House was for sale, quoting a price tag of £15,000,000.

Apart from three eateries in Hampstead (the former Cellier du Midi restaurant, a creperie stall next to the King William IV pub on the High Street, the still extant La Cage Imaginaire) and itinerant French onion sellers, who used to come to Hampstead from France with their bicycles garlanded with strings of onions, I had not considered that Hampstead had many French connections. However, seeing the convent and St Mary's and exploring their story, has shown me that France has had a significant place in Hampstead's history.

During the covid19 'lockdowns' in 2020, it was often impossible to enter churches because many of them were kept closed. On several occasions, especially when there were builders at work within a church, we were lucky enough to be able to enter. This happened at St Mary's, where De Gaulle attended mass in Hampstead. The church is located on Holly Walk about 180 yards north of St John's, Hampstead's Anglican Parish Church. It is set back from the road and its tall narrow façade is wedged between two terraced Georgian houses. The white painted façade with neo-classical ornamentation and a niche containing a large sculpture of the Virgin and Child, and a belfry with a single bell, has a Mediterranean look about it. It adds an exotic touch to its otherwise British surroundings. The façade was designed by the architect William Wardell (1823-1899), many of whose other creations are in Australia. Born a Protestant, he was influenced by his friend, the great Victorian architect Augustus Pugin (1812-1852), who converted to Roman Catholicism. Wardell followed in Pugin's footsteps and became a Catholic, building several Catholic churches in England before he moved to Australia in about 1858. In the 1840s, after becoming a Catholic, he became a parishioner at St Mary's.

Prior to the construction of St Mary's, the Roman Catholics in Hampstead worshipped in Oriel House in Little Church Row (now part of Heath Street south of the Underground station). When this became too small to accommodate the congregation, the present church was constructed in under a year, and was ready for use in August 1816. At that time, the congregation was led by the Abbé Jean-Jacques Morel. While he was still officiating at St Marys, a Papal Bull, the *Restoration of the Hierarchy to England and Wales*, was issued in 1850. Included in this document was permission for bells to be rung from Catholic churches in England (for the first time since the Reformation). It was this that led to the creation of the façade with a bell, designed by Wardell, which we see today.

Fortunately for us the church was open when we arrived. A couple of workmen were doing some repairs and did not mind us entering the small church. According to Nikolaus Pevsner and Bridget Cherry in their *London 4: North*, the interior was altered in 1878, and a sanctuary, as well as two side chapels, were added in 1907. The nave faces a *baldachino* supported by four pillars coloured black with gold-coloured decoration. It was designed by Adrian Gilbert Scott (1882-1963) in 1935. His family were parishioners of St Mary's. Adrian lived in Frognal Way in a neo-Georgian house called Shepherd's Well. Sir George Gilbert Scott (1811-1872), Adrian's grandfather, also lived in Hampstead, at

Admirals House close to Fenton House. There is a painting above the high altar that depicts the Assumption of the Virgin. This was painted by a student of Bartolomé Murillo (1617-1682) and presented to the church by one of its founders Mr George Armstrong. There is a stone effigy in the northern side chapel, the Lady Chapel. It depicts a figure with hands together as in prayer, with a lion at his feet. Although Abbé Morel had requested to be buried under a simple marble slab, this effigy of him was commissioned by the architect Wardell. The lion at the feet of the cleric signifies that he died outside the country of his birth.

Although the interior of the church is 19th century, it evokes the feeling of much older churches I have seen in Italy. As with the façade, the inside of St Mary's feels as if it is in a country close to the Mediterranean. While visiting its interior, I bought a copy of a booklet about the church, from which much of my information has been gleaned. The booklet mentions some notable members of the church's congregation, including General De Gaulle, the Duchess of Angouleme, William Wardell, the Gilbert-Scott family, the landscape artist George Clarkson Stansfield (1828-1878; he lived on Hampstead High Street), Baron Friedrich Von Hugel (1852-1925), and the novelist Grahame Greene (1904-1991).

Von Hugel, who lived in Holford Road, which runs east of Heath Street, was, like Greene, a convert to Catholicism. He was born in Florence, Italy, and moved to England when he was 15 years old. He was an influential religious historian and philosopher both inside and beyond the Roman Catholic Church.

He was a leading proponent of Catholic Modernism, which, according to Wikipedia:

"…is neither a system, school, or doctrine, but refers to a number of individual attempts to reconcile Roman Catholicism with modern culture."

Less cerebral than Von Hugel, but greatly skilled was Gino Masera (1915-1996), who worshipped at St Mary's. The booklet notes that when working at London's Savoy Hotel, Masera's:

"… artistic talent was revealed when he was asked to carve a block of salt for table decoration. He regarded the commission to carve the Stations of the Cross [in St Mary's] as a turning point in his career and went on to carve the statue of Christ the King which stands above the High Altar in St Paul's Cathedral."

Grahame Greene, an agnostic, became converted to Catholicism and was baptised in February 1926, partly because of the influence of Vivien Dayrell-Browning, whom he married in October 1927 in the Church of St Mary's in Hampstead.

St Mary's catholic church stands a few yards higher than a large burial ground, which lines the sloping east side of most of Holly Walk. This cemetery contains some interesting gravestones including those of the actor Anton Wohlbrueck (Walbrook) who died in Germany but whose ashes are buried in this cemetery; the cartoonist George du Maurier; and the Labour politician Hugh Gaitskell. This churchyard is that of the Church of England Hampstead parish church, St John-at-Hampstead, a pleasant edifice, designed by Henry Flitcroft (1697-1769) and others, and completed in 1747. It is surrounded by graves including that of the great artist John Constable, who figures in the next chapter.

ARTISTS IN HAMPSTEAD: ROMNEY, CONSTABLE, AND OTHERS

Since long ago, Hampstead and its rustic surroundings have attracted artists. This is well illustrated in a quotation from the life of Nollekens (see above), which reads:

"Wilson, Gainsborough, Loutherbourg, and Kirk for several years had lodgings at Hampstead, and made that spot the seat of their morning and evening study; and Collins and Linnell, now inhabitants, are constantly seen culling its beauties. It is also occasionally the residence of Beechey, Phillips and Westall; and I have seen Callcott, Arnald, the Reinagles, Burnet, and Martin enjoying its luxuriant windings. Old Oram, the landscape-painter, and member of the Board of Works, who was a man of some genius, inhabited the house south of Jack Straw's Castle. And it was to Hampstead that Hayley's friend, Romney, the painter, retired in the decline of his life"

I do not know exactly when Hampstead first attracted artists, but the historian Thomas Barratt suggests that it was by the mid-18th century, when landscape painting began to be favoured by British artists, many of whom resided in London. The Swiss artist Henry Fuseli (1741-1825) was frequently in Hampstead between 1764 and 1768, and there is an account, quoted by Barratt,

84

of at least one visit to the area by Sir Joshua Reynolds and Thomas Gainsborough:

"Hogarth and Sir Joshua Reynolds might have been seen at Hampstead in the old Wells days. The Bull and Bush became a popular house for London artists, wits, and people of quality. In "Wine and Walnuts, or After-Dinner Chit-Chat", by Ephraim Hardcastle, the pseudonym of W. H. Pyne, a well-known litterateur and artist of the period, there occurs a description of a gathering of wits at this old hostelry, when, in addition to the author, the party consisted of Reynolds, Gainsborough, Sterne, Garrick, Foote, Bunbury, Caleb Whitefoord, and others."

Here is a sample from Hardcastle's description of that meeting in the pub the political satirist Caleb Whitefoord (1734-1810) asked Joshua Reynolds (1723-1792), who painted his portrait in about 1773:

"… 'did you see that double-headed parsley in the garden, Reynolds?' 'No, I did not, it escaped me'. 'No, sir ! why, where were your chromatics ? — trees in miniature — a fairy wood, green as an emerald, and not see it! Yes, white-legged chicks and streaky bacon — Didst see the peas, Reynolds, twining up the lilliputian hop-poles?' — 'I did, sir,' answered Reynolds, smiling. — 'O! then be thankful to the Lord for preserving your optics. That's a blessing, at any rate'. 'What are you ruminating about, hey, friend Lawrence? — are you going to be dull because I lampooned the parsons, man? — come, give me thy hand. No, Sterne, God forbid I should speak disrespectfully of your cloth. I love a parson next to painting — that's gospel. I never set my foot in a parsonage house, if it be tenanted by a pious man, but I could weep.'"

Sterne was the author and clergyman Lawrence Sterne (1713-1768).

Amongst the many artists associated with Hampstead, two of those who have stood the test of time and spent long periods in the village are George Romney (1734-1802) and John Constable (1776-1837). In more recent times, Hampstead has also been associated with major 'modern artists' of the 20th century, who will be discussed in another chapter.

Romney had a house on Holly Hill. An old fire station with a tall clock tower, which was built in 1871 and used until 1923, stands on a corner at the southern end of narrow Holly Hill, opposite Hampstead Underground Station. Ascending steep Holly Hill, on our right is the house (number 16) where the painter Derek Hill (1916-2000) lived between 1947 and his death. A painter of portraits and landscapes, he was well regarded in Ireland. Close to his home, number 18 Holly Hill is named 'Sundial House' and has a heavily painted black sundial attached to its façade. It was once owned by Hill. A little further up the hill on the same side as Sundial House, there is a large house with white painted weatherboarding. This was the residence of a painter far better-known than Hill, the portraitist George Romney. He began to want to live away from central London, as Barratt related:

"…in 1792 he often rambled out in the direction of Hampstead. Finally, in 1793, he decided to set up a country establishment on the Northern Heights. In June 1793 he took a lodging at Pineapple Place near Kilburn … But it turned out to be a rather costly experiment, drawing him away a good deal from his sitters in Town …"

He lived and worked between Pineapple Place and his London abode in Cavendish Square. However, as Barratt noted, his work in 'town':

"...at last became so distasteful to him that he determined to have a country house and studio of his own, and pitched upon Hampstead as the ideal spot for his purpose—not too remote from Town, yet affording all the quietude and picturesqueness that could be desired. He made many visits to Hampstead before deciding upon a house, and finally, in 1796, purchased an old house and stable at the top of Holly Bush Hill."

Romney bought the property on Holly Hill and had it redesigned by Samuel Bunce (1765-1802) for use as a studio and gallery in 1797/8. When he lived there, he would have had an uninterrupted view over London. Now, buildings such as the massive Victorian building, replete with turrets topped with conical roofs, the former Mount Vernon Hospital, where tuberculosis used to be treated, and is now a block of flats, hide what was once a splendid panorama.

Close to the former hospital, and surrounded by a brick wall, stands Mount Vernon House, formerly known as Windmill House, which was built in about 1728. It had been home to the surgeon William Pierce (c1706 -1771); General Charles Vernon (died 1810), Lieutenant of the Tower of London from 1763 until 1810, who leased it between 1781 and 1800; and Edmund John Niemann (1813-1876) the British landscape painter, yet another of the many artists who have lived in Hampstead. On the outer wall, there is a plaque commemorating the physiologist Sir Henry Dale (1875-1968), who lived there. Dale first identified acetylcholine in 1914 and proposed that it might be a neurotransmitter, a substance that allowed nerve cells to communicate with one another and with muscle cells. In 1936, he and his collaborator Otto Loewi (1873-1961), whom he met at University College (London), were awarded a Nobel Prize for their work on the role of acetylcholine in neurotransmission.

Returning to Romney's home, in addition to a large picture gallery, one of the more interesting features that he built there was described by Barratt:

"One of his whims was the building of a dining-room close to the kitchen, "with a buttery hatch opening into it, so that the artist and his friends might enjoy beefsteaks, hot and hot, upon the same plan as the members of the Beefsteak Club were served at their room in the Lyceum"."

Although Romney had spent a great deal of money to create his Hampstead abode, to which he moved after having lived in Cavendish Square for at least 20 years, he was not entirely happy being so far away from the buzz of central London life. He sold the house in 1799. In 1807, the house was enlarged and became 'The Hampstead Assembly Rooms', where meetings and gatherings of various sorts were held. Later, in 1929/30, the house was remodelled and enlarged by the architect Sir Bertram Clough Williams-Ellis (1883-1978), who created the picturesque village of Portmeirion in western Wales, as well as enlarging Hampstead's Whitestone House in 1934.

In *Architect Errant*, the autobiography of Williams-Ellis, he wrote of Romney's former home:

"The fine old house, much altered and adapted to our curious habits, being far too large for needs or means, was proportionately delightful to inhabit, and with two ex-billiard rooms (it was once a club) at the disposal of the children and their friends, its size had its compensations ... I had taken the immense old picture-gallery as my studio ..."

Further on, the architect reveals something of the social life he enjoyed in Romney's former residence:

"It was a splendid house for large parties and we gave a lot of them – dances every so often, a show by Ballet Rambert ... We also gave a party to meet the Russian Ambassador, M. Maisky, who made a speech from the gallery balcony, and all sorts of odds and ends of meetings and conferences, mostly vaguely cultural."

Monsieur Ivan Maisky (1884-1975), Ambassador to the UK between 1925 and 1927, was not the only high-ranking Soviet official to visit Hampstead. As will be described in a later chapter, the village was also visited by the Bolshevik revolutionary and Soviet politician Maxim Litvinov. In 1931, Williams-Ellis visited the Soviet Union with his wife, a children's author with Communist sympathies, Amabel (1894-1984), who arranged the official invitation for her husband.

The most unusual guest in Romney's house came when it was occupied by Williams-Ellis. It was Betsy, a simian introduced to the house by the zoologist Sir Solly Zuckerman (1904-1993). Williams-Ellis wrote that Sir Solly:

"... wished one of his research baboons on to us, as he wanted to study its reactions to 'bright, intelligent young society' ... so his Betsy had quarters on the flat roof at the top of the house for several months. Not the social success we had hoped..."

Williams-Ellis and his family left Hampstead to live in Wales when WW2 broke out.

So, much has happened on this plot of land, which used to be the site of the stables of Cloth Hill, a house that existed in the 17th century before it was replaced by Romney's former Hampstead residence.

A small lane, Holly Mount, starts close to Romney's house. A few yards along it, stands the picturesque Holly Bush pub. Barratt related that in the late 18th century and early 19th, some meetings of the then flourishing Hampstead Dinner Club (founded 1784) were held in this hostelry, which is housed in a building constructed in the 1790s. He noted:

"The meetings of the Dinner Club served a very useful purpose, providing a gathering ground for the leading local lights, enabling them to express their views on the questions of the hour, and to encourage patriotic efforts in times of national trial—for those later Georgian days were days of anxiety and conflict, both abroad and at home. In October 1790, while discussing the probabilities of war, two of the members were prompted to make a bet on the subject, which was thus recorded in the minutes: "Mr.Creed lays a dozen of claret, that there will be war betwixt England and Spain within three months, and Mr. Bowles lays the contrary."

The building in which the pub is located was first built as a residence. It then housed some 'Assembly Rooms', before becoming a pub in 1928. It is a quaint place to enjoy a pint or two.

To the north of Romney's house is Fenton House, built about 1693. It was once owned by the Riga merchant PI Fenton, who bought it in 1793. Now maintained by the National Trust, it houses a fine collection of old keyboard instruments. In the 1960s when I first visited it, visitors were free to touch the instruments and make sounds or music. Now, this is forbidden unless you are a musician who has been given special permission to play them. Fenton House is next door to Bolton House and Volta House. These two and another, Windmill House, comprise a terrace constructed 1720-1730. The poet Joanna Baillie (1762-1851) lived in Bolton House between 1791 and 1851. Her guests at the house included John Constable, Walter Scott, William Wordsworth, Lord Byron, and John Keats. The street on which these buildings and Fenton House stand, Windmill Hill, was so named in 1709, probably because there had been a windmill nearby in the 17th century, if not before.

Windmill Hill is not more than three minute's walking distance from the first place that John Constable rented in Hampstead during the summer of 1819, Albion Cottage, which according to Wade, adjoined Whitestone House, on Whitestone Lane, close to Whitestone Pond. While he was there, he painted *Hampstead Heath, with the House Called 'The Salt Box'*, which is in the collection of the Tate Gallery. Whitestone House is next door to another residence, Gangmoor, built in the 18th century. With a fine view over the Heath, this was once the home of the cartoonist George Du Maurier (1834-1896) in the 1860s, and then later of the physiologist the late Professor Sebastian Dicker, who planted many saplings in the garden. These, which he dug up on his walks on the Heath, have now grown so large that the cottage cannot be seen from the road. Between the Pond and Romney's house, the terraced house that Constable rented in the summers of 1821 and 1822 still stands. Barratt related:

"It was at No. 2 Lower Terrace that the couple and their three children first took up their abode. The house was small; but comfortable and in close proximity to the picturesque scenes the artist wanted to study and depict. He kept on his studio in Keppel Street, but was as much as possible at Hampstead with his family."

In the last of a series lectures he gave to the Royal Institution in Albermarle Street in 1836, Constable emphasised his systematic approach to depicting nature, by saying:

"Painting is a science and should be pursued as an inquiry into the laws of nature. Why, may not landscape painting be considered a branch of natural philosophy, of which pictures are but the experiments?"

One of Hampstead's attractions for Constable was its wide expanse of sky, which, as Barratt wrote, the artist:

"… regarded as the keynote of landscape art, and so assiduously did he study cloud, sky, and atmosphere in the Hampstead days that Leslie, his biographer, was able to become possessed of twenty of these special studies, each dated and described. Constable was a man of Wordsworthian simplicity of character, fond of all things rural, and devotedly attached to birds and animals."

The website of Cambridge's Fitzwilliam Museum reinforces what Barratt wrote:

"While living at Hampstead, Constable made a series of oil sketches of the sky alone, each one marked with the date, time and a short description of the conditions. His interest in clouds was influenced partly by the work of the scientist Luke Howard, who had in 1803 written a pioneering study, classifying different types of cloud ..."

In *The Invention of Clouds* by Richard Hamblyn, a biography of the chemist and amateur meteorologist, who devised the modern classification of clouds (cumulus, nimbus, etc.), Luke Howard (1772-1864), it is noted that Constable, who was familiar with Howard's work, focussed his concentration:

"... on the extension of his observational range and clouds were the means that he had chosen for the task. After years of searching for an isolated image, seeking a motif upon which to weigh his technical advancement as a painter, he had found it at last in the unending sequences of clouds that emerged and dissolved before his eyes like images on a photographic plate."

During the summers of 1821 and 1822, Constable made over one hundred cloud studies on the higher ground of Hampstead and its heath. Writing in 1964 in his *The Philosophy of Modern Art*, the art critic Herbert Read (1893-1968), who lived in Hampstead, commented that Constable was:

"... rather a modest craftsman, interested in the efficiency of his tools, the chemistry of his materials, the technique of his craft. His preparatory 'sketches' are no more romantic than a weather report. But they are accurate, they are vividly expressed, they are truthful."

Read next contrasted Constable with Turner, pointing out that the former was far more attentive to depicting nature accurately than the latter, who became increasingly extravagant in his portrayal of it, increasingly moving towards what is now called 'expressionist'. Barratt wrote that although Constable admired Turner, he had no desire to imitate him and:

"He knew his limits, and recognised that within those limits were to be found subjects worthy of the highest aspirations. "I was born to paint a happier land," he wrote, "my own dear England; and when I cease to love her may I, as Wordsworth says, — 'never more hear er green leaves rustle or her torrents roar..'"

In 1827, having become wealthier, Constable rented a little house for him and his family to live long term. This was number 40 Well Walk. He wrote a letter to an acquaintance, Fisher, on the 26th of August 1827, in which he noted:

"We are at length fixed in our comfortable little house in Well Walk, Hampstead, and are once more enjoying our own furniture, and sleeping in our own beds. My plans in search of health for my family have been ruinous; but I hope now that our movable camp no longer exists, and that I am settled for life. So hateful is moving about to me, that I could gladly exclaim, 'Here let me take my everlasting rest!' The rent of this house is fifty-two pounds per annum, taxes twenty-five, and what I have spent on it, ten or fifteen."

Constable and his family were often troubled by ill-health. He lost his wife, who died of tuberculosis in 1828, leaving him to care for their seven children. A letter he wrote to his friend and biographer, the painter Charles Robert Leslie (1794-1859), from Well Walk on the 20th of January 1834 illustrates this:

"My dear Leslie. I have been sadly ill since you left England, and my mind has been so much depressed that I have scarcely been able to do any one thing, and in that state I did not like to write to you … Poor John has been very ill; walking in his sleep at school, he fell and brought on erysipelas; he was six weeks in bed, and on his return to Hampstead for the holidays, he took a rheumatic fever, and was confined for a month. I do not think I shall send the boys again to Folkestone."

Constable remained in Hampstead until his death and was buried in the churchyard of St John's parish church. The artist is known to have made a great number of paintings and sketches of Hampstead and its rural landscapes. Many of these can be viewed in art galleries in the UK.

Romney and Constable are probably the best-known of the pre-20th century artists, who lived and/or worked in Hampstead, but they were far from having been the only painters attracted to the area before 1900, as can be seen from what I quoted from the book about Nollekens at the beginning of this chapter.

MODERN ARTISTS AND THE ISOKON

My parents knew a painter, an emigrant from Germany, Walter Nessler (1912-2001). They bought several of his paintings, which used to hang in our living room. Born in Leipzig, a gentile opposed to the Nazis, he arrived in England in the 1937, soon after his work was pronounced 'degenerate' by the German authorities. At first, he was interned as an enemy alien in Huyton Camp near Liverpool during WW2. After the war, he bought a house in West

Hampstead, in which he had his studio. I suppose my parents must have known him because he had studied sculpture with Elizabeth Frink at the St Martins School of Art in 1959, when my mother, a sculptor and close friend of Frink, was also using the sculpture workshops at St Martins. Nessler, whom I met when I was a child, was one of many artists (and architects) who fled from Europe after Hitler's dictatorship commenced. Some of these people, far better-known than Nessler, spent some time in Hampstead. In 2020, the art historian Caroline Maclean, published her *Circles and Squares. The Lives & Art of the Hampstead Modernists*. Although she concentrates more on the lives and art of the Modernists than on Hampstead, it is a useful introduction to the artists who lived in the area during the first half of the 20th century.

Early in the 20th century, the Australian artist Henry Lamb (1883-1960), not a Modernist but a founder of the Camden Town Group of post-impressionist artists in 1911, had a studio at the top of the Vale Hotel in the Vale of Health. It was in Lamb's studio that the now better-known Stanley Spencer (1891-1959) created his oil painting, *The Roundabout*, in 1923. This fairground apparatus was in the grounds next to the hotel and is depicted as viewed from above. Spencer, who also had a studio in the hotel, painted at least one other picture of Hampstead, *The Vale of Health, Hampstead, London*, which is now in a museum in Glasgow. According to Spencer's biographer Kenneth Pople, Spencer first met Lamb in about 1913 at the hotel in the Vale.

In February 1925, Spencer married the artist Hilda Carline (1889-1950), sister of the war artist Richard Carline (1896-1980), and they lived for two years in the Vale of Health Hotel, where they shared a studio. Richard Carline lived in Hampstead's Downshire Hill (number 47), at which many of the local artists used to meet in the 1920s, several of whom, like Spencer, had studied at The Slade School of Fine Art in London. Richard Carline painted a picture depicting one of these gatherings. The following artists are shown in the painting: Stanley Spencer, James Wood, Kate Foster, Hilda Carline, Richard Hartley, Henry Lamb, and Anne and Sidney Carline. It was in Downshire Hill that the artist, writer, and promoter of the Surrealists, Roland Penrose (1900-1984), and his second wife, the photographer Lee Miller (1907-1977), lived at number 21. Penrose moved in during the 1930s, and by the start of WW2 he was living there with Miller. When the war broke out, Penrose joined the Air Raid Protection Force. Miller's biographer, Carolyn Burke, related:

"... Lee prepared for "siege, starvation, invasion." "I figured out that if it were coming to ... a diet of potatoes, field mice and snails ... I might as well make them taste nice, so the only hoarding I did was truffles – pimentos – spices and all things nice ..."

Meanwhile, Penrose, Burke wrote:

"... installed an air-raid shelter, painted pink and blue, in the garden, with a Barbara Hepworth sculpture near the entrance ..."

Near the house occupied by Miller and Penrose, St John's Downshire Hill is a lovely church with an elegant façade and some neo-classical decorative features.

Its construction was completed in 1823. It was built as a proprietary chapel, a chapel belonging to a private individual but open to the public. The church's website informs that:

"In 1813, the land on which the building stands was bought by a distinctive trio: builder William Woods, lawyer Edward Carlisle and James Curry, a Christian minister who financed the venture and would take charge of the church when the building was finished. St John's is one of a number of churches dating from the 18th and 19th centuries which were privately financed in this way, rather than being under the control of the parish church."

The church's freehold has passed through several owners since the building was completed. Currently, it is the only remaining proprietary chapel in the Diocese of London, and one of the few last surviving examples in the country.

Downshire Hill was home to at least two other artists. One was John Heartfield (1891-1968), who lived there between 1938 and 1943. On a commemorative plaque outside his house, he is described as "Master of Political Photomontage". Born in Germany as Helmut Herzfeld, he was an artist who employed art, and in particular photomontage, as a political weapon. He was anti-Nazi and fled Germany in 1933, arriving in England in 1938, having spent some time in Czechoslovakia. More recently, another artist, quite different from Heartfield, lived in Downshire Hill between 1979 and his death. He was the creator of The Muppets, Jim Henson (1936-1990). Between Heartfield's and Henson's houses, there is a superb example of adventurous 20th century architecture, number 49a Downshire Hill, The Hopkins House designed by Michael Hopkins in about

1976. In its sophisticated simplicity, it is a dramatic contrast to all the other buildings along the road. Lovers of contemporary architecture should wander down Keats Grove, which branches off Downshire Hill, to see another fine example of a recent residential edifice, almost opposite Keats House.

Heartfield's home on Downshire Hill has a peculiar feature, which might have been added long after he lived there. It is a weathervane. That is not a particularly unusual embellishment, but on closer examination, it is not a run-of-the-mill British weathervane. Weathervanes in England often have the four points of the compass abbreviated as NSEW, that is, north, south, east, and west. The one on Heartfield's former home has the letters NSOE. At first, I thought that the O was an abbreviation for the German for east, 'Ost'. If the weathervane was German, it should have had the letters NSOW. Then, I thought that the O might be an abbreviation for the word for west in Italian, Portuguese, Spanish or French. This makes sense because the other points of the compass in those languages are abbreviated: N, S, and E. I suspect that the weathervane was added after Heartfield's time.

Apart from Lee Miller, there was another photographer of note living in Downshire Hill, at number 9. This was the home of the writer and photographer Allen Chappelow (1919-2006). Amongst his publications was a biography of George Bernard Shaw, whom he met on a few occasions and photographed. Amongst Chappelow's many other achievements, he was on the first British students tour of the USSR made just after Stalin died, and the first trip made by a British tourists to Communist Albania after 1945. He visited the country again in the early 1990s after the end of its Communist era. In his later years, he became a recluse. Sadly, he came to an unpleasant end, bludgeoned to death in his home on Downshire Hill. His life and death and the unusual trial of his alleged murderer are described in a superb book, *Blood on the Page*, by Thomas Harding, who was brought up in Hampstead. The trial was starnge because some of it was held *in camera*, for reasons that have not yet been revealed, and might never be.

Returning to Hampstead's modern artists before WW2, the roundabout, painted by Spencer, was also painted by Richard Carline and Mark Gertler (1891-1939). The latter moved to Hampstead in late 1914. According to Caroline Maclean, Gertler, who studied alongside Spencer and Carline, moved into the studios near New End, Well Mount Studios, in 1915, and painted his well-known *Merry-Go-Round* in 1916. This painting, which is in the collection held by the Tate Gallery, was inspired by a special funfair that was held on Hampstead Heath in 1915 on behalf of wounded soldiers and sailors. The painting is believed to reflect that artist's reaction to war. He was a conscientious objector. Later, Gertler lived at several other addresses in Hampstead in addition to Well Road: The Vale of Health, 13a Rudall Crescent, and 53 Haverstock Hill.

The arrival of Lamb, and then artists such as Spencer, Gertler, and the Carlines, in Hampstead during the early part of the 20th century, heralded, and maybe also attracted, more artists, both British and émigré, to Hampstead in the period before WW2. Whether it was the availability of dedicated studio space or the presence of the earlier artistic arrivals, I cannot tell, but during the 1920s and 1930s, Hampstead became a magnet for artists, many of whom are included in Maclean's book about the Modernists. What is clear from her book, as well as that by Pople, is that there were complex interactions between the artists, both professional and social. One factor that attracted artists to Hampstead was the economic decline in the 1920s, which, as pointed out by Maclean, led to a fall in the cost of accommodation in and around Hampstead, making it more affordable for artists to live and work there.

Well Mount Studios, close to the former New End Hospital, looks like a small industrial unit with two sloping roofs each with large skylights along one side of Well Road. The studios were built in the late 19th century. The building's exterior is not particularly attractive, but its interior was tastefully renewed in 2003. These were not the only purpose-built artist's studios erected in late 19th century Hampstead. During the 1870s and 1880s, as Hampstead expanded, several large houses with studios and large north facing windows favoured by painters, were built for successful artists, many of them designed by the architects Battersbury and Huxley. In 1879, Thomas Batterbury built the Wychcombe Studios near to Englands Lane in Belsize Park, a southern part of Hampstead. They have double-height studio windows. In 1872, Battersbury built The Mall Studios close to Parkhill Road, just south of old Hampstead village. Initially, these were used by artists including Robert Macbeth (1848-1910), Sir George Clausen (1852-1944), Thomas Danby (c1817-1886),

Walter Sickert (1860-1942), and Arthur Rackham (1867-1939), the illustrator. The studios are described in Maclean's book:

"...they included small waiting rooms, costume rooms, a lobby and 'other necessary conveniences'. They had three skylights each and large north-facing windows... the dados, or lower parts of the wall, were originally painted different colours from the higher parts to offer a background to pictures..."

The sculptor Henry Moore (1898-1986) lived close to the Mall Studios at 11a Parkhill Road from 1929 until 1940. He had studied with Barbara Hepworth (1903-1975) at the Leeds school of Art. Between 1927 and 1939, Hepworth worked and lived at the Mall Studios, initially with her first husband, the sculptor John Skeaping (1901-1980) and then (after 1931) with her second, the painter Ben Nicholson (1894-1982), who died in Hampstead (at a house in Pilgrims Lane). Others who lived and worked at Mall Studios included the influential art historian and critic Herbert Read (1893-1968). Not far from the studios, the painter Paul Nash (1889-1946) lived at number 3 Eldon Grove between 1936 and 1939. Close by at 60 Parkhill Road the artist Piet Mondrian (1872-1944) lived and worked between 1938 and 1941. Prior to moving to Parkhill Road, Mondrian had lived with a remarkable engineer and furniture entrepreneur Jack Pritchard (1899-1992).

Jack and his family lived at 37 Belsize Park Gardens, having moved there from Platts Lane. Pritchard, who studied engineering and economics at the University of Cambridge, joined Venesta, a company that specialised in plywood goods. It was after this that he began to promote Modernist design. In 1929, he and the Canadian architect Wells Coates (1895-1958) formed the company, Isokon, whose aim was to build Modernist style residential accommodation. Pritchard and his wife, a psychiatrist, Molly (1900-1985), commissioned Coates to build a block of flats in Lawn Road on a site that they owned. Its design was to be based on the then revolutionary new communal housing projects that they had visited in Germany, including at the influential Bauhaus in Dessau.

The resulting Lawn Road Flats are close to both Fleet Road and the Mall Studios in Parkhill Road. Completed in 1934, they were, noted the architectural historian Nikolaus Pevsner, "… a milestone in the introduction of the modern idiom to London." He wrote that the edifice:

"…put on a forbidding face towards the street, with large unmitigated concrete surfaces … It is all in the spirit of revolution, unaccommodating and direct to the verge of brutality."

The open-air passages (outdoor corridors on each floor) linking the neighbouring apartments and the service elements of the building face the street. The windows on the side of the Flats away from the street face an untamed sloping area of vegetation, which to this day has remained undeveloped, and is now a nature reserve called Belsize Wood. I like the building's elegant, sculptural simplicity; it has stood the test of time and enhances its surroundings. In the basement space of the block, there was a refreshment area known as the Isobar, where food and drink were served to tenants and their guests. This and its furniture were designed by Marcel Breuer (1902-1981). Regularly, exhibitions were held in the Isobar and, according to an on-line article in *The Modern House Journal* these were attended by artists including Adrian Stokes, Henry Moore, Barbara Hepworth, Ben Nicholson and Naum Gabo. The article also noted that this refreshment area was frequented by modernist architects such as Erich Mendelsohn, Serge Chermayeff and, Wells Coates, as well as by left-wing politicians. Pritchard occupied the penthouse flat. In 1969, he sold the block, and now it contains accommodation for 25 keyworkers on a shared ownership basis and 11 flats are in private ownership. The block, first known as the 'Lawn Road Flats', is now called 'Isokon. Lawn Road Flats'.

T F T Baker, Diane K Bolton and Patricia E C Croot, writing in *A History of the County of Middlesex: Volume 9, Hampstead, Paddington*, noted that the Lawn Road Flats were built partly to house artistic refugees, who had fled from parts of Europe then oppressed by dictators, notably by Adolf Hitler. Some of them had been associated with the Bauhaus. These included the architect and furniture designer Marcel Breuer, the architect Walter Gropius (1883-1969), and the artist and photographer Laszlo Moholy-Nagy (1895-1946). All three are regarded as masters of 20th century visual arts.

Despite both having come from bourgeois backgrounds, the Pritchards aimed to free themselves from middle-class conventions. The concept and realisation of the Lawn Road Flats were important landmarks in their quest to achieve a new, alternative way of living. The atmosphere that prevailed in the community that either lived in, or frequented, the Lawn Road Flats and its Isobar was predominantly left-wing, and extremely welcoming to cultural refugees from

104

Nazi Germany. Probably, it had not been anticipated that the place would become a convenient place for Stalin's Soviet spies to use as a base. According to a small booklet about the flats, *Isokon The Story of a New Vision of Urban Living*, published in 2016, the flats were home to the following espionage agents, who had been recruited by Soviet intelligence agencies in Central Europe: Arnold Deutsch, Simon Kremer, Jürgen Kuczinski, and Brigitte Kucynski Lewis. Jill Pearlman, one of the book's several authors, noted that they found the Lawn Road Flats convenient for several reasons:

"Above all, they blended inconspicuously into the sociable community of tenants there. Many tenants too were refugees from Central Europe … Even the Lawn Road Flats building worked well for the spies. One could enter and exit any unit without being seen … no one could see in. At the same time, the cantilevered decks on each floor provided the tenants a perfect vantage point from which to survey the street below."

Two of the many people, who lived in the flats before the end of WW2 were the sculptor Henry Moore and novelist Agatha Christie (1890-1976). In his fascinating book *The Lawn Road Flats*, David Burke wrote that Moore was already living in one of the flats by September 1940. The flats are near the Belsize Park and Hampstead Underground stations, both of which have platforms far beneath ground level. These became very crowded at night when they were used to shelter civilians trying to avoid the bombs being dropped by the Germans. It was in these stations that Moore made many of his now familiar sketches of the conditions in these makeshift shelters. An article in the Tate Gallery's website noted:

"Moore's Shelter Drawings, which became official 'war art', transformed his reputation, bringing success at home and internationally. They depict a mass of almost skeletal figures huddled together in a nocturnal underworld. Angered by their poverty, Moore described the crowds he had witnessed sheltering from bombing raids in the London Underground as "the most pathetic, sordid, & disheartening sight".

Agatha Christie and her husband, the archaeologist Max Mallowan (1904-1978), took up residence in one of the Lawn Road Flats in 1941, when the Blitz was at is most intense. They had moved to London from Devon in mid-1940. Burke explained that prior to moving in, they had had a London residence first in Mayfair, and then after the bombing worsened, in Kensington's Sheffield Terrace. By March 1941, conditions in the Kensington area had become too dangerous and the couple moved to the relative safety of the Lawn Road Flats. They were introduced to the Pritchards and the Flats by one of its tenants, Mallowan's colleague the archaeologist Stephen Glanville (1900-1956). Agatha and Max spent a pleasant year in the Flats. Max was doing war work and Agatha was assisting medical work at University College Hospital. While at Lawn Road, Agatha was able to write several books and plays including her only spy novel, *N or M*.

The Lawn Road Flats were, fortuitously, well-designed to resist bomb damage. David Burke wrote that in 1938, JBS Haldane (1882-1964) published his book about air raid protection, *Air Raid Precautions*, in which he stated that ferro-concrete buildings with a steel frame were much more difficult to destroy than brick buildings. The Flats were built precisely this way and consequently were amongst the safest buildings in London during aerial bombardment. Many buildings around the block of flats were destroyed but the Isokon remained standing, albeit with a few windows shattered. Burke quotes one of the former tenants, a retired US intelligence agent who lived in the Flats from 1948, Charles Fenn (1907-2004), who summarised the joys of living in the Isokon Flats in the *Guardian* newspaper in 1992:

"This building ... turned its back on the street and its face to the wilderness, so that the widows looked out upon what seemed open countryside. As in a well-constructed yacht, the flats offered *multum in parvo*, and at what seemed a very low rent. Breakfast, if required, was served to each flat. Cleaners ... serviced the flats daily: shoes were cleaned each morning by the porter, the attached club served meals and drinks ... Close by were a tube station, a bus depot, Hampstead Heath, and excellent second-hand bookshops and junk-shops"

Today, the Isobar is no longer; it was converted into a flat. There is a small exhibition area in one of the garages of the flats. This is open occasinally, but I have yet to visit it.

Both Breuer and Moholy-Nagy were Hungarians, as was the architect Ernő Goldfinger (1902-1987). In 1934, he and his wife moved to London where they first lived in a modernistic block of flats in Highgate, Highpoint I, which had been designed by the Russian born Constructivist architect Berthold Lubetkin (1901-1990). Lubetkin had left the USSR in 1931 and settled in Hampstead alongside the artistic community associated with Herbert Read and others in or near the Mall Studios. The Goldfingers moved out of Highpoint and after living at various addresses away from Hampstead, they bought a plot at number 2 Willow Road, close to Downshire Hill. Goldfinger's original plans were rejected by the London County Council in 1936. A year later, he submitted another design, but this met with many objections to concrete buildings, including from Henry Brooke, Baron Brooke of Cumnor (1903-1984). who was then Secretary of the Heath and Old Hampstead Protection Society. However, various local residents, including Roland Penrose, were in favour of his design. The website of the National Trust, which now maintains the building that was finally erected in 1939, noted:

"Goldfinger explained that very little concrete would be exposed to view, and that it would conform to the surroundings and tradition of Georgian building in London. The houses were completed in the summer of 1939, shortly before the outbreak of the Second World War. Ironically, when 2 Willow Road was eventually handed over to us in 1993, it was by Peter Brooke, the then Heritage Secretary and the son of Lord Brooke, the property's most vocal opponent."

This modernist structure, a terrace of three residential units, met with the approval of the often-stern architectural critic, the historian Nikolaus Pevsner. He wrote of Goldfinger's home:

"Here is the contemporary style in an uncompromising form, yet by the use of brick and by sheer scale, the terrace goes infinitely better with the Georgian past of Hampstead than anything Victorian."

Goldfinger designed much of the furniture in his house, the middle one of the three homes in the terrace. In 1942, Goldfinger, who had Marxist sympathies, hosted an exhibition of leading artists in his house to raise funds for "Aid to Russia". The house contains his good collection of books and some 20th century art. Visitors are given a good, guided tour at the limited times when it is open.

By now, it should be evident that during the first half of the 20th century, Hampstead had, for several reasons, become a nucleus of visual artists of various kinds. The occasionally intimate relations between them, as exemplified by Barbara Hepworth and Ben Nicholson, have been described in the book by Caroline Maclean. After WW2, many of these creators had left Hampstead. Much of what I have described, possibly apart from what I know of Walter Nessler, is known to many and has often been written about, and it is this relatively recent connection with the development of modern art in Britain that adds to Hampstead's Bohemian reputation.

BOLSHEVISM AND HEATH STREET

I have already mentioned the Soviet Union's Ambassador, Ivan Maisky, visiting Williams-Ellis in his house on Holly Hill. This steeply inclined lane meets Heath Street near to Hampstead Underground station not far from Café Louis. One day in 2020, after having been confined to our locality (Kensington) for three months by strict 'lockdown' rules, we drove to Hampstead, and enjoyed cups of coffee at a tiny outdoor table at Louis. I looked across Heath Street from where we were sitting and stared at the Hampstead branch of Tesco's. This run-of-the-mill supermarket, rather surprising for upmarket Hampstead, is housed in a building with light red tiling and brickwork with stone window settings. Above Tesco's, there is an old sign in bas-relief that reads "EXPRESS DAIRY COMPANY LTD" and next to that, there is a plaque with the date "AD 1889". The year 1889 has had a special significance for me ever since I attended the Hall School, a prestigious preparatory school for boys near Swiss Cottage. The school was founded in 1889 and celebrated its 75th anniversary in 1964, while I was still studying there. Maybe because of this, my mind is always alert to that year. The founding of a preparatory school in 1889 is a relatively insignificant reason to remember the year. More importantly it was the 100th anniversary of the French Revolution and the year of the completion of the Eiffel Tower in Paris. Before sitting at that outdoor table at Louis in 2020, I knew about 1889 in connection with what I have mentioned already, but nothing about the former Express Dairy in Hampstead bearing the plaque with the date 1889. The other buildings on that stretch of Heath Street, which was built-up in the Victorian era, were, like the dairy, mostly constructed in the late 1880s.

For many centuries, Hampstead has been the haunt of people involved in creative pursuits. So, it was no surprise that the former Express Dairy opposite Louis had at least one interesting cultural connection. In February 1916, the

110

Bolshevik revolutionary Maxim Litvinov (1856-1951) proposed to his future wife Ivy Low in the café inside that branch of Express Dairy. Ivy, a novelist, was born, please note, in 1889 (she died in 1977). At the time he became acquainted with Ivy, Litvinov was with Lenin in London. Ivy did occasional typing for Maxim, and it was not long before they were attracted to one another. Passionate about cinema, he took her to watch films with him and one day he 'popped the question' in the Express Dairy. After they married, they lived in Hampstead until the outbreak of the Russian Revolution in October 1917. They did not return to Russia immediately because in January 1918 Maxim Litvinoff was made First Proletarian Envoy to the Court of St. James's.

According to Zinovy Sheinis in his biography of Maxim first published in 1988, Maxim often went to Hampstead to meet his friends the Klyshkos, who lived on Hampstead High Street. Nikolai Klyshko (1880-1937) was a Bolshevik revolutionary of Polish parentage, who had settled in London and was a fluent Russian speaker. For a brief period, Litvinov lived in Hampstead with Klyshko and his English wife. Sheinis wrote about Maxim's meeting with Ivy:

"They had met at a friend's house. Then at a gathering of the Fabian Society. Litvinov was impressed by her knowledge of Tolstoy and Chekhov. Putting on weight, red-haired, of average height, well-mannered, and not very talkative, he made a big impression on the young writer. Her mother, the daughter of a colonel in the British Army, naturally wanted a different match for her daughter and certainly did not want to see her married to an insecure emigre from Russia. As for his religious background, Ivy Lowe simply never gave it a thought. She was herself from a family of Hungarian Jews who had taken part in the Kossuth uprising; in her girlhood she had been a Protestant, then had been converted to Catholicism. The choice of religion was her private affair and concerned no one else."

After their marriage, they lived in a house, owned by Belgian refugees, in Hampstead's South Hill Park (number 86). While there, Sheinis related:

"Friends sometimes gathered there in the evenings to discuss the political news; then an argument would flare up, developing into a fierce squabble. It always seemed to Ivy that her husband and his guests would any moment start flinging chairs at one another. At the very height of the dispute, when it was almost at boiling-point, she would leave the kitchen, go into the room, and announce that tea or coffee was ready. The disputants would calm down and drink their tea in peace."

He also wrote that Ivy:

"… was not interested in and did not understand the political activities of her husband and his friends. To her, it was an alien world. In London, after the October Revolution, she asked her husband if he knew Lenin. Maxim replied that he had known Lenin for a long time. But she had no idea that letters from Lenin were coming to their house and that her flat was the headquarters of Bolshevik emigres."

Later, they lived in a tiny house in West Hampstead. After that, Litvinov, having become a Soviet diplomat, moved from Hampstead. Despite not being officially accredited by the British, Sheinis noted:

"The Litvinovs were even invited to receptions. Though Soviet Russia was not yet recognised, its powerful influence reached standoffish London, Ivy Litvinova recollected."

By 1921, the Litvinovs with their two young children, at least one of whom was born in Hampstead, settled in Moscow. Although Litvinov held high governmental posts in the Soviet Union and outside it (as a Soviet diplomat), he and Ivy, like so many other citizens in Stalin's Russia, were constantly in fear of being arrested and/or killed.

Almost opposite the former Express Dairy on Heath Street there is another building that bears a foundation stone with the year 1889. It is on the building that housed the Hampstead Liberal Club between 1889 and 1925. The stone was laid in July 1889 by the barrister and Liberal politician Sir Charles Russell QC MP. He was Charles Russell, Baron Russell of Killowen (1832-1900), an advocate of Irish Home Rule. He defended the Irish nationalist politician Charles Stewart Parnell successfully during the Parnell Commission trial (1888-89). The case ended in February 1889, a few months before he laid the foundation stone of the unremarkable building, which was designed by the architects, Spalding and Cross.

Litvinov and Maisky were not the only links between Hampstead and Soviet Russia. Another memorable personality, who shared this connection is discussed in the next chapter.

Branch Hill, according to Wade, was an old track to Childs Hill. Now the northern continuation of Frognal, it appears in several of John Constable's paintings. Recently, when we were walking along it, I spotted a commemorative plaque that I had not noticed before. Close to a house where the singer Paul Robeson (1898-1976) lived for one year, it commemorates a person, whom I had never come across before. The plaque reads:

"Alfred Reynolds, Hungarian poet and philosopher lived here 1980-1993"

Before discussing Reynolds, here is something about his erstwhile neighbour the bass-baritone Paul Robeson. Born in the USA, Robeson was extremely conscious of the often violent, hostility to black people in that country. In the 1920s he was a hit in the London premiere (1928) of the musical *Showboat*. Robeson and his wife Eslanda became frequent visitors to London, which they found much more congenial than the States, but by 1929 his allegiance to Communism attracted the attention of the British police. Despite this, the couple rented a house called The Chestnuts in Branch Hill, which faces a slope of Hampstead Heath that leads up to Whitestone Pond. While in Hampstead, Robeson and his wife were, according to Christopher Wade:

"...lionised in Hampstead by a distinguished crowd including his near neighbour, Ramsay MacDonald."

MacDonald (1866-1937), Britain's first Labour Prime Minister lived from 1925 until his death at number 103 Frognal, a Georgian house built in 1745 by Henry Flitcroft. Between 1916 and 1925, he had lived at Hampstead's number 9 Howitt

114

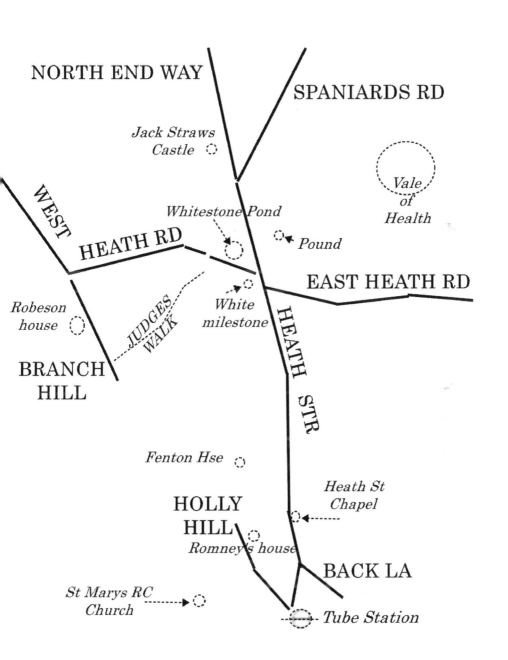

NORTH END WAY

SPANIARDS RD

Jack Straws
Castle ⟳

WEST

HEATH RD

Whitestone Pond

Pound

Vale
of
Health

EAST HEATH RD

Robeson
house ⟳

JUDGES
WALK

White
milestone

HEATH STR

BRANCH
HILL

Fenton Hse ⟳

HOLLY
HILL

Romney's house

Heath St
Chapel

BACK LA

St Marys RC
Church

Tube Station

115

Road. After its occupation by MacDonald, the house in Frognal was owned by the American screenwriter Donal Ogden Stewart (1894-1980) in the 1950s. The *Ham & High* newspaper noted on the 30th of October 2015:

"Hollywood legends including W.E.B Dubois, Charlie Chaplin, Ingrid Bergman and Katherine Hepburn visited him at the property when he lived there between 1953 and 1980."

The Robesons occupied The Chestnuts on Branch Hill between 1929 and 1930, before moving to number 19 Buckingham Street, near The Strand. In late 1934, Robeson made his first visit to the USSR. Professor Maxim Matusevich of Seton Hall University recorded in his article (https://blogs.shu.edu/) about this that Robeson:

"…fell in love with the land and its people. By all accounts, including his own, he received an exceptionally warm reception, which stood in grotesque contrast to the harrowing experience of his layover in the rapidly nazifying Berlin. During that first visit the Robesons stayed at the famed Hotel National, in the suite that a year earlier had been used as the living quarters of America's first ambassador in Moscow, William Bullitt. Robeson was familiar with the experiences of other African Americans who visited or resided in the Soviet Union during this era and whose experiences on such trips were almost universally and overwhelmingly positive."

Robeson, who suffered during the USA's McCarthy era, continued making visits to Russia well after the end of WW2.

Returning to Alfred Reynolds, sadly the two most knowledgeable Hungarians I knew, who might have known something about him are both dead: our family friend the philosopher Imre Lakatos (1922-1974), who lived in Hampstead Garden Suburb, and one of my father's co-authors, the economist Peter Bauer (1915-2002). Searches of the Internet revealed little other biographical information in English apart from what is noted on Wikipedia. Alfred Reynolds (1907-1993) was born Reinhold Alfréd in Budapest, Hungary (the Hungarians put their surnames before their first names). His mother was Jewish and his father Roman Catholic. After graduating from the University of Leipzig in 1931, he founded a magazine called *Haladás* ('Progress'), which published the works of various Hungarian poets and was closed by the police soon after it began. Next, he founded another journal, a monthly with leftish tendencies called *Névtelen Jegyző* ('Anonymous Chronicler'), which was also soon closed by the police. After a brief spell as a member of the Communist Party of Hungary and a spell of imprisonment in Hungary, Alfred moved to the UK, to London, in 1936. During WW2, he served in the British Army, joining the Intelligence Corps in 1944. When the war was over, he became a leading light in the Bridge Circle, a group of libertarians. The group produced a journal called *London Letter*, some of whose articles were published in a book called *Pilate's question: Articles from 'The London Letter', 1948-1963*, which was released in 1964 and contains articles by Reynolds. In 1988, he published another book in English, *Jesus Versus Christianity*. The aim of this book, according to its 'blurb' on the Amazon website, was:

"...to redefine the prevailing image of Jesus of Nazareth. The author considers that Jesus remains a living figure reminding us of our humanity – the kingdom of Heaven within us. He argues that we should free the image of doctrinal encumbrance."

Prior to his arrival in England, Reynolds published his writings in Hungarian and those of other Hungarian poets, mostly in the journals he founded. Many of his papers, publications, and other memorabilia are currently on display at the Petőfi Literary Museum in Budapest. That is all I can tell you about Reynolds who spent the last years of his life in a fine house that affords good views over Hampstead Heath.

JUDGES WALK

Almost opposite Reynold's former home, a short staircase with narrow steps of unequal height leads from Branch Hill to a tree-lined footpath called Judges Walk. This pathway overlooks a steep northwest facing declivity that falls away sharply from Whitestone Pond. This was once the head of a tributary of the River Brent, which flows into the River Thames at Brentford. Today, apart from much mud in wet weather, there is little obvious evidence of the stream. Judges Walk has not always had that name. It has also been known as Prospect Walk on account of the views that may be obtained from it, which must have been better in the past than now because the vegetation lining the path might have been less dense. Part of that view has also been obstructed by buildings on Branch Hill. In days gone by, Judges Walk was a popular place for promenading. Barratt, writing in 1912, noted:

"Judges' Walk is naturally much resorted to for the beauty of its view and its splendid grove of limes and elms."

In 1745 when Church Row became a street lined with 'better-class' houses and the parish church was being rebuilt, it became a more fashionable place to promenade than Judges Walk.

How did Judges Walk get its name? William Howitt, author of *The Northern Heights of London* wrote:

"This avenue derives its name from the tradition that during the great plague of London the judges removed from Westminster, and held their courts in this very airy spot."

This derivation has been questioned both by GE Mitton in *Hampstead and Marylebone* (published in 1902), who commented that:

"… derivations of this sort are very easy to make up and entirely unreliable", and by Barratt, who wrote:

"If, as tradition asserts, the judges held their courts here in the time of the Plague, that is good enough ground for the title; but as no actual proof of this has hitherto been brought forward it is at least open to doubt."

However, he did not totally discount a connection of the path's name with the judiciary:

"...since so many judges have lived in this charming locality and been accustomed to take their walks up and down its famous avenue, it is only natural and in the fitness of things that it should be called Judges' Walk."

Christopher Wade noted that Judges Walk acquired its present name in the early 20th century, after having had a variety of names including 'Prospect walk', 'King's Bench Avenue', and 'Upper Terrace Avenue'. Like others before him, he was doubtful about the Great Plague theory. He suggested that the pathway was named after the nearby Branch Hill Lodge (at the bottom of the staircase mentioned above), which was once known as 'Judges' Bench House'. The house, long-since demolished, stood on the site now occupied by the present, rather unattractive Branch Hill Lodge built in the 19th century, which was the home of John Lewis (1836-1928), the founder of the store chain John Lewis. His home became named 'Spedan Towers', maybe to honour his eldest child John Spedan Lewis (1885-1963), who formed The John Lewis Partnership in 1928 after his father had died in Hampstead. The older (now demolished) house was redesigned in 1745 by the architect Henry Flitcroft (1697-1769) for the Master of the Rolls, Sir Thomas Clarke (1703-1764). It was later occupied by at least other two senior members of the English justice system, Sir Thomas Parker (1695-1784) and then the lawyer Alexander Wedderburn the Earl of Rosslyn (1733-1805) before he moved into his estate next to the present Rosslyn Hill.

Apart from the view from Judges Walk, which has been painted by the John Constable, there is a building covered with wood cladding (clapboarding) that

120

can be seen by looking away from the declivity. Entered from Windmill Hill, this house, whose foundations were laid in the late 18th century, is currently named 'Capo di Monte', having previously been known as 'Upper Terrace Cottage' and 'Siddons Cottage'. The actress Sarah Siddons (1755-1831) stayed there between 1804 and 1805. Barratt noted that the house:

"…was occupied by Woodburn the printseller; also, in succession, by Copley Fielding the artist, and Edward Magrath, the first secretary of the Athenaeum Club."

On the 11th of November 1846 Edward Magrath (1799-1859) received a letter (reproduced on https://epsilon.ac.uk) in which the scientist Michael Faraday (1791-1867) wrote:

"…I think tomorrow is your day at Hampstead and so I intend (and my wife too if Miss Magrath is at home at present) to reach Hampstead tomorrow & supposing it not inconvenient perhaps even to lunch with you about half past 12 oclk. But do not derange any previous intention of your own: if we do not get a biscuit at your house, we shall at the next bakers. The weather has been so dry that I do not like to put off my intention."

The British Museum has a letter written in 1847 to Magrath, thanking him for a gift of a collection of sketches of Hampstead, which he gave as a gift to the Royal Academy.

Years later, Capo di Monte was home to the art historian Kenneth Clark (1903-1983), and later of the broadcaster Marghanita Laski (1915-1988). No doubt some of these residents of Capo di Monte strolled along Judges Walk to take the air and enjoy the view. This vista was described in a novel, *Interplay* (published 1908), written by the suffragette Beatrice Harraden (1864-1936), who was born in Hampstead:

"She sat in Judges' Walk, and surveyed from there the stretches of wood and copse with their varying shades of green, relieved by delicate tones of red and enhanced in beauty by the sombreness of many trees which, even as ball-room belles, preferred to make a later and more consequential entrance into the scenes of splendour."

The eastern end of the short Judges Walk is close to Whitestone Pond, which figures in the next chapter.

WHITESTONE POND

"Four miles from St Giles Pound" and "four and a half miles from Holborn Bars" - these words are carved on a weathered, white, stone milepost close to Whitestone Pond at one of the highest places in north London. This pond in Hampstead got its current name because of its proximity to this white milepost. Originally known as 'Horse Pond', it was a place where horses could drink and wash their hooves. The pond was supplied with ramps to allow easier access for the horses. Although there are few horses to be seen in Hampstead nowadays, these ramps were preserved when the pond's surrounding banks were extensively renovated in 2010. The pond used to be supplied by dew and rainfall but was later kept filled by water from the mains water supply, which is fortunate given how little rain falls during some periods of the year. Being a shallow pool in an exposed location so high above sea level (443 feet), it is often covered with ice in cold weather.

To the east of Heath Street, where it runs alongside the pond, and several feet below it on the ground that slopes down towards the Vale of Health, there is a square walled enclosure. This is marked on 19th century maps as 'pound'. It was, according to the hampsteadheath.net website, used:

"…to hold roaming pigs. Pigs used to be taken to the Heath by their owners to root about for food, but stealing resources from the Heath was a punishable offence. An elderly keeper of the manor of St John's Hampstead, one John Stevenson, used to round up the pigs and hold them in the Pound."

When I was a child in the 1960s, it was easily visible from Heath Street but today, it is hidden from view by trees, but can be seen from the air (e.g., using Google maps). Writing in 1912, Barratt noted:

"There is still a pound in the hollow opposite the Whitestone Pond, on the eastern side of the Spaniards Road. This dates from 1787; it took the place of another pound, for having removed which a man was "presented" at the Manor Court … It is worth while noting that the gate of the existing pound had for its side supports two jaw-bones of a whale; these, having become warped or insecure, were removed some years ago."

More easily visible than the pound is tall flagstaff standing a few feet west of the pond. This marks the spot where there was once a beacon that formed part of a network of beacons that could be lit to communicate with each other during the 16th century when the threat of invasion by the Spanish navy was feared. The

123

beacon by the Pond was the northernmost of a series of beacons which originated on the cliffs at St Margarets near Dover. This network can be seen on old maps such as that drawn by William Lambarde (1536-1601) in 1570, several years before the arrival of the famous Spanish Armada. Currently, the only purpose of the tall white pole is to fly the red and white flag of the City of London high above the pond.

High as the pond is, it is not the highest point in Hampstead. That honour goes to the small observatory on the top of the reservoir just south of the pond. This point is 449 feet above sea level. The reservoir, according to the website www.ianclarkrestoration.com, is a:

"… wonderful example of mid-Victorian architecture … The reservoir and railings were constructed in 1856 for the New River Company to serve Hampstead with the water being delivered by pipes from Highgate. The company was absorbed into the Metropolitan Water Board in 1902."

The small observatory, perched on the reservoir, is topped with a dome. It was established in 1910 by the Hampstead Scientific Society and can be seen best from Lower Terrace. The first secretaries of the Society were two keen astronomers, Patrick Hepburn and Philip Edward Vizard, who wrote a short Hampstead guidebook. The first telescope, a ten-and-a-half-inch reflecting telescope, was donated by Colonel Henry Heberden on condition that it could be used by members of the public. In normal times, the observatory is open to the public on clear nights. At the beginning of the 20th century, nights were much clearer than they became later, and valuable observations were made. As time passed, both dust and light pollution have rendered it far more difficult to make any observations at all. In addition to astronomical uses, the observatory is home to a collection of devices used in meteorology. The weather station at the observatory has the longest continuous record of climate measurements for any still extant meteorological site in Greater London, having begun in 1909.

Returning to the Pond, I remember that during my childhood, the traffic around it used to be terrible, especially during rush-hours. It became even worse when police officers arrived to try to control it. While I was studying at Highgate School, there was an extremely bright boy in my year group, 'Blanco-White' was his surname. During physics classes, he appeared not to pay attention to the teacher because he was too busy designing complicated electronic circuits. When we took our physics mock O-Level examination, he was the only person in the class to pass it, exceeding the pass mark by a large margin. One morning, Blanco-White arrived at school and showed us a complicated diagram. It was his proposal for a scheme that should allow traffic to flow smoothly around Whitestone Pond (where five major roads meet). It is a long time since I saw the scheme that he designed, but I would not be surprised if it was almost the same as the much-improved traffic flow system that exists today and was only instituted a few years ago.

EAST HEATH ROAD AND SOUTH END GREEN

East Heath Road runs eastwards at first, then south-eastwards, descending from Whitestone Pond towards South End Green. The road marks the eastern edge of the spread of Hampstead into Hampstead Heath. Except for three well separated blocks of flats, there are no buildings on the eastern (i.e., Heath) side of the Road. A winding lane leads off the road to of the Vale of Health.

The block of flats facing Whitestone Pond at the top end of East Heath Road ('EHR') is called Bell Moor. Built in 1929, this edifice stands on the site of the house where the historian Thomas J Barratt (1841-1914) lived from 1877 to 1914. He was Chairman of the Pears soap manufacturing company and a pioneer in brand marketing, as well as a historian of Hampstead. His *Annals of Hampstead*, published in 1912, is a detailed, beautifully illustrated, three volume account of Hampstead's history, to which I refer often. Barratt was the creator of the successful Pears soap marketing campaign that used the words: "Good morning. Have you used Pears' soap?" In addition to a plaque commemorating Barratt on Bell Moor there are two others. One of them records that the conductor Sir Thomas Beecham (1879-1961) lived there from 1937-1941 and the other is placed to record that the surface of the soil at Bell Moor is 435 feet above sea level or 16.5 feet higher than the top of the cross on the dome of St Paul's Cathedral.

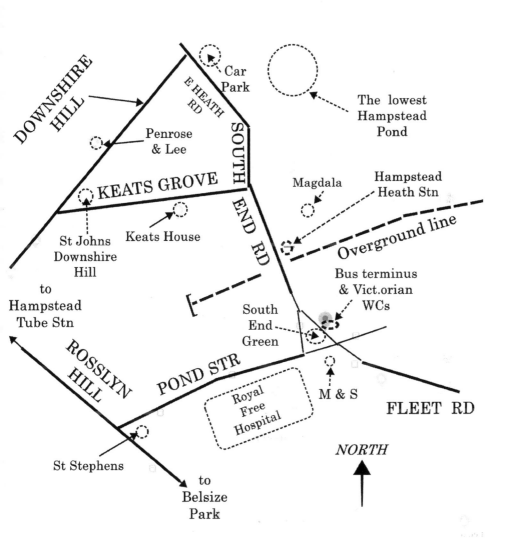

DOWNSHIRE HILL

E HEATH RD

Car Park

The lowest Hampstead Pond

Penrose & Lee

SOUTH END RD

KEATS GROVE

Magdala

Hampstead Heath Stn

St Johns Downshire Hill

Keats House

Overground line

to Hampstead Tube Stn

Bus terminus & Vict.orian WCs

South End Green

ROSSLYN HILL

POND STR

Royal Free Hospital

M & S

FLEET RD

St Stephens

NORTH

to Belsize Park

127

There are houses on the west side of EHR. The writer Katherine Mansfield (1888-1923) and her husband, the critic John Middleton Murry (1889-1957), lived at the end of a short Victorian terrace, at number 17 EHR (formerly 'Portland Villas'). Next door to this, there is a picturesque ivy-clad building, Heath Cottages, with one wall covered in wood cladding and a small balcony above one of its centrally placed pair of front doors. Barratt included a drawing of this building in his book but made no comment about it. A large house, The Logs, with an extravagant brick tower, eye-catching but not attractive, is reached further down EHR. This was built in 1868, designed by JS Nightingale for the drainage and water supply engineer and Justice of the Peace for Middlesex Edward Gotto (1822-1897). It has also been home to the comedian Marty Feldman and later the popular musician Boy George. The Logs neighbour, Foley House, has already been described.

Proceeding down EHR, we pass several large brick-built terraced houses and arrive at the corner of a lane called Heathside. A large house on the corner of this and EHR bears a plaque that notes that the composer Sir Arthur Bliss (1891-1975) lived here in East Heath Lodge from 1929 to 1939. It was in this house that the painter Mark Gertler painted the composer's portrait in 1932. During his residence on EHR, his musical compositions began to become less avant-garde, and Bliss became a musical successor to the composer Edward Elgar. I wonder whether living in a house with views over Hampstead Heath might have influenced his change in composing style.

East Heath Lodge, which was built in about 1785 by the local builder Henry White and modified in about 1820, is divided into two residences. Bliss occupied the eastern half of the building. A large bell hangs under a metal canopy outside the western half of the building, which bears the name 'South Lodge'. West of East Heath Lodge along Heathside, there are some large cottages built in about 1814. South of Bliss's former home, EHR is flanked to the east by a large public car park with a poor surface, the East Heath Car Park, which has parasitised part of the Heath. Below Heathside, there is a sloping, triangular grassy meadow that tapers to a point near Goldfinger's home and the meeting point of Willow Road, Downshire Hill, and EHR.

South of its meeting with Willow Road, EHR continues as South End Road. The houses lining the west side of it but set well back from it by long strips of beautifully cared for gardens are far older than Goldfinger's residence. All of them were built by the mid-19th century and most of them had been in place long before that time. Many of the dwellings have names: Hartley House (no. 103), where the architect Oswald Milne (1881-1968) once lived; Heath Cottage (no. 101); Guernsey Cottage (no. 93), home of JE Wallis, the 19th century translator of Heinrich Heine's *Book of Songs*; Bronte Cottage (no. 89), home of the artist Mary Hill (1870-1949); St Johns Cottage (no. 87); Rose Cottage; Leighton House (no. 73); and Russell House (no. 71) is an early 19th century house with a late 19th century enclosed veranda by Charles Francis Annesley Voysey (1857-1941), one of his earliest projects. Beyond these, there is Keats Grove, across which a line of shops commences. One of these used to be the premises of Rumbold's bakery, which is mentioned in a piece about David Morgan and the nearby Magdala pub, published in *Camden New Journal* during April 2019. In this article, Morgan spoke about Rumbolds as well as Hampstead in general:

"… his working-class family lived in Hampstead before it became affluent. "People always say to me I can't have an accent like this and be from Hampstead," he said. "I say we were one of the original families there, long before the other lot moved in. "My grandads were born in the 1880s when Hampstead wasn't even part of London … I remember Mr Rumbold's bakery, opposite the Barclays in Heath Hurst – they served bread, proper bread. Bank holidays, there were stallholders running all the way up East Heath Road ...""

South End Road leads into South End Green, which is no longer particularly green. According to the website of The Magdala pub (friendsofthemagdala.co.uk), the Green was visited by the playwright Richard Brinsley Sheridan (1751-1816), who:

"…one night after a drink-fuelled session at a friend's house in the Vale of Health, he managed to walk down the hill as far as the corner of the present Pond St and South End Rd before collapsing in a heap. The local watch arrested him and marched him back to the lock-up in Hampstead Village. When they demanded his name he announced loftily that he was 'William Wilberforce'."

From the Green, Fleet Road and heads southeast towards Chalk Farm, and Pond Street ascends west to Rosslyn Hill. At South End Green, there was once a cinema. A correspondent, Gary McDonald, told me it was originally the 'Hampstead Picture Playhouse' (opened 1914), and then it was taken over in 1965 by Classic Cinemas, and in 1985 it was the sold to Canon and renamed

'Canon' then 'Virgin' in 1995. They sold it and it was then named ABC. It could seat 1500 people. This cinema with many names closed in 2001 and its site is now occupied by a Marks and Spencer's food store. Sainsbury's hoped to open a store in South End Green, but it met with protests as recorded in the *Ham and High* in January 2015, which summarises other attempts to open supermarkets in the area:

"Oscar winner Emma Thompson has added her name to the swelling campaign to stop a Tesco store opening in Haverstock Hill. The star joins fellow acting greats Dame Janet Suzman and Tom Conti, along with comedian James Corden in backing a petition against the supermarket giant which has more than 2,000 signatures. Protesters say the planned shop on the site of the former HSBC bank, in Haverstock HIll will destroy the community feel of the high street by driving out much-loved independent shops, cause traffic chaos and is not needed when there are already two other Tesco stores nearby ... Dame Janet Suzman is due to speak at a public meeting next Tuesday January 20 at 8pm at St Stephen's, in Pond Street. In July she was part of a successful campaign to stop Sainsbury's opening a shop in South End Green."

Reading this made me wonder how Tesco'

Hampstead Heath Overground Station is across the Green. It is close to a pub with fake half-timbering called the Garden Gate. In 1855, a pub on this site was called 'The Perseverance'. It was renamed 'The Railway Tavern' by 1871 and got its present name recently. The Magdala pub on South Hill Park is also close to the station. It was outside this pub that Ruth Ellis (1926-1955) shot her boyfriend on the 10th of April 1955. She was later executed by hanging and was

131

the last woman in the UK to be hanged for murder. The architecturally unremarkable pub is named after the Battle of Magdala that occurred in 1868 during the Abyssinian War.

South End Green no longer contains a pond. Until 1835, when it was drained and filled-in, there was a pond at the eastern (lower) end of Pond Street, which leads west from the square. This became South End Green, and, in the 1880s, assumed importance when it became the terminus for a tramway. Later, a huge tram depot was built in a plot of land enclosed by terraces of houses lining the following roads: Agincourt, Fleet, and Cressy. The depot's entrance was a gap between two houses on Cressy Road. On a corner where Pond Street enters the Green, there used to be a café, 'Prompt Corner' which was popular with chess players. This has gone, only to be replaced by another café where chess is hardly ever played. Both establishments are in the building that used to house a bookshop where the writer George Orwell (1903-1950) worked during 1934 and 1935.

The green, which was once the terminus of a tramline, is still the end point for a bus route, number 24. There is small area where the busses park whilst their drivers take a break. Near this, there are subterranean public toilets. The 'gents' is magnificent, with its white glazed brick walls decorated with bands of light green bricks, its long narrow, black and white chequered floor, its polished dark wood cubicles, and its row of tall, white urinals all topped with grey (flecked with white streaks) granite separators. Although there is electric lighting, a dusty skylight admits some natural light. These toilet facilities, both the men's and the ladies', were constructed in 1897 for the benefit of passengers using the tramway. Stephen Emms, writing in the *Kentish Towner* in October 2013, noted that the gent's underground facility at South End Green was a pick-up place used by homosexuals. He noted:

"But most memorably South End Green is the only public toilet still in use known to have been visited by iconic 1960s playwright Joe Orton. Apparently it was his "favourite pick-up point" too""

The lost pond was the lowest of a series of interlinked Hampstead Ponds. The Hampstead Ponds, now three in number, are fed by streams that rise near the Vale of Health, which is northwest of the uppermost pond, the Mixed Bathing Pond. The latter flows into the second pond and then down into the first, the lowest. These streams, along with those that flow into the Highgate Ponds, are sources of the water that flows in the now subterranean River Fleet, which empties into the Thames under Blackfriars Bridge. Northeast of the upper pond, that which is used by swimmers, is Viaduct Pond. This is so named because it is traversed by a brick viaduct, built between 1844 and 1847. This structure was to have been the grand entrance to an estate of residential villas that Sir Thomas Maryon-Wilson had hoped to build on the Heath but was prevented by local opposition.

The idea of damming the streams on the Heath to make the ponds might have been conceived as early as 1589 but it was only in 1692 that the Hampstead Water Company leased the springs that now feed the ponds. The latter, which were used as freshwater reservoirs, were created by damming the streams in the early 18th century. The pond at the Vale of Health was created later, in 1777. Water from these ponds/reservoirs was supplied to users in north London via wooden pipes created by boring holes in elm tree trunks. The Highgate Ponds, which also supply water to the Fleet, were also created by the Hampstead Water Company. In 1856, the New River Company acquired Hampstead Pond number 1 and the Vale of Health Pond, which were by that time becoming less savoury as far as water quality was concerned. Four years later, the Hampstead Junction Railway Company opened what is now Hampstead Heath Overground Station. Trains travelling east from this station towards Gospel Oak pass below a part of Hampstead Heath, Parliament Hill, from the summit of which there a lovely view of central London. The station is just south of a pond, which was filled in in 1892. There was another pond in South End Green, also filled-in long ago, where a 19th century drinking fountain now stands. This disused neo-gothic drinking fountain was erected by "Miss Crump of Hereford House" to honour the memory of her cousin William Warburton Pearce, who died in 1872, and another of her cousins, James Bradley Chamberlain, who died in 1880. The fountain was designed by JH Evins. Hereford House may well have been near South End Green, where the present Royal Free Hospital now stands.

Pond Street, which leads uphill from South End Green to St Stephens on Rosslyn Hill, is lined on its north side by old buildings and on its south side by the enormous Royal Free Hospital, which is housed in aesthetically indifferent buildings constructed in the early 1970s. The hospital was founded in 1828.

Until it moved to its present site in Hampstead, its headquarters were in Grays Inn Road, in buildings that are now part of the Eastman Dental Hospital. I was born (not without some considerable difficulty) in the Grays Inn Road premises. The present site of the hospital is on land that was previously occupied by the Hampstead General Hospital, which was founded in 1882 by Doctor William Heath Strange (1837-1907). This hospital, which was taken over by the National Health Service in 1948, was demolished in 1975. It occupied the site of the present hospital's often crowded visitors' car park, which is frequently busy because many of the families of the hospital's patients are too prosperous to consider using the very adequate public transport that serves the Royal Free.

The Royal Free has sad memories for me. Both my mother, and her brother, my uncle Felix, who lived opposite the hospital in Fleet Road, and their sister, spent the last few weeks of their lives in beds in the hospital's wards, and died in them. They were all born in South Africa. I used to visit them often. On the day that Felix died, a kindly nurse from Zimbabwe gave him a piece of the South African dried meat called 'biltong'. Thus, Felix, who despite being 'white' was an African at heart, died having had a final taste of his native land. One small consolation about visiting patients at this hospital is that the wards' windows (in a building that sticks out of the landscape like a 'sore thumb') provide superb views of Hampstead and its surroundings.

The aesthetically pleasing northern side of Pond Street is a welcome contrast to the hospital's side. The imposing Roebuck pub whose façade is crowned by a triangular pediment was in business in 1871, if not before. It is not marked on a detailed map surveyed in 1866, reflecting that Hampstead had not yet spread so far from the village centre. However, Pond Street antedates the pub. It had that name already in 1484. Downhill from the pub, there is a series of residential buildings that look much older than it. They may well be 18th century structures, which replaced earlier buildings. One of the former inhabitants of this side of Pond Street was the biologist Julian Huxley (1887-1975), who lived at number 31 between 1943 and his death. His father the writer Leonard Huxley (1860-1933) lived at 16 Bracknell Gardens (west of Frognal) between 1916 and his death. His sons, Julian, and his brother the writer Aldous Huxley (1893-1963), also lived there briefly.

When I attended the Hall School in nearby Swiss Cottage, one of my fellow pupils was a son of the sculptor Daphne H Henrion (1917-2003). For a time closely associated with the writer Arthur Koestler, she translated, and created a title for, his novel now known as *Darkness at Noon*. In 1947, Daphne married FHK 'Henri' Henrion, and then for the following twenty years they lived in Pond Street. I recall that there used to be one of her sculptures in the front garden of their Pond Street house, which they left in the 1970s. The piece is no longer there.

A real treat for lovers of Victorian architecture stands at the corner of Pond Street and Rosslyn Hill: the church of St Stephen. Built in 1870 and designed by Samuel S Teulon (1812-1873), who died in Hampstead, the church is rich in intricate stone detailing, but often closed. It overlooks a triangular green space on the east side of Rosslyn Hill, Hampstead Green. A few yards north of Hampstead's former Town Hall, this green area, according to Christopher Wade, was:

"… riddled with streams, so the foundations [of the church] were never easy. But here Teulon, the rogue architect of over a hundred churches, created his *magnum opus* – and died, exhausted, soon after."

Across Rosslyn Hill on the corner of Lyndhurst Road, and opposite St Stephens, stands an unusual church. It is brick-built with vast tiled roofs. Star-shaped in plan, this used to be Lyndhurst Congregational Church. Between 1884 and 1930, the Reverend Robert F Horton (1855-1934) was its full-time minister. The roughly hexagonal church, which was designed by Alfred Waterhouse (1830-1905) who designed London's Natural History Museum, was built in 1884. It could accommodate 1,500 people, seated. Today, the church's deconsecrated premises house recording studios.

SIR HARRY AND ROSSLYN HILL

Losing an election or being dismissed from office are probably the worst things that can happen to politicians in Britain today. Several centuries ago, politicians risked a far worse fate: decapitation. Such was the ending suffered by a 17th century politician who chose to live in Hampstead, close to Westminster yet surrounded by countryside. Sir Henry Vane (c1612-1662), who is often referred to as 'Henry Vane, the Younger' or 'Harry Vane' was born into a wealthy family. He completed his education in Geneva, where he absorbed ideas of religious tolerance and republicanism. His religious principles led him to travel to New England. Between May 1636 and May 1637, he served as the 6th Governor of the Massachusetts Bay Colony. While in America, he raised a large amount of money to be used for the establishment of what is now Harvard University. Soon, he came into conflict with other colonists. Barratt wrote:

"…he soon found that his own ideas of religious independence and those of his friends were not in harmony. Their "tolerance" was shown in a cruel and rigid intolerance of everything that did not fit in with their own narrow Calvinistic views; Harry Vane stood for a larger humanity."

Harry returned to England and became a Member of Parliament as well as Treasurer to the Royal Navy (in 1639). He was knighted by King Charles I in 1640.

When the conflict between the Royalists and the Parliamentarians broke out in about 1642, it was hoped that Harry would stick with the Royalists, but he did not. He became a supporter of the Parliamentarians. During the Commonwealth that followed Cromwell's victory in the Civil War (1642-1651), he regained his position of a treasurer to the navy. Harry's views on various things differed from those of Oliver Cromwell. By this time, Harry had moved to a house in Hampstead, Vane House, where, it is believed, he used to meet with Cromwell, Fairfax, and other prominent Parliamentarians. The poet and supporter of the Parliamentarians John Milton (1608-1674) was also a visitor at Vane House.

Barratt relates that when the question of executing King Charles I was being decided:

"…Vane refused to be a party to the sentence, and retired to his Raby Castle property in Durham, one of the estates his father settled on him on his marriage in 1640."

And CV Wedgwood, writing in her *The Trial of King Charles*, noted that just before the trial of the King, Vane was:

"… still in London; he still zealously attended to his duties as Commissioner of the Admiralty, but he would not take part in the proceedings against the King, which he judged illegal. Added to his dislike Army's action, he had another, more personal, for staying away; as the son of a Court official, he felt a genuine compunction about shedding the blood of the King."

Vane had married Frances Wray, daughter of Sir Christopher Wray, who was a Parliamentarian. Harry became concerned when Cromwell barred him from the dissolution of the so-called 'Long Parliament' in 1653. Barratt explained:

"When Cromwell violently broke up the Long Parliament, his most active opponent was Sir Harry Vane, who protested against what he called the new tyranny. It was then that Cromwell uttered the historic exclamation, "O Sir Harry Vane! Sir Harry Vane! the Lord preserve me from Sir Harry Vane!" Vane was kept out of the next Parliament, and, still remaining at Raby, made another attack on Cromwell's Government, in a pamphlet entitled *The Healing Question*. This was a direct impeachment of Cromwell as a usurper of the supreme power of government, and led to Vane being summoned before the

Council to answer for his words." Harry's actions led to his imprisonment on the Isle of Wight."

Following Oliver Cromwell's death in 1658, Harry returned to public life and his home in Hampstead. He was striving for Britain to become a republic rather than a continuation of the dictatorial Protectorship established by Cromwell and briefly continued by his son Richard. When King Charles II was restored to the throne, ending the Protectorship, Harry, who had not been party to, or in favour of, the execution of Charles I, was granted amnesty and hoped to live in retirement, contemplating religious matters that interested him, in his Hampstead residence. But this was not to be. Although the King was happy to forgive Harry, some of his advisors were concerned that, to quote Barratt:

"Vane's ultra-republicanism was probably more objectionable to Charles II than it had been to the Protector, and Charles had not been established on the throne more than a few months when the arrest of Sir Harry Vane was ordered."

Harry was taken from his garden in Hampstead by soldiers on an evening in July 1660. After a short spell in the Tower of London, Harry spent two years as a prisoner on the Isles of Scilly. In March 1662, he was brought back to the Tower and faced trial at the King's Bench. The charge against him was:

"…compassing and imagining the death of the king, and conspiring to subvert the ancient frame of the kingly government of the realm…"

The judges in this unfair trial had no option but to find him guilty. He was executed at the Tower.

I would not have been aware of this remarkable man had I not spotted a brown and white commemorative plaque in his memory on an old brick gate post on the west side of Rosslyn Hill, just where it becomes Hampstead High Street. The gatepost and a short stretch of wall, set back from the road, are all that remains of Harry's Vane House, which was demolished. It was still standing in 1878, by which time it had been heavily modified and, according to Edward Walford's *Old and New London*, published in the 1880s, his house was:

"…occupied as the Soldiers' Daughters' Home. Vane House was originally a large square building, standing in its own ample grounds."

This was connected by a covered arcade to a school for soldier's daughters. The building which housed the school still stands on Fitzjohns Avenue and has been renamed Monro House. Writing in 1900, there was still something to be seen of Sir Harry's home as noted by Mrs Caroline A White in her *Sweet Hampstead and its Associations*:

"It is generally believed that the fine old red-brick mansion to the left of the road as you ascend Rosslyn Hill, now the 'Home of the Soldiers' Daughters,' is the veritable house which the unfortunate Sir Harry Vane built for himself on Hampstead Hill, a place in which he had hoped to pass the declining years of his life in peace. Of the original house only an old staircase leading to the garden exists, but the interior of the mansion has suffered so many changes…"

Later, she quotes a book by Eliza Meteyard (1816-1879), *Hallowed Spots of Ancient London* (published 1870) in which Harry Vane's last moments in Hampstead were described or (most probably imagined):

"…the famous avenue was the scene of Sir Harry's arrest. Here on the evening of an early day in July, 1660, just as the sun was setting, Sir Harry walked and meditated, as was his wont, till the glowing splendour of the western sky gradually faded, as did the sounds of the cotter children at their play, the barking of a sympathetic dog, or some broken scrap of hymn, and still Sir Harry continued to pace beneath the elm-trees, the sweetness and the stillness deepening with the twilight, when the measured tramp of soldiers on the hill, some of whom marched straight to Vane House, whilst others guarded the exits, struck terror into the hearts of his humble neighbours, who, before night settled fully down, saw Sir Harry taken from his home, a prisoner on his way to the Tower, whence, after two years of torturing uncertainty, and removals from one place of captivity to another, he came forth on another summer's day, June 14, 1662, to die by the hand of the executioner on Tower Hill, another martyr to the liberties of his country."

The avenue mentioned in this extract was an avenue of elms that disappeared long before 1900. The heavily modified Vane House, in which Sir Harry resided, was demolished in 1972. Near to gatepost mentioned above, there is an estate called Vane Close. So, Harry's name lives on in Hampstead.

Pilgrims Lane meets Rosslyn Hill opposite Vane Close. According to GE Mitton in *Hampstead and Marylebone* (published in 1902), Rosslyn Hill was originally named 'Red Lion Hill' after a pub that used to stand on this thoroughfare near the western end of Willoughby Road, but it was no longer in existence when Mitton was writing. Rosslyn Hill is named after Rosslyn House, a mansion with extensive grounds that lay between Rosslyn Hill and the present Fitzjohns Avenue. It was once the home of Alexander Wedderburn, 1st Earl of Rosslyn (1733-1805), who was a lawyer and politician. He served as Lord High Chancellor of Great Britain from 1793 to 1801. Lyndhurst Avenue marks the northern boundary of the now non-existent Rosslyn estate.

The Red Lion no longer exists. Neither does the police station that once stood on its site. Today, a pink granite drinking fountain stands by the side of the pavement close to where the pub used to be. It was probably constructed in the third quarter of the 19th century. Inscribed with quotations of a Christian nature, it provides a tap and basin for humans and below it at floor level another for animals. The lower basin is surrounded by the words: "The merciful man is merciful to his beast". The fountain, which is out of action currently, bears no clue to which organisation placed it there. Further down Rosslyn Hill, we reach the corner of Pilgrims Lane, a street that leads northeast to Willow Road. On a map surveyed in 1895, most of what is now Pilgrims Lane, was then named 'Worsley Road'. In 1964, the Labour politician and for some time Leader of the

143

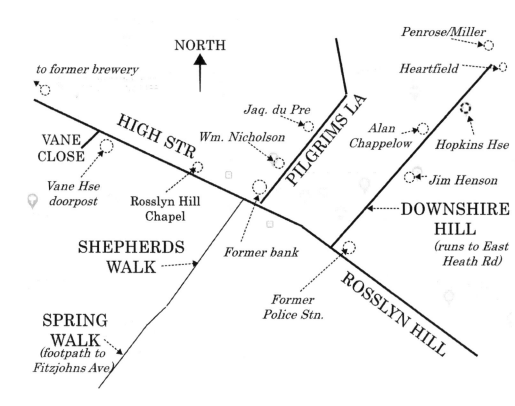

to former brewery

NORTH

Penrose/Miller

Heartfield

Jaq. du Pre

PILGRIMS LA

Wm. Nicholson

HIGH STR

VANE
CLOSE

Vane Hse
doorpost

Alan
Chappelow

Hopkins Hse

Jim Henson

Rosslyn Hill
Chapel

DOWNSHIRE
HILL
(runs to East
Heath Rd)

SHEPHERDS
WALK

Former bank

SPRING
WALK
(footpath to
Fitzjohns Ave)

Former
Police Stn.

ROSSLYN HILL

144

Labour Party Michael Foot (1913-2010) and his wife began living on Worsley Road, and in 1970 they persuaded Camden Council to change its name to Pilgrims Lane. Before that, only a short, curved stretch of the street near Rosslyn Hill had its present name. The lane was not named after religious travellers but in memory of Charles Pilgrim or his father James (died 1813), who had once owned part of the local Slyes Manor, which used to be on the west of Hampstead High Street.

A former branch of Lloyds Bank stands on a corner of Rosslyn Hill and Pilgrims Lane. The entrance to this handsome building is on its corner. It is surmounted by a hemi circular pediment in which there is a bas-relief crest bearing the letters "LBL". Above this there is a sculpture of a beehive, the symbol of industriousness. The hive was a symbol for Lloyds Bank from 1822 until 1884, when the bank took over Barnetts Bank in 1884 and then adopted Barnetts' symbol: a black horse. 'LBL' stands for Lloyds Bank limited. The bank building, now converted to a block of flats, was designed in 1894/95 by Horace Field (1861-1948), who designed several banks for Lloyds. For some time, Field had his architectural practice in Hampstead, where his father, also an architect, had worked. The architectural historian Nikolaus Pevsner described the Queen Anne-revival type of building as "… accomplished Wrennaissance style …" Writing in the *Architectural History (Vol 53, 2010)*, Timothy Brittain-Catlin noted that the building:

"… included two residences, a shop and offices, and the bank evidently shared the concerns of other residential landlords. The minutes note its refusal to grant a tenancy in 1913 because suffragette material was to be sold from the premises in question."

The painter and printmaker Sir William Nicholson (1872-1949) lived in the building between 1904 and 1906. His son was the well-known artist Ben Nicholson (1894-1982), who married the sculptor, Barbara Hepworth. Part of Ben's education was in Hampstead at Heddon Court School, which later relocated to Mill Hill. A short distance away from the former bank there is an unexceptional house on Pilgrims Lane, where the 'cellist Jacqueline du Pré (1945-1987) lived between 1970 and 1975. In February 2017, Moray Welsh, writing in the *Ham and High*, noted:

"The steps up to the Lloyds Bank building on Hampstead High Street are relatively new and fairly innocuous, but they bear testimony to one of the great tragedies of modern British music-making. Because it was on her way into the bank that the cellist Jacqueline du Pre, who lived nearby in Pilgrims Lane, first fell down and realised there was something seriously wrong. It turned out to be multiple sclerosis."

Opposite the bank building is number 2a Pilgrims Lane, a big house largely hidden by a high wall. Its door bears the name Rosslyn Hill House. It is probably early 19th century. It was the home of Edward Henry Nevinson (died about 1850 in Hampstead), Paymaster to the Exchequer. At one time, this was the home of another Nevinson, the journalist and essayist Henry Woodd Nevinson (1856-1941). He married the British suffrage campaigner Margaret Wynne Nevinson (née Jones; 1852-1932). Their son, the artist Christopher RW

146

Nevinson (1889-1946), was born in their family home in nearby Keats Grove. He was studying at the Slade at the same time as Mark Gertler. A biographical note on the Tate Gallery website relates:

"When he left the Slade, Nevinson befriended Marinetti, the leader of the Italian Futurists, and the radical writer and artist Wyndham Lewis, who founded the short-lived Rebel Art Centre ... At the outbreak of World War I, Nevinson joined the Friends' Ambulance Unit ... For a very brief period he served as a volunteer ambulance driver before ill health forced his return to Britain. Subsequently, Nevinson volunteered for home service with the Royal Army Medical Corps. He used these experiences as the subject matter for a series of powerful paintings which used the machine aesthetic of Futurism and the influence of Cubism to great effect. His fellow artist Walter Sickert wrote at the time that Nevinson's painting La Mitrailleuse, 'will probably remain the most authoritative and concentrated utterance on the war in the history of painting.'"

So, Nevinson was yet another 20th century artist associated with Hampstead.

Proceeding a few yards down Rosslyn Hill, we arrive at a large redbrick building with white stone trimmings on the south corner of Downshire Hill. This was built as the 'Hampstead Police Station and Magistrates' Court' in 1913 and designed by John Dixon Butler (1861-1920), who, so the historicengland.org.uk website noted:

"...was appointed Architect and Surveyor to the Metropolitan Police in 1895, following the retirement of his father, who had held the post since 1881. Dixon

Butler was articled to his father, John Butler, and hence had an excellent education in the design and planning of police-related buildings…"

The building, which ceased being used as a police station and court in 2013, has been re-purposed. However, a doorbell next to a side door on the Downshire Hill side of the edifice is still labelled "Magistrates".

The Rosslyn Hill Chapel, a Victorian gothic edifice, is set back from Rosslyn Hill on a plot between Pilgrims Lane and Willoughby Road. It was built in 1868 on a site where there had been various buildings used for worship by Dissenters since about 1692. The present building replaced an earlier chapel constructed in 1828, and this had replaced an even earlier structure. The novelist known by her pen name George Eliot (1819-1880) is said to have attended services in the chapel. Until 1885, the chapel grounds were entered from Pilgrims Lane. Then after two buildings were demolished on Rosslyn Hill, the space occupied by them became a garden with a path leading from the road to the chapel,

Approximately 80 yards up the High Street (the continuation of Rosslyn Hill) from Willoughby Road, stand the remains of the premises of the former Hampstead Brewery, founded in 1720 by John Vincent (died 1755). In about 1713, Vincent, already a landowner, acquired the Jack Straws Castle pub near Whitestone Pond. The old brewery can be recognised by an archway decorated with sculptures depicting sheaves of barley and an inscription that reads: "Established 1720. BREWERY. Rebuilt 1869". The archway is at the street entrance of a covered cobbled lane that leads to a converted Victorian industrial building, now named Clive House, which stands in a yard, which also contains an old well-head. Vincent founded the brewery behind a pub called the "King of Bohemia's Head" in 1720. In 1733, he was granted a 33-year lease of a spring by the trustees of an estate in Hampstead, where it was located, and other wells including some with curative mineral waters. The spring was used only to supply the brewery and a few adjoining houses and was of little value to anyone other than the brewer.

In addition to the brewery, Vincent acquired much other property in Hampstead including several pubs. On his death in 1755, Vincent's brewery and other properties passed to his younger son Robert, who is thought to have continued running the brewery with his elder brother Richard. Richard entered Wadham College, Oxford, in April 1736 and became a barrister (Inner Temple) in 1743. In 1787, Robert's widow Elizabeth became involved in running the business and some of the Vincent family's pubs in Hampstead including the 'George', the 'Black Boy', and the 'Coach and Horses'. She retained an interest in the brewery until 1812, when it had already been taken over by Messrs Shepheard and Buckland (in 1797). The brewery was rebuilt in 1869 with two shopfronts on the High Street, and by the 1880s, it was owned by Mure & Co. In 1928, the company had 184 employees, but it closed in about 1931. Reffell's Bexley Brewery acquired it in 1931. By 1959, the brewery buildings had become quite dilapidated; they were being used for motor repairs. Later, the structure was converted for use as office space and an attractive group of residences were built within the former brewery's compound. The main brewery building is now named Clive House. It is currently the offices of the Pears Foundation, which its website explained is: "…an independent, British family foundation, rooted in Jewish values, that takes £15 - 20 million of private money every year and invests it in good causes."

The Brewery's grounds were adjacent to the site of a church and its hall, which has is now occupied by residential dwellings. Some of the hall's original windows topped with ogival arches have been retained. This building is labelled as 'Trinity Presbyterian Church' on a map surveyed in 1866. It was founded in 1844 and had its roots in Calvinist theology. The church was opened in 1862 and demolished in 1962. Shops were built on its site and the hall was converted into Trinity Close, a residential building complex

.

NEW END, CHOLERA, AND GROVE PLACE

This chapter includes a discussion of outbreaks of illness which occurred in the past. In many countries today, millions of people live with plague and illness and might even accept it as a part of daily life. In the present century, this was not the case in the UK until the arrival of covid19. Back in the 19th century when transmission of disease was poorly understood and living conditions in the UK were less hygienic than today, disease was rife, and epidemics were not unusual. Related to this, there is a carved stone plaque high on a wall of a house, currently Heathside Preparatory School, on a lane called New End. The plaque reads:

"This building was erected by voluntary contributions for a dispensary and soup kitchen. It was intended as a thank-offering to Almighty God for his special mercy in sparing this parish during the visitation of cholera in the year 1849. The site was purchased in 1850 and the building completed in 1853. He shall deliver thee from the noisome pestilence. Thomas Ainger M.A. incumbent"

Thomas Ainger (1799-1863), who was born in Whittlesea, Cambridgeshire and studied at Cambridge University, was awarded 'perpetual curacy' of St John-at-Hampstead in 1841, a position he held until his death. He was, according to a Cambridge University website:

"An energetic parish priest and poor-law guardian; helped to found schools and a dispensary; enlarged his church and promoted the building of new churches in the district around Hampstead."

It was not everyone in Hampstead, who was spared from cholera. One of those, who was afflicted, not in 1849 but five years later, unwittingly made a great contribution to science. Today, we can have injections that radically reduce the chances of suffering from cholera, but that was not the case back in 1849, when the mechanism by which the disease spreads was not yet understood. One case of the disease, which significantly helped to further knowledge of its mode of spread, occurred in Hampstead in 1854. Dr John Snow (1813-1858), who was a pioneer in the fields of hygiene and anaesthesia, suspected that cholera was spread via drinking water. He demonstrated that cases of the disease were clustered around water sources. During an outbreak of cholera in 1854 in London's Soho district, which was centred around a pump in Broad Street, now

Broadwick Street, he found that by removing the handle from the pump so that the locals could no longer draw their drinking water from there, the local outbreak of cholera was ended. The pump in Broad Street was only three feet away from a leaking cess pit and its water was contaminated by waste matter. Snow theorised that the cause of cholera was not as previously had been thought a 'miasma' (something in the air), but something in drinking water. Stephanie Snow wrote in volume 31 of the *International Journal of Epidemiology*, 2002): "In 1849, the London Medical Gazette had suggested that in regard to Snow's theory, the experimentum crucis [i.e., critical experiment] would be that the water conveyed to a distant locality where cholera had been hitherto unknown produced the disease in all who used it. One of the cholera victims Snow had traced through his Broad Street investigation was a widow who lived in Hampstead. She had a regular delivery of water from the Broad Street pump as she preferred its taste. Her last delivery was made on 31 August and by 2 September, having drunk the water, she had died from cholera. Snow regarded this as 'the most conclusive' of circumstances in proving the connection between the water pump and the cholera outbreak."

The widow had lived at 'West End', which during 19th century was the name of what is now West Hampstead. John Snow had been alerted to her existence by Reverend Henry Whitehead (1825-1896), a vicar in London's Soho district, who was at first sceptical of Snow's theory of the water-borne transmission of cholera and favoured the idea that cholera existed as an airborne 'miasma'. Although Snow and Whitehead differed on their ideas on the transmission of cholera, they decided to work together. Peter Daniell and David Markoff provide more detail about the widow in Hampstead in their website (www.choleraandthethames.co.uk):

"Whitehead was able to tell Snow about a widow living in Hampstead, who had died of cholera on the … 2nd September [i.e., 1854], and her niece, who lived in Islington, who had succumbed with the same symptoms the following day. Since neither of these women had been near Soho for a long time, it was impossible that they could have contracted the disease through breathing in the polluted air of the area. Intrigued, Dr Snow rode up to Hampstead to interview the widow's son. He discovered from him that the widow had once lived in Broad Street, and that she had liked the taste of the well-water there so much that she had sent her servant down to Soho every day to bring back a large bottle of it for her by cart. The last bottle of water—which her niece had also drunk from—had been fetched on 31st August, at the very start of the Soho epidemic. This was just the sort of evidence he needed to prove the argument of the miasmatists wrong."

The plaque in New End suggests that Hampstead Parish was 'spared' from the cholera in 1849, which was almost true. In that year, Hampstead, which then had a population of fifteen thousand, had 8 deaths from cholera per 10,000, whereas many areas of London reported between 100 and 200 deaths from cholera per 10,000 (1000 to 2000 per 100000, figures far higher than the worst covid19 death rates in London).

If I had not noticed the plaque in New End, I doubt that I would have become aware of the West Hampstead widow's role in the unravelling of the mystery of cholera. Below the plaque and on the same wall, there is a pink granite object, which looks like a broken drinking fountain. This bears the date '1859', five years after the large outbreak in Soho. Incidentally, it was in that year, that Joseph Bazalgette (1819-1891) began his programme of improving London's sewerage system. This helped to reduce the out breaks of cholera, but there was at least one more in the East End of London in 1866.

Near New End, I spotted an intriguing plaque on a building on Grove Place, a short street running southwest from Hampstead's steeply inclined Christchurch Hill. The building containing numbers 29-31 Grove Place has often attracted my attention because its roof is topped with a couple of small cupolas, each supported by four slender, carved wooden pillars. The edifice bears a metal plaque, which is in an excellent state of preservation. It bears the words:

"This stone was laid by Mrs Sarah A Gotto on the 13th of July 1886 being the 50th Yr of the reign of her majesty Queen Victoria"

Elsewhere on the wall facing Grove Place there is a metal shield, painted black, which bears the following: "1871. SPPM". I was puzzled by this because SPPM means 'St Pancras Parish Middlesex' and 1871 was some years before the stone was laid by Mrs Gotto, and moreover the building was not in that parish. Christopher Wade noted that in 1970 it was converted into flats. It had been built in 1895 as Bickersteth Hall, a hall for the nearby Christ Church. It was named after a former vicar, who later became the Bishop of Exeter. This was Edward Bickersteth (1825-1906), who had been vicar of Christ Church in Hampstead from 1855 to 1885. Wade adds that it is confusing that the 1871 St Pancras shield and the 1886 Mrs Gotto plaque have been placed on the building. So, it seems that Mrs Gotto might have had little to do with laying the first brick of the building, *unless* the construction of the hall commenced in 1886. I wondered who she was.

Wade describes Sarah Gotto as "Mrs Edward Gotto". Edward was Edward Gotto (1822-1897), a civil engineer and architect who entered a partnership with Frederick Beesley in 1860 to create the engineering firm of Gotto and Beesley, which flourished for 30 years and carried out drainage works and water supply projects in towns all over the world. According to an obituary, Mr Gotto lived in Hampstead in a house called The Logs on East Heath Road. Built in 1868, The Logs, was as I have described elsewhere, much later home to the comedian Marty Feldman and the singer Boy George. Edward's wife Sarah was born Sarah Ann Porter (1829-1901). She and Edward had eight children, one of whom was Harold Ralph Gotto, who was born in 1868 in Hampstead and later became a major in the British Army.

FITZJOHNS AVENUE AND SWISS COTTAGE

Before the 1880s, the only main roads connecting Hampstead with 'the rest of the world' were Hampstead High Street and Heath Street. The former linked Hampstead to London via Camden Town, and the latter to Hendon and Highgate. There was no road connecting Hampstead directly with Swiss Cottage until Fitzjohns Avenue was built in the late 1870s, when urban development around Swiss Cottage and Hampstead began in earnest. By the end of that

155

decade, people had bought plots along the avenue and employed architects to design the grand buildings that still line it. The tree-lined thoroughfare has been compared with Paris and was described by *Harper's Magazine* in 1883 as "… one of the noblest streets in the world". Well, it is reasonably elegant, but I have seen many far nobler avenues during my travels.

I will now describe a route from Hampstead to South End Green via Swiss Cottage. The section of the present Heath Street between the Hampstead Underground Station and the top end of what is now Fitzjohns Avenue used to be known as 'Little Church Row' prior to the existence of the avenue. The currently named 'Monro House' stands at the top end of the steeply sloping, straight Fitzjohns Avenue. This Victorian institutional building with some neo-gothic features was designed by Edward Ellis (1817-1890) in 1869. Standing on land once owned by Sir Harry Vane, it was then 'The Royal Sailors' Daughters' Home' (and school), which was formerly housed in nearby Frognal. Facing it across a long garden was the former Royal Soldiers' Daughters's Home. That was housed in the now demolished former home of Sir Harry Vane on Rosslyn Hill. Currently, Monro House is used by the Borough of Camden to provide 'sheltered housing' for the over-60s.

A little further down the avenue, stands St Anthony's Junior School. This is a red brick building of no special architectural merit, which is marked on a map surveyed in 1912. This 'preparatory school', whose aim is to prepare boys for entry to Public Schools (i.e., private secondary schools), was founded in

Eastbourne by Richard Patton in 1898. It moved to its present location in 1952. It is a Roman Catholic school primarily, but it accepts boys of other faiths. During my time at another nearby 'prep' school ('The Hall', see below), St Anthony's often challenged my school at sports matches. However, I never took part in these matches because sport has never been my 'forte'.

Further down the hill, the narrow Shepherds Path, which leads to Lyndhurst Terrace, was once called 'Shepherds Walk'. Before building plots were laid over parts of it, this used to continue to Rosslyn Hill. Its name derives from that of a local landowner called 'Shepherd'. This path is close to the location of the now non-existent, Shepherd's Well, which is described in the next chapter. A little south of the path, but across the avenue, there is a huge neo-gothic style house, 'The Tower' (number 55 Fitzjohns Avenue). This 'baronial' creation was built in 1880 for HF Baxter to the designs of John T Wimperis (1829-1904). The tall tower is decorated with bartizans, overhanging corner turrets such as are found in old castles. This house is one of several magnificent 19th century constructions lining the avenue. Further downhill at numbers 40-42 Fitzjohns Avenue, there is another building that, like The Tower, appeals to fantasy. Named 'Palm Court', it has two palms growing beside its main entrance. Apart from these plants, there is little to convince the viewer that he or she is anywhere but in Hampstead. Lower down, the building that houses North Bridge House Primary School (nursery branch) has a very fine decorated porch in wrought iron and glass. Number 3, almost at the bottom of the avenue, was once the home of the Hungarian-born Jewish portrait painter Philip de László (1869-1937). It cannot have harmed his career prospects when, in 1900, he married a member of the banking branch of the Guinness family. He lived in Fitzjohns Avenue from 1927 until his death.

Next, we slip into Freudian territory. The Tavistock Centre, which houses The Tavistock and Portman Trust was completed in 1967 to the designs of FAC Maunder, who trained at the School of Architecture at Durham University during the late 1930s. Its geometric simplicity provides a complete architectural contrast to the decorative buildings along the rest of Fitzjohns Avenue. It was constructed on the site of a part of the Marie Curie Hospital (for the radiological treatment of women suffering from cancer and allied diseases), which was bombed in 1944. The main part of the hospital used to stand where Lyndhurst Road meets Fitzjohns Avenue.

The Tavistock Centre's excellent website informs that it has:

"…been at the forefront of exploring mental health and wellbeing since the First World War."

Now part of the National Health Service, the Tavistock Clinic, originally housed in Tavistock Square, was founded in 1920 by Dr Hugh Crichton-Miller (1877-1959). Using new psychological and psychiatric techniques, alternatives to traditional asylum treatments, Crichton-Miller, although influenced by Sigmund Freud (1856-1939) and Carl Jung (1875-1961), employed treatments based on his own extensive clinical experience. The Tavistock had already combined with the Portman Clinic by the time that the building in Fitzjohns

158

Avenue was completed, although there had been close associations between the two long before that. The Portman, established in 1931, offered:

"...clinical services for people who suffered from problems arising from delinquent, criminal, or violent behavior, or from damaging sexual behavior or experiences. The Clinic also offered training and consultation for professionals working in forensic mental health."

Its early vice-presidents included well-known personalities such as: Sigmund Freud (1856-1939), Karl Jung (1865-1961), the 'sexologist' H Havelock-Ellis (1859-1939), and the author HG Wells (1866-1946).

In memory of the man, who had so much influence in twentieth century psychology and psychiatry, there is a statue of Sigmund Freud in a garden at the corner of the Tavistock Centre's site, where Fitzjohns Avenue meets Belsize Lane. Dressed in a jacket and seated, Freud peers down, somewhat distracted in thought, at passers-by. The bronze statue was created in about 1970 by Oscar Nemon (1906–85), who was born in Croatia. Nemon first met Freud, who posed for him, in 1931, and thereafter produced a series of portrait heads of the founder of psychoanalysis. His final portrait of Freud, a statuette of Sigmund seated, was begun in 1938 (in London) and was to have been the basis of a full-scale work to be sited at Vienna Psychoanalytic Society. This study led to the present statue, which was first located outside Swiss Cottage Library, before being moved to its present site in 1998.

Sigmund and his daughter, the psychoanalyst Anna Freud (1895-1982), moved to London in 1938, after the Nazi Germans annexed Austria. The large red brick house where Sigmund lived for the last year of his life (and Anna until her death) is near the Tavistock Centre at number 20 Maresfield Gardens, a 'tributary' of Fitzjohns Avenue. This building in the 'Queen Anne Style', constructed in 1920, now houses the Freud Museum, which was opened to the public in 1986. The exhibits include many of Freud's possessions which he brought from Vienna, including his famous Psychoanalytic Couch.

Moving from Freud's home along Maresfield Gardens towards Fitzjohns Avenue, we pass number 6, which bears a plaque commemorating that this and its neighbour were the original home of Westfield College, which was founded in 1882 for giving higher education to women. A college that was part of the University of London, it later moved from Maresfield Gardens to a site on Kidderpore Avenue (near Finchley Road) in Hampstead. The college became coeducational in 1964 and merged with Queen Mary College in 1989. The college buildings on Kidderpore Avenue have been demolished and replaced by apartment blocks. Number 4 Maresfield Gardens, built in 1881, was the home of Cecil Sharp (1859-1924) between 1918 and his death. Sharp, the father of British folksong revival in early twentieth century Britain, was no stranger to Hampstead. Between 1896 and 1905, he was the Principal of the Hampstead Conservatoire of Music, which used to be housed in part of what is now the Central School of Speech and Drama (see below). The conservatoire had earlier provided him with a home elsewhere in Hampstead, at number 27 Church Row.

Built more recently built than most other buildings in Maresfield Gardens, the Roman Catholic Church of St Thomas More is set back from its neighbours. It is worth climbing the few steps to its entrance to see inside its oval interior with fine stained-glass windows by Alfred Robin Fisher above the main altar. The church was designed in 1968 by Gerard Goalen (1918-1999), who designed many other Roman Catholic churches. It occupied land which was once part of Philip de László's back garden. Although it is now over 45 years old, the brick lined interior of the church has a very modern feel. Like so many relatively recently constructed Roman Catholic churches, a pleasing contemporary design conducive for contemplative activities has been chosen for St Thomas More in preference to old-fashioned traditional designs.

Returning to Fitzjohns Avenue, at its southern end, there is an octagonal drinking fountain with a sharply pointed tiled roof. It is almost opposite the Freud sculpture. Made in a pinkish stone in the 'arts and crafts' style, this fountain was donated by the widow of "The late Samuel Palmer of North Court Hampstead" in 1904. Samuel, who lived at nearby 40 College Crescent (known as 'North Court') and died aged over 80 in 1903, was involved in the business of the famous Huntley & Palmer biscuit company. Today, the fountain no longer issues water. On some days, a flower-selling stall is set-up next to it.

A few yards south of the fountain, across a busy road junction there is the Odeon-Imax cinema built in 1937 to the designs of Harry Weedon (1887-1970).

Next to, and dwarfed by it, there is a building that looks like a Swiss alpine chalet. When my late mother used to go past this in the bus travelling between Golders Green and the West End, there was a conductor who used to shout: "Swiss Sausage" when his bus sailed past this curious building. It houses the pub called 'Ye Olde Swiss Cottage'. Ever since the 1840s, soon after the construction of Finchley Road in 1826, there has been a pub housed in a building resembling a Swiss chalet. Each time it has been rebuilt it has been designed to resemble a Swiss alpine residence. Finchley Road was originally a turnpike, a toll road that bypassed the steep hills of Hampstead. The Swiss Cottage pub was built right next to the former Junction Road Toll Gate. The whole area around the pub has assumed the name 'Swiss Cottage'. The Odeon's southern neighbour is a huge art deco block of flats, Regency Lodge, designed by Robert Atkinson (1883-1952) and AFB Anderson and built in 1937-38 with its own underground garage.

On Finchley Road, just north its meeting with Fitzjohns Avenue, there stood the Cosmo, a wonderful Central European restaurant much favoured by emigrees from Germany and other parts Central Europe. It first opened as a coffee bar in 1937 and closed in 1998. One of the many people who dined in Cosmo was my cousin the ecologist Peter Bunyard, who used to be taken there as a small child by his mother the photographer Anneliese Bunyard (1913-1949). She arrived in London from Germany in 1936 and lived just south of Swiss Cottage, which is a part of Hampstead where many refugees from Hitler's Germany settled when they arrived in London. In 1942, Anneliese and another photographer, also a German Jewish refugee, Inge Ader (born 1918), opened the Bunyard Ader

Photographic Studio on Finchley Road in a building, now demolished, almost opposite the former Cosmo restaurant. An article on the website of the Ben Uri Research Unit noted that the two women:

"... opened the Bunyard Ader photographic studio on the Finchley Road, north London, in the area nicknamed 'Finchleystrasse' owing to the large influx of German-speaking refugees ... Bunyard specialised in portraiture and Ader in advertising and fashion photography but they signed all their work with the collective signature 'Bunyard Ader'. Their subsequent commissions creating advertisements and photography spreads for Vogue, Tatler and Harper's Bazaar are a testament to both their individual and collaborative photographic skills. Their studio also undertook family, society and professional portraits. They sought to employ fellow immigrants whenever they could and also photographed immigrant actors at the Austrian exile theatre Das Laterndl and at the Embassy Theatre (a repertory company in Swiss Cottage which gave work to immigrant actors)."

My cousin Peter told me that in the Embassy Theatre's foyer there are some of his mother's photographs displayed in frames.

Between 1960 and 1965, I went to a school between Swiss Cottage and Belsize Park. During the summer terms, we were taken to the Swiss Cottage Baths, which were housed in an Edwardian (or late Victorian) building on the west side of Finchley Road. It stood between Swiss Cottage Station and Goldhurst Terrace, next to which stands the former 'John Barnes' department store. The latter is an example of art deco architecture (designed by TP Bennett and built in 1935) and now a branch of Waitrose. All that I can remember about the old pool's building was that its interior walls were decorated with coloured tiling. During the 1960s, it was closed and demolished. Its site is occupied by a poor replacement, an incongruous tall, dull, 'sixties' block, the ground floor of which was for a time home to first a branch of Sainsburys, then of Iceland. The old pools were replaced by a new swimming pool complex east of the Odeon. This was opened in 1964. What was then the 'new pool' has since been rebuilt and replaced by an even newer sports complex. The 'latest' swimming pool and sports centre stand on the site of the 1964 pool building next to Swiss Cottage Central Library, which was also built in the early 1960s. I remember that when it opened in 1964, it was considered a revolutionary design. Not only was its architecture, designed by Basil Spence (1907-1976), wonderfully original, but its facilities seemed (to me, then aged 12) to be miraculous. Even now, so long after its construction, the library remains an eye-catching example of good 20th century design.

The library and sports centre are part of a leisure complex, which includes greenery (lawns and trees), water features, sculptures, an occasional market, and a theatre. Originally, they were intended to form part of a new Hampstead Civic Centre, a plan that was abandoned in 1965, when local authorities underwent revision: the previously 'independent' Borough of Hampstead became part of the newer and much larger Borough of Camden. Across a green space opposite the northern end of the library, there is an abstract sculpture called *The Hampstead Figure*. Made in bronze by the surrealist sculptor FE McWilliam

164

(1909-1992) in 1964, the piece depicts a reclining female figure. It was commissioned as part of the ensemble of civic buildings for the Borough of Hampstead, planned by Sir Basil Spence and others.

When I went to school during the first half of the 1960s, The Hampstead Theatre Club, now 'The Hampstead Theatre', was housed in temporary accommodation between Eton Avenue and College Crescent, at the southern end of Fitzjohns Avenue. In 1962, it moved from its original home in Hampstead's Holly Bush Vale into what looked to me like a giant shoebox, a prefabricated portable building. It remained in its temporary accommodation for about forty years until its new building was completed in 2003. The attractive new theatre, which maintains some of its predecessor's external rectangularity, was designed by Bennetts Associates. Stepping into its multi-level foyer areas is a visually exciting experience. This is in no little way due to the way that the metal-clad rear wall of the auditorium projects into the foyer, making it a dramatic sculptural feature. The main auditorium is well-designed. The seats are well raked, comfortable, and none of them has a poor view of the stage. The theatre continues to be one of the more interesting places to watch, mostly contemporary, drama in London.

Outside the northern side of the theatre, there are often street market stalls. They sell everything from foods, prepared and otherwise, to clothes and second-hand books. On Wednesday, there is a 'farmers' market' held along this stretch of road. During the 1970s, I remember that there were odd market stalls set up occasionally south of the theatre outside the swimming pool and library. They might have been commercial, but they looked quite 'alternative', very informal, and a bit bohemian. A college friend of ours used to make wooden toy rocking-horses and colourful quilt covers to sell there to generate a bit of pocket money.

The Royal College of Speech and Drama occupies an old building on Eton Avenue (named after Eton College, a large landowner in Swiss Cottage). It is almost opposite the Hampstead Theatre. The college was founded by the English teacher of speech and drama Elsie Fogerty (1865-1945) in 1909. Initially, it was housed in the Royal Albert Hall. In 1957, it moved to its present location in the Embassy Theatre, a repertory theatre, in Swiss Cottage, which opened in 1928. Prior to that, the building was the home of 'The Hampstead Conservatoire', a private music college, one of whose directors was Cecil Sharp (see above). The building, which was built in 1880, has undergone many internal changes.

I used to walk past the Royal College and then along Adamson Road every school day between 1962 and 1965. This was the route that I followed from the bus stop at Swiss Cottage Station to the Hall Senior School, which is housed in a red brick house on Crossfield Road. This was built to the designs of ER Robson (1836-1917), architect to the London School Board. Like other schools that Robson designed, The Hall is in the Queen Anne style, which he favoured because he felt it was more suitably enlightened and secular than Gothic Revival. It was built shortly after 1878, when houses begun to be constructed on

166

the recently laid-out Crossfield Road. It was briefly a school for girls, before taken over as a boys' preparatory school, The Hall. This was founded by the Reverend Francis Wrottesley as the 'Belsize School for Boys' in 1889 in a nearby building, his home at number 18 Buckland Crescent.

When I attended the senior school, the classrooms were arranged around a large wood-panelled central hall (with a first-floor gallery) that was decorated with the crests of the many Public Schools, for which we were being prepared. The boys used to enter the school under an archway at the bottom of some steps on the left side of the façade. The bricks beside the archway used to be pockmarked with small hemispherical concavities, where boys had rotated the edges of coins to grind away the soft bricks. On a recent visit, I noticed that these bricks have been replaced. I suppose there are now school rules that forbid damaging the bricks with coins, or that the pupils have more sophisticated ways of distracting themselves.

In the early 1960s, the Hall Junior School was housed in a large Victorian villa standing at the junction of Buckland Crescent and Belsize Park. This appears in a painting, *A Street Scene in Belsize Park, a House at Hampstead, London*, by Robert Polhill Bevan (1865-1925; a founder member of the Camden Town Group of artists), which is now in the Museum of London. From 1900 to 1925, Bevan lived nearby in a house in Adamson Road, number 14, which might explain why he created so many paintings of Hampstead and its environs. Older than the senior school's building, the Junior School's building appears on a detailed map surveyed in 1866, well before Crossfield Road and Eton Avenue existed. I entered the Hall Junior School in 1960. It was a kindly place, with acceptable food. Fish and chips were served once a week. When we entered the building, we had to take off our 'outdoor' shoes and replace them with 'indoor' shoes. After a few terms, we transferred from the Junior School to the larger Senior School in Crossfield Road.

When I was a pupil at The Hall was, it was one of the best preparatory schools in London, but it was rather elitist. Many of the students were boys, whose parent(s) had achieved something that made them worthy of an entry in *Who's Who*. I was in that category. There were also several sons of multi-millionaires, including several Greek shipping magnates, and a member of the family that created Tesco's. I remember waiting for my bottle of free mid-morning milk alongside a member of the Royal Family, a cousin of Queen Elizabeth II, who was in my academic year. Although a viscount at the time, he was, like the rest of us, addressed by his surname, Lascelles, without his aristocratic title. During my time at The Hall, my fellow pupils included several, who have now become well-known, including: the actor Simon Cadell; the composer Robert Saxton; and the historian Christopher Tyerman. Others who were educated at The Hall, but not when I was there, to name but a few, included: the communist intellectual James Klugman; the politician Clement Freud; the politician Oliver Letwin; the judge David Neuberger; the playwright Peter Shaffer; the poet Stephen Spender; and the food critic Giles Coren.

The food we were served in the Senior School was far less tasty than that which we had enjoyed in the Junior School. Many of the teachers were less friendly than those in the Junior School. Miss McDonald gave us singing lessons. She made those boys, who were not talented singers (including me), sit on the floor of the so-called 'Billiard Room', which had windows overlooking Crossfield Road. We were known as 'the mice'. To entertain the rest of the class, who had good voices, she would make the tuneless and usually shy 'mice' sing unaccompanied. It was in this room, which contained a vast billiards table, that in January 1965 we watched the funeral of Winston Churchill on a small black and white television. Miss McDonald's unsympathetic approach barely matched the cruelty displayed by some of the male teachers. Mr Rotherham, a small plump man with a red face who taught us Latin, used to grab boys by their hair and then drag them up and down the classroom. This 'punishment' was known by the pupils as a 'Rozzie haircut'. Mr Packhard, another language teacher whose fingers were twisted because of rheumatism or arthritis, used to show off by trying to write on the blackboard with both hands simultaneously. If a boy annoyed him, he used to give the culprit's ear a sharp 'blip' with one of his deformed digits. Mr Bathurst, who taught history, was prone to tweaking boys' ears or rapping their knuckles with the edge of a ruler. Unrelated to this, in those days teachers smoked in front of us in class. The school was so examination-oriented that we were not given homework to take home. Instead, we spent an hour at the end of the school day, completing 'homework' assignments under examination hall conditions. To be fair, we received a very solid academic grounding, and were well-prepared for the entrance examinations for admission to good private secondary schools.

Some of the boys were so bright that they completed the entrance examination's curriculum several years before they were old enough to be able to enter secondary school. They were kept occupied intellectually by being taught advanced Latin and Greek, as well as philosophy. I was not one of these geniuses. I passed the Common Entrance Examination in 1965 and gained admission to the school of my choice, Highgate School. On my last day at the Hall, the then headmaster, Mr Cooper, asked me whether I was sad to be leaving his school. When I answered "no, not at all", his face dropped. The school continues to thrive today, and its pupils still wear the pink and black uniforms decorated with a Maltese cross. Once when I was getting off the bus at Golders Green, some boys, seeing me in my pink blazer with its prominent black Maltese cross, shouted "Nazi" at me, the cross signifying to them its German military usage.

Sometimes I travelled between the Hall and Golders Green by taking the Underground from Belsize Park Station. Belsize Park was originally a part, a sub-manor, of the Manor of Hampstead consisting of several farms. Its name derives from that of a house built in the 17th century by the Royalist soldier and courtier Daniel O'Neill (c1612-1664) for his wife Katherine Stanhope, Countess of Chesterfield (1609-1667), who was the first woman to hold the office of Postmaster-General, a position she inherited after O'Neill's death. He

170

was her third husband. To reach the station, I used to walk away from Swiss Cottage along Belsize Park, which becomes Belsize Avenue before it reaches Haverstock Hill. Where the two roads meet, stands what used to be Hampstead Town Hall. This grand red brick building with white stone trimmings was built in 1878, seven years before Hampstead was made a part of London. The edifice, designed by HE Kendall (1805-1885), District Surveyor for Hampstead from 1844, and his nephew Frederick Mew (1832-1898), is no longer a town hall. It is now used for cultural purposes and is known as 'Hampstead Town Hall Centre'. Incidentally, Mew's daughter Charlotte Mary Mew (1869-1928) was a poet of some renown. A short distance from the old town hall and up Haverstock Hill, we reach St Stephens church and Pond Street, an area already described.

SHEPHERDS WELL

In many people's minds, the name 'Tyburn' evokes thoughts of martyrs and executions. For, amongst the trees growing by the River Tyburn, there were many killings carried out in mediaeval and later times. Eventually, the place where these often cruel, fatal punishments were performed was moved westwards near to where Marble Arch stands today. Amongst those who lost their lives, there were many unfortunate Roman Catholics, who were regarded as traitors because they wished to adhere to their religion. Today, the Tyburn Convent and Church stands at the eastern end of Bayswater close to the site of Tyburn Tree, the location of the executions. The River Tyburn, now no longer visible, is one of London's many lost rivers (i.e., rivers that have been covered over by urban developments). It flowed across what is now Oxford Street somewhere west of Marylebone Lane and east of Marble Arch, and then southwards towards Green Park, and then down to the River Thames. According to Nicholas Barton in his informative *The Lost Rivers of London*, the Tyburn has or had one source at Shepherds Well in Hampstead and another in the grounds of the former Belsize Manor (on the present Haverstock Hill). The stream flowed south through Swiss Cottage towards Regents Park. There, it is carried in a pipe across the Regents Canal towards Marylebone Lane.

Various footpaths lead away from the east side Fitzjohns Avenue. These paths bear the names Spring Path, Spring Walk, and Shepherd's Path. They are all just north of Lyndhurst Road. Near the corner of Lyndhurst Road and Akenside Road, which runs south from it, there is a circular stone plaque bearing the words:

"For the good of the public this fountain is erected near to the site of an ancient conduit known as The Shepherd's Well"

The drinking fountain, which was placed by the Metropolitan Drinking Fountain and Cattle Trough Association close to this plaque, has been removed, leaving only a metal base plate affixed to the pavement. The drinking fountain is said to have been near the conduit known as Shepherd's Well, but I wondered where exactly it was located.

A glorious Victorian gothic building called Old Conduit House stands between the site of the circular plaque and the corner where Lyndhurst Road meets Lyndhurst Terrace (formerly known as 'Windsor Terrace'). This building might

172

possibly have been named in memory of the Shepherd's Well water conduit. It was built in about 1864. A detailed map, surveyed in 1866, marks the building and, more interestingly, a spot labelled 'Conduit Wells', which was in what was then open country a few yards west of Old Conduit House, near where Fitzjohns Avenue (not yet built in 1866) meets Lyndhurst Road. Edward Walford writing in his *Old and New London* published in the 1880s revealed:

"Down till very recently, Hampstead was separated from Belsize Park, Kilburn, Portland Town etc. by a broad belt of meadows, known as Shepherds' or Conduit Fields, across which ran a pleasant pathway sloping up to the south-western corner of the village, and terminating near Church Row."

This pathway ran along the course of what has become Fitzjohns Avenue. Walford continued:

"On the eastern side of these fields is an old well or conduit, called the Shepherd's Well, where visitors, in former times used to be supplied with a glass of the clearest and purest water. The spring served not only visitors but also the dwellers of Hampstead with water, and poor people used to fetch it and sell it by the bucket."

From this description, it seems likely that what was marked on the 1866 map as 'Conduit Wells' might have been the Shepherd's Well. A map dated 1860 shows 'Shepherd's Well' in the same spot as the Conduit Wells on the 1866 map. Walford added that unlike other springs around Hampstead (e.g., The Chalybeate Well in Well Walk), the water of the Shepherd's Well did not have a high mineral content. The probable location of the former Shepherd's Well is close to the Junction of Lyndhurst Road and Fitzjohns Avenue, probably a short distance southwest of the end of Shepherd's Path. Some of the water that fed the Shepherds Well also flowed into the Tyburn, making it one of the river's many sources. Mrs Caroline White, writing in 1900, noted that Shepherds Well:

"... supplied Hampstead with water, employing a body of local water-carriers, who made a living by vending tall pails full to the householders at a penny a pail. The last of these old water-carriers died an inmate of the workhouse at New End about 1868."

CHURCH ROW

My parents were what one might call 'foodies' today. In the 1960s, when I was a child, they occasionally enjoyed evening meals in Hampstead. In those days, they were keen on a restaurant, Le Cellier du Midi, in Hampstead's Church Row. They spoke highly of it but never took me there; maybe they considered me too young to enjoy fine French food. Years later in the late 1990s, friends of my parents invited my wife and me to have dinner at the Cellier du Midi, a place that I had been dying to try for many years. Frankly, the food at the meal was quite disappointing. I could not imagine that my parents would have tolerated such poor cooking; the place had gone downhill. In June 2014, the Cellier, which first opened in the 1950s, ceased operating. Now, there is a different eatery operating in its former basement premises. The Cellier has disappeared but many other, much older, landmarks remain in Church Row.

The area through which Church Row runs began to be developed, along with other plots west of Hampstead High Street, soon after 1710, when Richard Hughes of Holborn began buying up the land. From this date onwards, houses began being built along what began to be called Church Row from 1728. There are still many attractive 18th century buildings lining this tree-lined thoroughfare that leads from Heath Street to St John's parish church. The Row extends to Frognal, but west of the churchyard, the houses are not as old as those to the east of it. Church Row has been described by Christopher Wade as "… the best showpiece in Hampstead". In its early days, Barratt related:

"A promenade in Church Row was akin to a walk in the Mall of St. James's Park. All the "somebodies" of Hampstead, residents and visitors, congregated there, and the Church Row houses were regarded as distinguished dwellings. Most of the people who lived in them were well-to-do merchants and professional men from the city, including several traders with the Orient, men who knew the Levant -and the Indies"

The Row has been home to many noteworthy people including: the writer Anna Letitia Barbauld (1743-1825) and her niece Lucy Aikin (1781-1864); the lawyer and the first historian of Hampstead John James Park (1795-1833) and also his father, the antiquary Thomas Park (1759-1834); the writer and son of Sir Oswald Mosley, Nicholas Mosley (1923-2017); the judge Geoffrey Hutchinson (1893-1974), who was a member of Hampstead Borough Council; the writer HG Wells; the artist William Rothenstein; the Labour politician Sir Frank Soskice (1902-1979); and the architect of Liverpool's Anglican cathedral, Giles Gilbert Scott (1880-1960), who was born in a house on this street. This list is far from complete, but it shows that Church Row attracted the 'great and good'. The main point is that the part of it running between the church and Heath Street it is extremely attractive.

I had never heard of Anna Barbauld until I began writing this book. Barratt noted she:

"… was already a writer of some standing, having published a volume of poems a dozen years earlier, followed by other works, some in prose and some in verse, that were more than well received. The goodness and the sincerity of Mrs. Barbauld's life seem to have been happily reflected in her writings."

Mrs Barbauld was active politically. For example, in 1791, she published her *Epistle to William Wilberforce Esq. On the Rejection of the Bill for Abolishing the Slave Trade*, in which she voiced her opinions on the sadness of the slave trade and the harm it would do the cultural and moral future of the British people if it were not abolished. Her husband, Rochemont Barbauld (1749-1808), was the descendant of a Huguenot family. He was appointed head of the Unitarian congregation that worshipped in a small chapel on nearby Rosslyn Hill (see above). The Barbaulds supplemented their income by renting rooms to bright pupils, whom they had previously taught at a school, which they had run near Diss in Suffolk before they moved to Hampstead.

At the west end of the wider eastern half of Church Row stands the church of St John-at-Hampstead ('St John's'). There has been a church at this location since before 1333, but the present building, designed by Henry Flitcroft and John

Sanderson, was dedicated in 1747. A copper spire was added in about 1783 and the church was enlarged in 1843. With barrel-vaulted ceilings over both the nave and the side aisles and a first-floor gallery, it has a pleasing neo-classical interior. It is entered through a pair glass doors etched with religious images and placed in about 1995. St John's churchyard, which surrounds the church, is entered from Church Row through a pair of decorative cast-iron gates, which used to stand at Cannons, the home of the Duke of Chandos in little Stanmore (Middlesex) and was demolished in 1747 when the family fortunes were lost after the South Sea Bubble burst. The churchyard is filled with gravestones and other funerary monuments. As mentioned already, the painter John Constable rests there. Amongst the multitude of noteworthy people interred around St John's in its graveyard and its annexe north of the church are: the novelist Walter Besant; the writers Eleanor Farjeon and Penelope Fitzgerald; the actor Gerald du Maurier, father of the author Daphne du Maurier; Gerald's father, the writer and cartoonist George du Maurier; the philosopher CEM Joad; the politician Hugh Gaitskell; Arthur and Sylvia Llewellyn Davies, whose children inspired JM Barrie to write *Peter Pan*; and the architect George Gilbert Scott junior. These are but a few of the many well-known people, who are interred in the churchyard.

At the upper end of the sloping annexe to the churchyard, there is an ensemble of gravestones remembering the lives of the Matthews family. Bert Matthews (1884-1974), a local rat catcher, was Hampstead's Pearly King for 40 years. In 1905, Bert married Becky in Hampstead Parish Church. They lived in Perrins court, which is almost opposite Church Row, but across Heath Street. Three years before his marriage, Bert became involved in charity work. He and his wife became Pearly King and Queen of Hampstead. The 'Pearlies' dress up occasionally in clothes that have been covered with mother-of-pearl buttons and, so attired, they collect money for charity. Like royalty, the Pearly Kings and Queens pass on their titles to their offspring. Although dressing up in the pearly button covered costumes is part of the fun, the Pearlies are dedicated to raising money for charitable causes. Three generations of the Matthews family are buried near to the Holly Walk edge of the cemetery: the bodies of three generations of Hampstead's Pearly royalty rest together.

Near to the Matthews's burial plot, lie the remains of one of Hampstead's many artists, Randolph Schwabe (1883-1948). He was born in Eccles near Manchester. His paternal grandfather was born in Germany and migrated to England. At the age of 14, Randolph enrolled at the Slade School of Fine Art and showed great skill in drawing, painting, and etching. During WW1, he was an official war artist. Following the end of the war, he taught fine art at both the Camberwell and Westminster schools of art. In 1930, he became the prestigious Slade Professor of Fine Art at University College and then Principal of the Slade. When war broke out in 1939, he became involved in official recording of the war, receiving a special commission to document the bomb damage to Coventry Cathedral. In addition to teaching, Schwabe was a prolific book illustrator. For health reasons, he moved to Helensburgh in Dunbartonshire, where he died whilst still Principal of the Slade. He was cremated, and his ashes were scattered in the cemetery in Hampstead, where a beautiful stone sculpture of a woman with bowed head, created by Alan Durst (1883-1970) commemorates him. Schwabe lived close to the cemetery in Church Row (at number 20).

Another memorial that particularly intrigued me is an ostentatious monument commemorating some aristocrats. It is in memory of three female members of the family of Frederick Ramon de Bertodano y Wilson, 8th Marquis de Moral (1871–1955). Born in Australia, Frederick went to England in 1895, where he trained as a lawyer. He served as an officer in the British Army in southern Africa during both the Matabele War (1896-1897) and the 2nd Anglo-Boer War (1899-1902). Then, he returned to England in 1905. In 1907, he married Lady Ida Elizabeth Dalzell (1876-1924), who is buried in the cemetery along with their daughter Marie Stephanie Stewart (1911-2009), née de Bertodano. However, Frederick Ramon is not buried in Hampstead but in Harare, Zimbabwe. He retired to what was then Southern Rhodesia in 1947, In 1906, Frederic was listed as being a Fellow of The Royal Geographic Society living at 43 Belsize Square, which is on the edge of Hampstead. Maybe this is why some members of his family are buried in St John's churchyard.

GRACIE FIELDS, FROGNAL WAY, AND FROGNAL

Short Frognal Way runs south along the eastern boundary of St John's churchyard and then heads west until it meets Frognal. In 1934, actress and entertainer Gracie Fields (1898-1979) commissioned a house to be built for herself and her first husband, Archie Pitt, on Frognal Way. This was five years before she moved to the Italian island of Capri. The house, with its roof covered by interlocking curved green tiles (pantiles) and a centrally located gable, which resembles those found in houses built by the early Dutch settlers in the Cape of Good Hope, is by no means a masterpiece from the architectural viewpoint. However, two of the other houses on this short private road are of special interest to connoisseurs of architecture.

Standing on raised ground above the north side of Frognal Way is number 9, the Sun House. This was designed by the modernist architect Maxwell Fry (1899-1987) and built 1934-35. Fry and his wife, the architect Jane Drew (1911-1996), later worked with Le Corbusier on his 1950's project to build Chandigarh, the new capital of the Indian state of the Punjab. Maxwell was originally trained in the classical style, but soon began working with noted exponents of modernism including Walter Gropius, Le Corbusier, and Pierre Jeanneret. His early compositions, which were in the neo-classical style, include Margate Station (1924-26), which is a far cry stylistically from the Sun House in Hampstead. It is difficult to believe that the same person had designed both. The architectural historian Nikolaus Pevsner (1902-1983), himself a resident of Hampstead and much admired by Maxwell Fry, wrote of the Sun House:

"... an object lesson in façade composition. White rendered walls, three-storeyed window bands of different heights, large first-floor balcony on thin steel supports and then a broad projection at the r. end on the first floor, and a narrow one on the l. on second floor level. The effect is surprising and shows what a design of quality can make of relatively elementary material ..."

Next door to Sun House is number 5, which being in the neo-Georgian style, is a complete contrast to its modernistic neighbour. Designed by and for Adrian Gilbert Scott (1882-1963), it was built in 1930. Adrian was related to the other members of the Gilbert Scott family, who were architects, and lived in Hampstead. His grandfather father, George Gilbert Scott (1811-1878), lived in Admiral's House, a building dating back to1700, on Admiral's Walk

There is another treat for lovers of modernism in Frognal Way. It stands where this short unpaved road meets the main road, Frognal. The façade of this building, number 66 Frognal, reminds me of paintings by the Dutch artist Piet Mondrian. The house was constructed in 1937 and was designed by Amyas Connell (1901-1980), Basil Ward (1902-1976), and Colin Lucas (1906-1984). Their architectural practice was short-lived (1933-1939), but highly creative and productive. According to the website themodernhouse.com, they:

"… were among the foremost exponents of the International Style in Britain. Their architecture largely comprised cubic sculptural forms made from reinforced concrete and an emphasised horizontality."

To quote Pevsner, the house they designed on the corner of Frognal Way was:

"… the extreme idiom of the day, now something of a classic. The design was perhaps a little too concerned to 'épater les bourgeois' [i.e., 'to shock the bourgeois']. The design has been diluted by alterations …"

Some of these alterations were approved by the original architects, others not. Despite the alterations, the building remains a stunning and pleasing architectural statement, and is a house in which I would be happy to reside. The architectural critic Ian Nairn (1930-1983), who both admired and criticised Pevsner's approach to architectural writing, wrote that in his opinion it was the best house built in Britain before WW2.

Regarding the other buildings in Frognal Way, Nikolaus Pevsner and his co-author Bridget Cherry summarise them beautifully:

"Otherwise Frognal Way has an assortment of interwar villas from Neo-Georgian to Hollywood Spanish-Colonial and South African Dutch (with pantiles) …"

The latter mentioned is the house that Gracie Fields had built. Opposite the Sun House, there is a house with two wings and a centrally located entrance, number 4, whose architectural style Pevsner has described as "Hollywood Spanish Colonial.". It has three windows above the front door and above these there is a curious roundel with a bas-relief depicting a man wearing a skull cap and a winged cloak. On either side of him there is a single flower. The roundel is dated 1934, the same year as the Sun House and Gracie Field's home were built. Its significance eludes me.

Today, Frognal, where General de Gaulle resided for a few years (see above), is the name of a winding lane that stretches uphill from Finchley Road to the short Frognal Rise, whose continuation is a short lane called Branch Hill (see above). In the past, the name referred to a small settlement not far from the western part of Hampstead's Church Row. Christopher Wade wrote that there was never a resident lord of the manor in Hampstead, but that the settlement called Frognal was the lord of the manor's farm. By the 1880s, all signs of farming had disappeared from this locality. In addition, he considered that the name 'Frognal', which means 'the place of frogs', might have been chosen because there were once many ponds around the hamlet of Frognal. A lane, now part of the present thoroughfare named Frognal, linked it to Hampstead. Frognal was mentioned in the early 15th century as a 'customary tenement': land held by tenants of a lord, who were economically dependent on him and his protection, but unlike Free tenants, they had no recourse to the protection provided by common law. By the 16th century, there was a small cluster of houses in the part of Hampstead now called Frognal. By then, the name probably also referred to a lane that ran from manor farm buildings to the parish church in Hampstead (now, St John's). Various substantial residences were built in the area during the 18th century, including the one designed by Flitcroft (see above). A few of these older houses remain standing today.

The road that led from old Frognal to Hampstead village was extended southwards to Finchley Road in 1878. It is on this newer stretch of road that the University College School stands, some of whose buildings were built between 1906 and 1907. The school was founded in 1830 as part of University College in Gower Street. It moved to Hampstead in 1907.

Amongst the several famous people who have lived in Frognal over the centuries (including for example: the poet Stephen Spender: the pathologist Sir Bernard Spilsbury; and the book illustrator Kate Greenaway), the best known is the author and lexicographer Samuel Johnson (1709-1784). Johnson's

183

biographer, James Boswell (1740-1795) wrote in his *The Life of Samuel Johnson*:

"In January 1749, he published 'THE VANITY OF HUMAN WISHES', being the Tenth Satire of Juvenal imitated ... Mrs Johnson, for the sake of country air, had lodgings in Hampstead, to which he resorted occasionally, and there the greatest part, if not the whole, of this Imitation was written."

The house where Mrs Johnson enjoyed the country air is believed to have been in Frognal. Barratt related:

"Sometimes while she was resting comfortably in bed at Frognal, Johnson, unable to pay the coach fare to join her, was walking about all night in the streets of London; for he could not afford the luxury of a Town lodging for himself as well as that at Hampstead for his wife. The Mitre [a pub or tavern] would have his company until a late hour on these nights, and now and then Goldsmith or some other friend would offer him the hospitality of his chambers. In the early morning he would trudge valiantly off to Hampstead, arriving there long before the coach. His weekly day or days off duty would of course be spent with his wife; and at convenient times he would accompany her to the Wells, possibly coming across Richardson, by whose generosity he was once freed from detention in a sponging-house for a debt of five pounds eighteen shillings."

A sponging-house was a place where debtors could be held for a short term. The house occupied by Mrs Johnson is believed to have been the older part of Priory Lodge opposite the present Frognal, as is mentioned by Mrs Caroline White in her *Sweet Hampstead and its Associations*:

"Mr. G. W. Potter reminds me that a very interesting discussion and much correspondence has recently (May, 1899) taken place as to the house inhabited by Dr. Johnson, the result being that Park's account is believed to be quite correct, viz., that it was the last house south in Frognal. Park's father had lived for years in Hampstead, and at the same time as Dr. Johnson; he must, therefore, have given his son accurate information on the point. The house in question is now called Priory Lodge ..."

Park's father, referred to above, was the antiquary Thomas Park (1759-1834), who resided in church Row, and would have been a child when Johnson lived in Frognal. The building no longer exists but is illustrated as it was in 1911 in Barratt's book published the next year. University College School was built just south of the site of Priory Lodge. On a map surveyed in 1912, Priory Lodge is marked a few yards southwest of the southwest corner of St John's church. It is no longer marked on a similar scale map surveyed in 1934.

Just below University College School, Frognal intersects Arkwright Road, on which the Camden Art Centre is located. It is housed in a Victorian gothic building, erected in 1897, which was the Hampstead Central Library that functioned until 1964. In 1965, the abandoned library became a nucleus for local artists and artistic activity, The Hampstead Arts Centre, which was given its present name, The Camden Art Centre in 1967. Soon after its creation, the centre became an important hub for artistic education and activities as well as interesting exhibitions. In 2004, the centre underwent a major refurbishment, which was supervised by Tony Fretton Architects. Today, it is a very pleasant place to visit. Its exhibition spaces are large and airy. It has a fine bookshop and a lovely café with food and beverages that offers seating both indoors and outside next to a well landscaped hillside garden.

Returning to the upper end of Frognal to where it becomes Frognal Rise, there is a small road, Oakhill Way, which in places becomes a narrow footpath. It follows an ancient track that ran to what is now West Hampstead. It reaches Oakhill Park, where Wade noted that once the actor Peter Sellers (1925-1980) lived in a block called Northwood Lodge. Near the gate posts that mark the beginning of Oakhill Way at its eastern end, there is a house bearing the date 1878 and called Combe Edge. One of its walls has a plaque commemorating Elisabeth Rundle Charles (1828-1896), who lived there from 1874 to 1896. A writer, Charles is best known for her novel about Martin Luther, *The Chronicles of the Schönberg-Cotta Family*, published in 1862, which can be read online (www.gutenberg.org), if you have nothing better to do. This house is close to a gothic revival gatehouse on Frognal Way, which overlooks a large area of allotments, and was designed by SS Teulon. The gatehouse is beside a road that passes Spedan Towers, already described in connection with Judges Walk, and leads to an architecturally interesting modern council estate called Spedan Close. It was designed by the architects, Gordon Benson, Alan Forsyth, and Borough Architect Sidney Cook. Each of the residential units, which are arranged in groups along three parallel terraces, one above the next on the slope of a hill, has its own roof garden. Completed in 1978, it was at that time the costliest council housing estate ever built in the country. Spedan Close leads from the estate to the houses where, as already described, Alfred Reynolds and Paul Robeson lived on Branch Hill. The latter leads to West Heath Road, which is a subject in the next chapter.

WEST HEATH ROAD AND PLATTS LANE

Huge, fierce looking dogs roam freely in the grounds of a huge mock Tudor house overlooking Hampstead Heath. Several notices on the outer wall of the property read: "Do not enter. Large dogs may be running free". The mansion dominates the corner of West Heath Road and Platts Lane. Approach one of the metal gates, designed to prevent an outsider from viewing the house properly, and within seconds one of those canines will meet you on the other side of the gates and bark menacingly. I did manage to peer through the railings and the shrubbery within them to catch a glimpse of a huge sculpture of a seated lion sitting close to the steps leading to the house's front door. I had often driven past this house without stopping and wondered about it. One day, I walked up to it and read a plaque posted on its boundary wall:

"Francis Owen Salisbury (1874-1962) 'Frank'. Artist. Mural and Portrait painter, recorder of scenes of magnificent pageantry and historic event. Stained glass artist. Lived here."

Born in Harpenden (Hertfordshire), he was the son of a craftsman, who worked in plumbing, decorating, and ironmongery. He was apprenticed to a stained-glass company when he was 15, and then entered Heatherley's School of Art as a part-time student. A skilled artist, Frank won a scholarship to the Royal

187

Academy Schools, where he won two silver medals. Soon, as related on the National Portrait Gallery's website, he:

"…acquired a considerable reputation. He exhibited at the Royal Academy from 1899 to 1943 and his career as a portrait painter also flourished in the United States. His sitters include five presidents of the United States, five British prime ministers and many members of the British royal family, including the official coronation portraits of King George VI."

Frank painted more portraits of Winston Churchill than any other artist. His portrait of Franklin D Roosevelt is the official portrait of this president hanging in the White House. He was the first person to paint a portrait of the young lady, who is now Queen Elizabeth II. He painted many of the most famous and infamous personalities of the first half of the twentieth century. His skills were not confined to portraiture as the commemorative plaque reveals.

He was highly successful in the USA and by 1932, he was able to move into his impressive mock-Tudor mansion, Sarum Chase, overlooking the heath. The house was designed by Frank's nephew Vyvyan Salisbury (died c1982). Following Frank's death, the property was bequeathed to the British Council of Churches, which soon sold the house and its contents. The house has since been used as a background for photo and film shoots. In Disney's 1996 film, *The 101 Dalmations*, Sarum Chase was used as the exterior of Cruella de Vil's home. By 1974, the house was home to St Vedast's School for Boys, part of the School of Economic Science, which has links with a branch of Hindu philosophy. In 2005, the building was sold and is now, or has been, the home of a property developer and major donor to charities. So, there you have it. If I have aroused your curiosity, that is good but do not try to enter this heavily guarded premises as did a little dog called Chewy, who found its way through a hole in the fence and met his sudden end in the garden of Sarum Chase in September 2016, as was reported in the *Ham and High* newspaper.

Platts Lane winds its way from Sarum Chase on West Heath Road downhill to Finchley Road. It follows the route of an old track between Hampstead Heath and West End (now West Hampstead). This track was already in existence by the mid-18th century. According to Christopher Wade, the thoroughfare was first called Duval's Lane to commemorate a 17th century French highwayman. Louis (alias Lodewick alias Claude) Duval (alias Brown) who was famed for being gallant towards his victims, many of whom he robbed on Hampstead Heath. Barratt related:

"It used to be told that, after stopping a coach and robbing the passengers at the point of the pistol on the top of the Hill, he would, having bound the gentlemen of the party, invite the ladies to a minuet on the greensward in the moonlight."

Duval was hung at Tyburn soon after 1669. Over time, this track's name became corrupted to Devil's Lane. A pious local resident, Thomas Pell Platt (1798-1852), put an end to that name after he had built his home, Childs Hill House, nearby in about 1840. Platt graduated at Trinity College in Cambridge in 1820 and became a Major Fellow of his college in 1823. While at Cambridge, he became associated with the British and Foreign Bible Society and was its librarian for a few years. He was also an early member of The Royal Asiatic Society (founded 1823) as well as a member of The Society of Antiquaries of

London. In 1823, he prepared a catalogue of the Ethiopian manuscripts in a library in Paris. In addition, he did much work with biblical manuscripts written in the Amharic and Syriac languages. Apart from being a scholar, he was an intensely religious man. He died not in Hampstead but in Dulwich.

Platt lived near the lane named after him for quite a few years. The same cannot be said for a later resident of Platts Lane, Tomas Garrigue Masaryk (1850-1937), who was born in Moravia (now a part of the Czech Republic). Masaryk added the name Garrigue to his own when he married the American born Charlotte Garrigue (1850-1923) in 1878. A politician serving in the Young Czech Party between 1891 and 1893, he founded the Czech Realist Party in 1900. At the outbreak of WW1, he decided that it would best if the Czechs and Slovaks campaigned for independence from the Austro-Hungarian empire. He went into exile in December 1914, staying in various places before settling in London, where he became one of the first staff members of London University's School of Slavonic and East European Studies, then later a professor of Slavic Research at Kings College London. Masaryk first lived in a boarding house near Whitestone Pond, at number 4 Holford Road. In June 1916, he moved from there to number 21 Platts Lane, which was near to the former Westfield College, where his daughter Olga was studying. The house, the whole of which he rented, became a meeting place for the Czechoslovak resistance movement in England. Masaryk stayed in Platts Lane until he departed for Russia in May 1917. It is possible that he returned there briefly when he made a visit to London in late 1918. On the 14th of September 1950, the Czechoslovak community affixed a metal plaque to the three-storey brick house on Platts Lane, which was built in the late 1880s. It reads:

"Here lived and worked during 1914-1918 war TG Masaryk president liberator of Czechoslovakia. Erected by Czechoslovak colony 14.9.1950"

Masaryk only used the house between 1916 and 1917. The year that the plaque was placed was a century after Masaryk's birth year. The day chosen, the 14th of September, was that on which he died in 1937.

Not far from Masaryk's Hampstead home, there is an undistinguished looking house on West End Lane, just south of West Hampstead Underground station. It used to be called The Czechoslovak Club before it became the Czechoslovak Restaurant and now Bohemia House. Here you can see a portrait of Masaryk and enjoy yourself sampling Czech beers and food. The restaurant is part of the Czechoslovak National House, which was founded as a club in 1946.

The houses where Czechoslovakia's freedom fighter lived in Hampstead still exist. However, that is no longer the case for another freedom fighter and founder of a new nation, who lived near Platts lane on West Heath Road. He was the wealthy barrister and founder of Pakistan, Muhammad Ali Jinnah (1876-1948). In the 1930s, Jinnah practised law in London. One of his biographers, Hector Bolitho (1897-1975) wrote (in 1954):

"One day in June 1931, when Jinnah was walking in Hampstead, he paused before West Heath House, in West Heath Road. It was a three-storied villa, built in the confused style of the 1880s, with many rooms and gables, and a tall tower which gave a splendid view over the surrounding country. There was a lodge, a drive, and eight acres of garden and pasture, leading down to Childs Hill. All are gone now, and twelve smaller, modern houses occupy the once-pretty Victorian pleasance. Nearby lives Lady Graham Wood, from whom Jinnah bought the house; and she remembers him, on the day when he first called, as 'most charming, a great gentleman, most courteous…'

… In September 1931 Jinnah took possession of West Heath House, and he assumed the pattern of life that suited him. In place of Bombay, with the angers of his inheritance for ever pressing upon him, he was able to enjoy the precise, ordained habits of a London house. He breakfasted punctually and, at nine o'clock, Bradbury was at the door with the car, to drive him to his chambers in King's Bench Walk. There he built up his new career, with less fire of words, and calmer address, than during the early days in Bombay."

It was at West Heath House that Jinnah entertained Liaquat Ali Khan (1895-1951), another of Pakistan's founding fathers and its first Prime Minister, who had arrived from India. Bolitho wrote:

"A great part of the fortunes of Pakistan were decided on the day, in July 1933, when Liaquat Ali Khan crossed Hampstead Heath, to talk to his exiled leader."

Bolitho recorded that Liaquat's wife recalled the occasion:

"Jinnah suddenly said, 'Well, come to dinner on Friday.' So we drove to Hampstead. It was a lovely evening. And his big house, with trees—apple trees, I seem to remember. And Miss Jinnah, attending to all his comforts. I felt that nothing could move him out of that security. After dinner, Liaquat repeated his plea, that the Muslims wanted Jinnah and needed him."

Miss Jinnah was the lawyer's sister, Fatimah. At the end of the evening, Jinnah said to Liaquat:

"'You go back and survey the situation; test the feelings of all parts of the country. I trust your judgment. If you say "Come back," I'll give up my life here and return.'"

Jinnah returned to India in 1934, and Pakistan was created in August 1947. Judging by Bolitho's description, Jinnah's Hampstead house could not have been very far from the house which Masaryk rented in Platts Lane, which, like Jinnah's garden, is close to, or more accurately on, Childs Hill. I have found West Heath House marked on a map surveyed in the 1890s. It was located on the west side of the northern part of West Heath Road, about 430 yards north of Masaryk's residence on Platts Lane.

WEST HAMPSTEAD

Platts Lane runs from West Heath Road to Finchley Road. Its continuation after Finchley Road is winding Fortune Green Road, which leads to West End Green in West Hampstead. West End Green was known as 'Le Rudying' (a name given to a woodland clearing) in the 14th century. By 1534, the settlement around the Green was known as 'West End', which remained separated from the rest of Hampstead by open countryside until the late 19th century. Currently, this green is a part of the district of West Hampstead. Mill Lane runs westward from West End Green to Shoot Up Hill, which is a stretch of Edgware Road that follows the route of the Roman Watling Street. Although not named until later, Mill Lane existed in the Middle Ages. A detailed map published in 1870 reveals that at that time, there were scarcely any buildings along it. It was not until the later that Mill Lane began to be lined with houses and shops. A pub on the lane, The Alliance, bears the date 1886, suggesting that before that time there was not sufficient local population to warrant building such a large hostelry.

Once, I was walking along Mill Lane in West Hampstead when I spotted a plaque almost hidden in the porch of a narrow doorway at number 54. It commemorated a craftsman who used to work in the building. I wondered why anyone had bothered to put up a notice to remember him. With frosted glass windows facing the street, number 54 is now the office of St Johns Wood Cars, a taxi and private vehicle hire company. The commemorative plaque that I noticed is close to the doorway that gives access to a staircase that leads to the upper floors of the building. The wording on it reads:

"Clifford Norman Bowler, watchmaker and jeweller, lived & worked here. 1899-1993. A Mill Lane tradesman for over 67 years."

Well, 67 years is a long time, and no doubt Clifford (1899-1993) was a well-known local. Articles published on the internet reveal that that he was a remarkable member of his profession. He was born in Northumberland in July 1899 and served in the Machine Gun Corps during WW1. By 1926, he was on the Electoral Register, registered as residing at 54 Mill Lane, and in 1929 he married Mabel in nearby Willesden. His shop used to be painted red and has been immortalised in a documentary film shot for Channel 4 by a local filmmaker, Conrad Blakemore, who currently teaches at the City Lit college in

London. His short film, *The Watchmaker*, a working day in the life of Clifford Bowler, can be viewed on YouTube. In it, Clifford, a charming old man, explains that he left the army in 1919 and began learning watch-repairing in Manchester. Faced with a wage cut, he asked his brother, who was already living in London, to find him some premises. The shop he acquired in Mill Lane was already a watch and clock repairing business. The £100 he paid for it included much equipment required for his trade.

Clifford's father was a professional banjo and mandolin player. Clifford and Mabel had two children. One of them, Norman Clifford Bowler (born 1932), has followed in his grandfather's footsteps by having a career in entertainment. Between 1961 and 2012, he appeared in many plays mainly on television. Although his watch repairer father probably had nothing to do with India, Norman forged a connection with that far-off country. In 2011, Norman Clifford recorded *The Rime of the Ancient Mariner* by Samuel Taylor Coleridge (1772-1834) in Bristol. The recording was made by Norman Clifford to raise money for a school, The Aikiyam School, in the settlement of Auroville, which is close to the city of Pondicherry, a former French colony, in the south of India. A website www.lanternmanproductions.bandcamp.com, that gives access to the recording also notes:

"After falling ill a number of years ago, Norman, as part of his recuperation began to spend time in the warmer climes of Southern India with his wife, Diane. As a result, he became directly involved with The Aikiyam School as a teacher of English and Drama. As the years have gone on, Norman spent more and more time in India, only returning to England to spend time with family and friends, and raise money for the school with poetry readings and personal appearances."

Clifford is privileged to have met the Indian freedom fighter and spiritual leader Sri Aurobindo (1872-1950) and The Mother (Mirra Alfassa; 1878-1973), Aurobindo's spiritual companion/muse, and there exists a recording in which he describes his impressions of her. When I chanced upon the almost hidden memorial to a watch and clock repairer in Mill Lane, little did I expect to discover a connection between a non-descript shop in West Hampstead and the south Indian utopian settlement of Auroville, where we have visited friends a few times.

West Hampstead is no longer an isolated settlement. It is yet another of London's numerous suburbs. It has several churches as well as a synagogue. The latter's website reveals:

"At the beginning of the nineteenth century, there were very few Jewish people living in the Hampstead area. The Jewish population of London was mainly centred around the city. In 1879 the Jewish population of Hampstead began to increase, following the movement of Jews first westward to the West End and Bayswater, and then northwards to St. John's Wood and Hampstead."

The synagogue, which is on Dennington Road and at first sight looks like a church, is close to West End Lane. It was designed by the architect Delissa Joseph (1859-1927) and consecrated in 1892.

Another place of worship, St James Church, is worth entering because it is not what it seems from its external appearance. This large parish church, built mainly with red bricks, was erected in about 1887. It was designed by Arthur William Blomfield (1829-1899), the fourth son of CJ Blomfield, Anglican Bishop of London between 1828 and 1856, who encouraged much new church building during the 19th century. This building could seat 1000 people and has some fine 19th century stained-glass windows. On entering the church through its electrically operated glass sliding doors, you will be surprised by what you find beneath its hammer beam timber ceiling. The west end of the nave is occupied by a post office, the first main branch of a UK post office ever to be housed within a church. One side aisle of the church contains a children's 'soft play' area, appropriately named 'Hullabaloo'. The floor of the nave is filled with tables and chairs occupied by people of all ages, some enjoying refreshments from the church's Sanctuary Café. All these things that you would not normally expect to find inside a church are part of The Sherriff Centre, a community organisation that began operating in 2014. The Centre's activities also include a stationery store, a free food bank, live music, as well as other events, free wi-fi, debt advice, and more. Jesus is said to have thrown the moneychangers and others involved in commercial activity from the Temple in Jerusalem (*The Holy Bible*, John, Ch 2, v 13-16). However, He might have approved of the commercial activities within St James because profits from the sales outlets in the Centre are used to help finance charitable work. In addition to everything that I have already described about the activities within St James, there is one more thing to mention. Despite the things that you might not expect to find inside a church, regular religious Church of England services are also held there. It is wonderful that St James, instead of becoming yet one more barely used

Victorian church in London, has become a vibrant and beneficial part of a local community, catering to more than only its by now small congregation.

SHOOT UP HILL

The Romans built good, mainly straight, roads when they occupied Britain. Watling Street, which linked Dover (in Kent) and Wroxeter (in Shropshire) via London, was no exception. London's Edgware Road, part of the A5 main road, follows the course of Watling Street. It connects Marble Arch with Edgware and beyond. A short section of this road travels over a hill between Kilburn Underground station and the start of Cricklewood Broadway, about 840 yards away. This aesthetically unremarkable stretch of the former Watling Street is called Shoot Up Hill. The east side of this road was the western edge of the former Borough of Hampstead. It is hard to imagine that this non-descript portion of one of London's main thoroughfares has anything to do with old Hampstead.

Also known in the past as 'Shuttop' or 'Shot-up', Shoot Up was the name of a mediaeval manor or an estate, which connected with the Manor of Hampstead. The land with the name Shoot Up (or its variants) was part of the Temple Estate, which was granted to the Knights Templars in the 12th century. In 1312, the Pope dissolved the Order of the Templars and transferred its possessions to the Knights Hospitallers of St. John of Jerusalem. By the 14th century, the Watling Street marked the estate's western boundary, as well as that

198

of the Manor of Hampstead. The Hospitallers were dissolved in 1540 by King Henry VIII. One of the king's officials involved in the dissolution of religious orders such as the Hospitallers was Sir Roger de Cholmeley (c1485-1565). Benjamin Dabby relates in his book, *Loyal to The Crown. The Extraordinary Life of Sir Roger Cholmeley*, that in 1546, Sir Roger was granted the:

"… the lordship and manor of Hampstead Midd. [i.e. Middlesex], and lands in the parishes of Wyllesden and Hendon, Midd. …"

He was granted these lands, which he had helped to take from the Hospitallers. Dabby wrote that his newly acquired estate was known as 'Shut Up Hill' or 'Shoot Up Hill' Manor and that it consisted of:

"… some two hundred acres of arable land, fifty acres of meadow, two hundred of pasture, one hundred and forty of wood, and one hundred of waste, in the parishes of Hampstead, Willesden, and Hendon."

It was a valuable estate, and being a landowner gave him enhanced status in court circles. Income from this estate helped finance the school that Sir Roger created shortly before his death. That school, founded in 1565 was Highgate School, which I attended between 1965 and 1970. Unlike others of his status, Sir Roger was uneasy about the signing of the document that brought the unfortunate Lady Jane Grey to the throne. This hesitancy allowed him to escape execution when Queen Mary succeeded her as monarch. Instead, he was imprisoned briefly and fined. The Shoot Up manor (or estate), which remained in the northwest corner of Hampstead Parish, passed through various owners after the death of Sir Roger. Until the 19th century when most of it was developed for building, there was little in the way of buildings on the land. A history of the area (www.british-history.ac.uk) revealed:

"There is unlikely to have been a dwelling house on the Temple estate earlier than the one which the prior of the Hospitallers was said in 1522 to have made at his own expense, a substantial dwelling house with a barn, stable, and tilehouse. It was probably on the site of the later Shoot Up Hill Farm, which certainly existed by the 1580s, on Edgware Road just south of its junction with Mill Hill Lane. The farm buildings remained until the early 20th century."

A map surveyed in 1866 shows that what is now Edgware Road was built-up as far as the railway bridges where Kilburn station is located, but north of this, Shoot Up Hill ran through open country, passing a flour mill ('Kilburn Mill') where the current Mill Lane meets the Hill, on the west side of the road. Today, Shoot Up Hill is lined on its eastern side by large dwelling houses, mostly divided into flats. The western side is occupied mainly by large purpose-built blocks of flats. One of these architecturally undistinguished blocks is appropriately named Watling Gardens. As for origin of the name Shoot Up Hill, this is unknown.

St Cuthbert's Road runs from Shoot Up Hill east to Fordwych Road. It was on this road that the modernist artist David Bomberg (1890-1957), who studied at The Slade, lived at number 10 from 1928 to 1934. It was while living there that he made two visits to Spain where he experimented in new ways of depicting what he saw. St Cuthbert's parish church is also on Fordwych Road. What you see today was designed by Jeremy A Allen and constructed in the late 1980s on the site of an earlier brick church designed by William Charles Street

(1835-1913) and erected in 1882. All that remains of this is a large bell that is displayed in front of the present building. Street's church was built to replace an earlier edifice constructed with sheets of iron.

Until this point, the book has been exploring aspects of Hampstead's past and present. The next few sections of this volume are about some of its environs: Primrose Hill, North End, Golders Green, and Highgate.

PRIMROSE HILL

Primrose Hill is south of Hampstead village and southeast of Swiss Cottage. On the south slope of the hill, there is a pair of parish boundary markers. One of them, dated 1854, marks the boundary of the former civil parish of St Pancras, and the other, dated 1830, refers to St Johns Hampstead, which was in the civil parish of Hampstead. Thus, although distant from old Hampstead and mostly in the former Borough of St Pancras, a part of the hill was within its parish. It is a delightful place to enjoy fresh air and has been home to several notable figures. From its summit at 210 feet above sea-level, it is possible to enjoy a superb panorama of London. At its peak, a circular concrete platform is surrounded by a low wall inscribed with words, which the poet William Blake (1757-1827) told the lawyer, diarist, and a founder of University College London, Henry Crabb Robinson (1775-1867):

"I have conversed with the spiritual Sun. I saw him on Primrose Hill"
In one of his poems, Blake wrote:

> "The fields from Islington to Marybone,
>
> To Primrose Hill and Saint John's Wood,
>
> Were builded over with pillars of gold,
>
> And there Jerusalem's pillars stood."

In the centre of the platform, there is a round commemorative metal plaque containing a bas-relief portrait surrounded with words in the Welsh language. It was placed to remember Iolo Morganwg (1747-1826), who was born in Wales as 'Edward Williams'. He was a poet and antiquarian, who both wrote and collected poetry in the Welsh language. He had a great interest in reviving and preserving the literary and cultural heritage of his native land. His integrity as a scholar was somewhat undermined by the fact that he had forged several manuscripts that he claimed were of mediaeval origin. Nevertheless, he was involved in the early revival of Druidism. In 1792, he founded the 'Gorsedd Beirdd Ynys Prydain' (Gorsedd of Bards of the Island of Britain). The Gorsedd, which still meets today, is a society of poets, writers, musicians, artists, and other individuals, who have made notable contributions to the Welsh nation, language, and culture. Every year, the Gorsedd assembles at a festival of Welsh culture, now known as the Eisteddfod. According to the website of the Royal Parks, Primrose Hill was the site of the first ever Gorsedd, which was held on midsummer's day, 21st of June 1792.

The gardens on the south side of Elsworthy Road back on to the northern base of the hill. It was on this road that my parents, newly married in 1948, lived briefly in a flat that they rented from the economist Ronald Coase (1910-2013). 46 years later, my father and my stepmother bought a house on the road, where he lived until he died, aged 101. Elsworthy Terrace, a cul-de-sac, leads from Elsworthy Road to the edge of Primrose Hill. The first female botanist to be elected a Fellow of the Royal Society, Agnes Arber (née Robertson; 1879-1960), lived at number 9 between 1890 and 1909, when she married the paleobotanist Edward Alexander Newell Arber (1870–1918). The Terrace leads to one of the many footpaths that form a crisscrossing network all over the grassy hill amongst its well-spaced trees of different shapes and sizes. Many of the paths meet at the treeless top of the hill.

Primrose Hill, first opened to the public in 1842, was part of land appropriated for hunting by King Henry VIII. The earliest mention of its name was in the 15th century. In October 1678, the body of the anti-Catholic magistrate Sir Edmund Berry Godfrey (1621-1678) was found on Primrose Hill, marked with signs of strangulation and other bruises. The identity of his killer(s) remains a mystery. The hill was also the site of duels including one in about 1813 when the Italian patriot Ugo Foscolo (1778-1827) faced Mr Graham, the editor of the Literary Museum.

The Victorian gothic St Marks Church near Primrose Hill is flanked on two sides by the Regents Canal and on another by a short street, St Marks Square. The church, which is not particularly attractive, was consecrated in 1853, damaged during WW2, and rebuilt by 1957. The northern edge of the church's ground is on Regents Park Road. Heading west from the church, we reach number 52 Regents Park Road, where the author and art historian my friend Michael Jacobs (1952-2014) lived as a 'house-sitter' during the 1970s. The road flanks the eastern edge of Primrose Hill before curving eastwards, where it is lined with shops and eateries. Since 1979, a Greek Cypriot restaurant called Lemonia has been flourishing in Regents Park Road. Originally, this was housed in premises on the south side of the road. In 1992, it moved across the road into larger premises, a former pub, the Chalk Farm Tavern, to which the bodies of workers were brought after an accident during the construction of a railway tunnel beneath Primrose Hill in the 19th century. Nearby, is the independent Primrose Hill Books shop, a handy source of reading matter for the local inhabitants, many of them with intellectual leanings, real or imagined. These long-established businesses are amongst shops offering a wide variety of goods, as well as cafés, restaurants, and a pub.

The philosopher Friedrich Engels (1820-1895) lived almost opposite Primrose Hill at number 122 Regents Park Road. A colleague and friend of Karl Marx, he lived in this large house between 1870 and just before his death. His residence had been chosen for him by Jenny (1814-1881), wife of Karl Marx and mother of his six children. Every Sunday, Engels used to hold an 'open house'. All visitors were welcome. Liberal amounts of food and drink would be available and there was music and singing. According to Tristram Hunt, a biographer of

204

Engels, the visitors included, for example, leaders of European socialism such as Karl Kautsky, William Morris, Wilhelm Liebknecht, Keir Hardie, Eduard Bernstein, and Henry Hyndman, who nicknamed Engels 'The Grand Lama of Regents Park Road'. He also received visitors from Russia, including founders of Russian Marxism, such as George Plekhanov and Paul Axelrod, as well as Sergey Stepnyak-Kravchinsky, the terrorist author of *Underground Russia*. The congregation of so many socialists at his home attracted the attention of the police, who frequently kept number 122 under surveillance.

East of Engels's former home, there is a building set back from Regents Park Road. Its red brick façade is topped with a green tiled pediment with white lettering that reads: "Chalk Farm Garage. Proprietors. The Flight Petroleum Co Ltd". The ground floor rooms of this building, which included the workshops of the garage are closed in with modern glazing. Now used as the art gallery of the Freelands Foundation, this used to be a local petrol filling station. Flight Petroleum is a company that still exists. It is based in Mississippi (USA). Before becoming a gallery, the former filling station was a branch of the Bibendum company that sold wines and spirits. Almost next to the former garage, a few feet west of it, there is a curious looking white building, that was never a dwelling or a shop. Old maps marked this as a 'chapel'. An extremely detailed map of 1895 reveals that this was in the grounds of the 'Boys' Home Industrial School'. The school's grounds occupied much of the land at the corner of Regents Park and King Henrys roads, which meet at an acute angle. The former filling station stands on the site of the entrance to the courtyard around which the school's buildings were arranged. The school was originally founded by the physician and social reformer George William Bell (1813-1889) as the 'Home for Unconvicted Destitute Boys' in 1858. It was originally in some houses on Euston Road, where the British Library stands now. Later that year, it became a certified 'Industrial School', which admitted boys sent by the courts for their protection, as well as those who came voluntarily. In 1865, the school had to move because its premises were about to be demolished to build a railway goods shed.

The school moved to new premises on Regents Park Road, initially a row of three houses. The chapel, one of whose pediments bears the letter 'T', was added after the school received a donation from a generous donor and it was later superseded by the establishment of the St Marys Church on the northeast corner of Primrose Hill. In 1868, a new school room was built on the northern side of the school's yard. This was raised on arches, the spaces beneath them being used to store materials such as wood that was used in some of the practical classes taught in the establishment. By the 1890s, the school occupied the buildings that now form the corner of Regents Park and King Henrys Roads. The boys learnt a variety of skills including carpentry, brush making, tailoring, shoemaking, and so on. They were also hired out to local residents, as Edward Walford described (writing in 1882):

"A large quantity of firewood is cut on the premises, and delivered to customers, and several boys are employed by private families in the neighbourhood in cleaning knives and shoes. The amount of industrial work done in the Home is highly satisfactory. The products of the labour of the boys and their teachers —

clothes, shoes and boots, brushes of every kind, carpentry and firewood—are sold, and contribute to the general funds of the institution ..."

I wonder whether any of these highly productive young boys ever did jobs for the household of Friedrich Engels, who lived close by. At the same time as they were beavering away, so was Engels. According to the website www.marxists.org, during his residence on Regents Park Road, not far from to the school, he:

"... wrote many of his famous works at number 122—*The Housing Question* (1872), *Anti-Duhring* (1877-78), the revised form of three chapters of this book published as *Socialism, Utopian and Scientific* (1880), *Origin of the Family, Private Property and the State* (1884), *Ludwig Feuerbach* (1888)."

Engels died in 1895. The school closed in 1920. Today, there is no memorial to the school where it used to stand, but Engels's house is marked by a circular plaque. Both the school and Engels were involved in social reform and the welfare of the oppressed, but few today would associate this pleasant bourgeois thoroughfare with such historical activities.

Another famous writer, the American poet Sylvia Plath (1932-1963) lived briefly in picturesque Chalcot Square, which is a few yards south of Regents Park Road. There is a plaque on number 3 that records that she lived there between 1960 and 1961. Married to the poet Ted Hughes (1930-1998), the couple moved into the top floor flat, somewhat cramped accommodation, in January 1960. It was here that their daughter Frieda was born a few months later. Plath described the square as:

"…overlooking a little green with benches and fences for mothers and children … five minutes' walking distance from Primrose Hill and beautiful Regent's Park"

It is still an attractive square, made even more appealing by the variety of colours of the 19th century houses surrounding it. The Hughes's moved to larger accommodation in nearby Fitzroy Road, where she took her own life. Although Sylvia lived longer at Fitzroy Road than at Chalcot Square, her children decided it would be best to commemorate her time in the square. When the plaque was placed on the house on Chalcot Square in 2000, her daughter Frieda was asked why it was not placed on the house in Fitzroy Road. She replied, according to the *Ham and High* newspaper: "My mother died there … but she had lived here."

Plath lived for only a year in Chalcot Square, but the Filipino national hero Dr Jose Rizal (1861-1896) spent even less time in the neighbourhood, in number 37 Chalcot Crescent, a sinuous thoroughfare. He stayed in London from May 1888 to March 1889. He had come to the metropolis for several reasons: to improve his English; to study and annotate a work by Antonia de Morga (1559-1636) about the early Spanish colonisation of the Philippines; and because London was a safe place to carry out his struggle against the Spanish, who were occupying his country. At Chalcott Crescent, he was a guest of the Beckett family. While lodging with the Becketts, Jose had a brief romantic affair with Gertrude, the oldest of the three Beckett daughters. When her love for him became serious, Jose left London for Paris. Before he left, he gave the Beckett girls three sculptures he had made in London.

Rizal was a remarkable man with many skills. Born in the Philippines, he was an ophthalmologist by profession and fought vigorously for reform of Spanish rule in the Philippines. Amongst his other abilities were novel and poetry writing; philosophy; law; art including drawing, painting, and sculpting; ethnology and anthropology; architecture and cartography; history; martial arts; and magic tricks. Apart from his brief fling with Miss Beckett, he had numerous other affairs all over the world. After staying in many places in different continents, he returned to the Philippines, where his involvement in activities against the Spanish rulers caused him to be arrested and executed by Filippino soldiers in the Spanish army on the 30th of December 1896.

Another reformer and patriot lived near Regents Park Road. He was Dr Bhimrao Ramji Ambedkar (1891-1956), who championed India's dalits ('untouchables') and formulated the Constitution of India. Between 1920 and 1922 while he was studying at the London School of Economics and for the Bar, Ambedkar lived in a house at 10 King Henrys Road near Regents Park Road. In 2015, the house was bought by the Government of Maharashtra and was then converted into a memorial to Ambedkar. It is open to the public. Visitors can learn about Ambedkar from the well-captioned photographs on the walls of the rooms that they can wander through. The upper floor contains a re-construction of Ambedkar's bedroom including a four-poster bed, some of the great man's books, and an old pair of spectacles, which might have belonged to him. Other rooms contain shelves of books and various memorials to Ambedkar. There is also a commemorative plaque to India's present Prime Minister Narendra Modi, who inaugurated the memorial house in November 2015. The garden contains statue of Ambedkar clutching a book (the Constitution) in his left hand. A few years ago, neighbours of the Ambedkar house complained about it, concerned that it would attract swarms of tourists. Well, I suspect that the real reason was a racist fear that their precious street would, heaven forbid, be swamped by crowds of Indians. This was unlikely to happen, just as there are but few Marxist tourists swarming around Engels's former home.

NORTH END

AND

GOLDERS GREEN

NORTH END AND GOLDERS HILL PARK

Hampstead village is separated from places north of it by a largely uninhabited range of hills covered with woods, parks, and heathlands. Before the Underground railway reached Golders Green in 1907, there was little more than open fields and a few houses between Hampstead and its northern neighbours Hendon and Finchley. One road crossed the hills from Jack Straws Castle (near Whitestone Pond) to North End, a small settlement next to the Old Bull and Bush Pub. The architectural historian Nikolaus Pevsner, who lived in North End, described it as: "… once an isolated hamlet among woodland on the Hampstead border…" In the 10th century, this area was known as 'Sandgate'. Today, this picturesque locality retains its isolated feeling.

The centre of Hampstead High Street is 340 feet above sea level; Jack Straws Castle, half a mile away, is 440 feet; the Bull and Bush at North End, less than half a mile from Jack Straws, is 370 feet; and Golders Green Underground station, another half mile further on, is down at 226 feet. So, travelling between Hampstead and Hendon or Finchley involved negotiating quite a steep hill. In the 1730s, a cutting was made to ease the road's gradients, and it is through this, with its high sided, nicely planted banks, that the road, now named North End

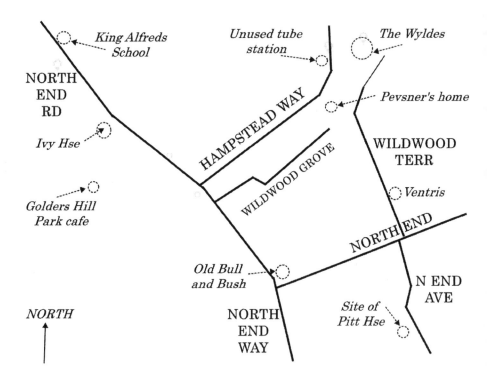

King Alfreds School

Unused tube station

The Wyldes

NORTH END RD

HAMPSTEAD WAY

Pevsner's home

Ivy Hse

WILDWOOD GROVE

WILDWOOD TERR

Golders Hill Park cafe

Ventris

NORTH END

Old Bull and Bush

N END AVE

NORTH

Site of Pitt Hse

NORTH END WAY

Way still runs. North of the Old Bull and Bush, the road is called North End Road. Before dropping steeply towards Golders Green, where it becomes Golders Green Road, the ancient thoroughfare skirts the eastern edge of Golders Hill Park, now officially a part of Hampstead Heath.

Before reaching the park from Hampstead, North End Way passes woods on the edge of West Heath. According to an article in *Heath Vision: Hampstead Heath in the 21st Century* (published by The Heath & Hampstead Society):

"Homosexuals currently use the West Heath during the night and day for their activities – at night there are several thousand."

North of West Heath, the road reaches the front entrance of Inverforth House. Next to it, Inverforth Close, a small private road open to pedestrians, leads off North End Way. At the end of it, there is a delightful garden with a wooden pergola, The Hill Garden, which is open to the public. It was once part of the gardens of Inverforth House. The present house was built in 1895 in a 'neo-Georgian' style to the designs of the architectural practice of Grayson and Ould. Between 1896 and 1904, Ronald Fisher (1890-1962) lived there as a child. He was one of the 'fathers' of modern biological statistics.

Between 1904 to 1925, The house was owned by William Lever, Viscount Leverhulme (1851-1925). He was one of the first men to produce soap on an industrial scale (in 1884) and was an enlightened industrialist. He built Port Sunlight near to Birkenhead to house his workers in pleasant surroundings. The house's library was designed by built by William and Segar Owen of Warrington, who also designed buildings at Port Sunlight. In 1955, Inverforth

House became a convalescent home of the (now closed) Manor House Hospital, and that is how I remember it from my childhood. The hospital was not part of the NHS. It was privately run by trade unions. The edifice ceased being a hospital in 1999. Now, the house contains privately owned, luxury flats; it has become a 'gated community'.

The gardens of Inverforth House were laid out from 1906 onwards by Thomas Hayton Mawson (1861-1933), garden designer, landscape architect, and town planner. According to one source (www.historic-uk.com), Lord Leverhulme wanted the pergola:

"...to be the setting for extravagant Edwardian Garden parties, while at the same time being a place where his family and friends could spend long summer evenings enjoying the spectacular gardens."

In 1960, the London County Council ('LCC') bought the Pergola and associated garden areas, which had by then become very dilapidated. In 1963, part of the gardens was opened to the public, and called the 'Hill Garden'. In later years, successors to the LCC have repaired to woodwork and brickwork of the extensive terraces and pergolas and maintained the gardens superbly.

Golders Hill Park, north of Inverforth House has an entrance on North End Road. The park occupies the grounds of a large estate created in the 1760s by Charles Dingley (1711-1769). He made his money in the Russian sugar trade and other enterprises. He was an enthusiastic supporter of the politician William Pitt the Elder (see below). One of the later owners of this estate, John Coore, hired the great landscape artist Humphry Repton (1752-1815) to landscape the grounds. The penultimate owner of the estate was Queen Victoria's surgeon Sir Thomas Spencer Wells (1818-1897), inventor of the still frequently used artery forceps, now named after him. After his death, the estate with its Victorian Golders Hill Mansion was sold first to the soap magnate and historian, Thomas Barratt (1841-1914), from whose works I have often quoted in this book. He sold it to a committee who wanted to save the grounds from being built over. In 1898, the grounds were opened to the public as a recreational park. The Victorian mansion, which stood close to North End Road, was destroyed by enemy bombing in 1941. This building was across North End Road from a large building (on the corner of Hampstead Way), which is marked on 19th century maps as 'Manor House'. Between 1917 and 2000, its grounds were used to house the Manor House Hospital. As a child, I used to walk past the hospital, which with its numerous ageing temporary-looking out-houses was not particularly attractive. The hospital has since been replaced by an unappealing looking apartment complex. At various times, the hospital had departments in Inverforth House and across North End Road in Ivy House.

When I was a child, my parents frequently took me to Golders Hill Park. We used to enter it from West Heath Avenue. Close to this entrance, there are tennis courts where my parents used to play. Opposite the courts, but beyond the edge of the park, there is a shoebox shaped residential building, whose upper storey walls are vast panes of glass. When it was built in 1961 by the architect Anthony Levy, who lived there, it was easily visible from the park. So exposed to view was its interior that its then occupants hung ugly white curtains to conceal their

215

lives and living quarters. Now, trees and plants have grown up around it so that it is hardly visible from either the park or the nearby streets.

For me, Golders Hill Park's main attraction is its small 'zoo'. A large upper enclosure – more like a big field than a cage – is home to a herd of deer. And, on my last visit there (in 2020), I spotted a creature in the field that looked to me like an ostrich; it was a rhea. A lower enclosure, which is divided into smaller cages and paddocks, open to the elements, contains a variety of creatures, both feathered and four-legged. As a child, I remember that there were wallabies on display as well as flamingos. The wallabies are still there along with a pair of ageing donkeys, but the flamingos have gone. Recently, I saw some ring-tailed lemurs sunning themselves in a cage. Once, there were a few muntjac deer in the paddock where the wallabies live. Some ibis had replaced the flamingos and on my last visit, I saw a caged kookaburra.

On a lawn in between the tennis courts and the animal enclosures, there is a sculpture that looks like an avant-garde bus shelter. It is *Gazebo*, sculpted by Wendy Hall in 1983. High above this sculpture near the top of a lovely curving grassy slope, there is a bandstand. This has been there for a long time. It is marked on a map that was surveyed in 1912. When I was young and living about a mile away in Hampstead Garden Suburb, I used to hear occasional brief snatches of music coming from the bandstand on weekend afternoons in summer when I was playing in our garden. The structure is well-maintained. A weathervane was added to it in 2012 to celebrate the 60th anniversary of the reign of Queen Elizabeth II. There is a huge old tree standing next to the bandstand. As it is surrounded by a sturdy cast-iron fence, I imagine that it is of some considerable vintage.

Descending the slope from the bandstand, we reach a small clump of trees that has been named 'The Stumpery', a term borrowed from Victorian times. This small, sloping wooded area contains a collection of fantastic looking stumps from dead trees and a narrow brook along whose banks numerous ferns grow. A winding path climbs gently through this sylvan glade, a vegetarian version of Jurassic Park. It emerges on to a small single-arched stone bridge spanning one end of a pond, which is linked by a rivulet to others downstream. The pond has been in existence for a long time. It appears without a bridge on an 1860 map, but there is a bridge on a map surveyed in 1894. So, it is likely that this is a feature of the gardens of Golders Hill House from before the time that the park was opened to the public. The pond attracts all kinds of ducks and other waterfowl and runs along one side of a square garden with walls on three sides. This is now a well-maintained flower garden. The enclosure containing it can be seen on an 1860 map, and an 1893 map shows that then it contained some glasshouses (for raising plants), which no longer exist. The later map shows some buildings to the west of the enclosure. These are still present.

Above the pond, stands the attractive, and popular, 'Refreshment House' with seating, both indoor and outdoor (on a terrace that overlooks much of the park). Established in 1973, the establishment is housed in a wood and glass building with elegantly simple modern architecture. Food and drinks are available here, as well as a good selection of ice-creams. Close by, a scantily clad sculpted stone figure sits holding a bowl to his lips. This is *Diogenist* created by Mark Batten (1905-1993) His obituary writer in *The Independent* newspaper wrote:

"His most famous work, The Diogenist, in Hopton-wood stone … established its author beyond all doubt as the leading, and indeed the only master in Britain of this most exacting technique. Indeed, I had to travel as far as Yugoslavia before I came across it again."

The boundary between the Boroughs of Camden and Barnet runs through Golders Hill Park, placing the houses in North End just within Camden and the former Borough of Hampstead. A notice marking the beginning of the Borough of Barnet stands on North End Road next to a house with some crenellations and mock Tudor features that neighbours the park. Built by John Coore in 1786, this has long been known as 'Ivy House'. Between 1840 and 1851, it was home to CR Cockerell (1788-1863), an archaeologist, architect, and writer. In 1851, and in poor health, he and his family returned to London, where they had a house in Chester Square. In 1912, the Russian ballet dancer Anna Pavlova (1881-1931) moved into Ivy House and lived there until her death. During the 1950s, the house became part of Manor House Hospital (see above). Then, more recently Ivy House was home to a Jewish cultural centre. Now, it is a girls' school, 'St Anthony's School for Girls'.

Moving northwest along North End Road, away from North End hamlet and Golders Hill Park, we reach the gates of King Alfred's School. Founded in 1898, this co-educational 'progressive' school moved from its original site in

Hampstead to its present position on the former Manor House estate in 1919. It appealed to parents who wished their children to have a less conventional educational experience than was otherwise available. Today, I believe that it is less unconventional than it used to be when I was a child. One of its buildings was designed by my late uncle, the structural engineer Sven Rindl (1921-2007). Further down towards Golders Green on Wellgarth Road, stands a large building (built 1915), which used to house a nursery training college, and then, in later years, a youth hostel. Now, it is a block of flats. After the sculptor Barbara Hepworth gave birth to triplets in 1934, she put them in the Wellgarth nursery college to allow herself time for working on her art.

Returning uphill towards North End, we pass a large, detached house with bow windows, but little else of architectural interest: 145 North End Road. It bears a blue plaque commemorating the fact that the writer Evelyn Waugh (1903-1966) lived there. The house was built by his father in 1907. Waugh wrote in his autobiographical *A Little Learning*:

"I was four years old when my father built his house in what was then the village of North end, Hampstead. He was, in fact, the first of its spoliators. When we settled there the tube reached no further than Hampstead…"

All went well until, as I mentioned at the beginning of this book, the Waugh's postal district was changed from Hampstead to Golders Green:

"Eventually (I think after the first war) our postal address was altered from Hampstead to Golders Green. My father deplored the change, and, as far as possible, ignored it, because Hampstead had historical associations, with Keats and Blake and Constable, while Golders Green meant, to him, merely a tube station."

Waugh also mentioned:

"… there was in North End Road, a few hundred yards below us, a row of seedy old proletarian dwellings named 'the Terrace'. These were my mother's especial care, and I am sure she was a welcome visitor there."

This terrace still exists. Further down North End Road from the Waugh's house, the row of unexciting inter-war suburban dwellings is interrupted by a short terrace of slightly more attractive 19th century terraced dwellings. This appears on old maps (e.g., 1896) as 'Golders Hill Terrace'. It was built in about 1874. At that time, there were few other buildings between these houses and Brent on the edge of Hendon.

Returning uphill past King Alfred's we reach Hampstead Way, a road that leads into Hampstead Garden Suburb (its construction began in the first decade of the 20th century). A few yards along the road on the left, there is a small well-secured enclosure containing a low building with heavy steel doors and topped with a nasty looking spiky railing to deter intruders. This structure marks the entrance to an Underground station at which no trains ever stop. It lies on the Northern Line between Hampstead and Golders Green stations and was to have been called either 'North End' or 'Bull and Bush'. Most of the subterranean parts of the station – its platforms, stairways, and lifts – were built long before the surface access building was constructed in the 1950s. During the Second World War, the station was used to store archives, which were only accessible from inside the tunnels, and, during the subsequent Cold War, the unfinished station was designated for civil defence purposes. Passengers travelling on the tube in the dark tunnels between Golders Green and Hampstead can just about discern the platforms of what would have been one of London's deepest Underground stations.

Opposite the Underground access hut, there is a wood-clad (clapboard) building on high ground. This is part of Wyldes Farm (see below). Incidentally, many clapboard covered houses were built in and around Hampstead, presumably because timber was readily available in the woods that surround the village. Near the junction of Hampstead Way and Wyldes Close, there is a building bearing a small bas-relief depicting two naked boys carrying a plank and one carrying an axe. This is affixed to the wall of a house, built in 1915 by T Laurence Dale where the Scottish architect Thomas Smith Tait (1882-1954) lived for some time from 1929 onwards. Just beyond the Close, a rough path heads uphill from Wildwood Road into a wooded part of Hampstead Heath. It curves to the right, and provides a good view of Wyldes Farmhouse, also called the 'The Wyldes'.

On 19th century maps, what is now the Wyldes was surrounded by 'Heath Farm'. This delightful ensemble of rustic buildings comes as a great surprise to anyone used to the often-mundane suburbs of northwest London. Much of the exterior of these buildings is clapboard. According to Nikolaus Pevsner, some parts of the buildings are as old as 17th century. The newer parts are 18th century. Two commemorative plaques can be seen from the footpath. One states that the painter John Linnell (1792-1882) lived at The Wyldes (in a part of it rented from the farmer who owned it), and that the artist and poet William Blake (1757-1827), stayed here occasionally. The author Charles Dickens (1812-1870) also stayed here for five weeks in 1837. At that time, he was busy writing episodes of *Oliver Twist* and *The Pickwick Papers*. In 1884, Charlotte Wilson (1854-1944), an English anarchist and collaborator of the Russian Peter Kroptkin (1842-1921), moved into the Wyldes. There, she presided over meetings of the Hampstead Historic Club, which was also known as 'The Karl Marx Society'. Its meetings were attended by left-wing sympathisers people such as: George Bernard Shaw, Ford Madox Brown, Sydney Webb, and Annie Besant. There is no plaque commemorating Wilson's time at the Wyldes.

The other of the two plaques states that the architect and town-planner Sir Raymond Unwin (1863-1940) lived at the Wyldes between 1906 and 1940. It was from this house that he planned the development of the nearby Hampstead Garden Suburb. Close to the farm, and in complete contrast to its rural appearance, there is a terrace of four, unattractive but imposing, tall brick buildings on Wildwood Terrace. When I was at the Hall School in Swiss Cottage between 1960 and 1965, I used to visit one of my friends, Nicholas Hodgson, who lived in one of these houses. He was a grandson of the architectural historian the German Jewish Nikolaus Pevsner, who lived in this terrace between 1936 (three years after coming to England from Germany) and his death in 1983. I never met the great man. These four houses do not appear on a detailed 1863 map, but they do on an 1894 map. The same is true for the row of 19th century terraced houses that lie alongside Wildwood Grove, which is below the Pevsner dwelling, and can be reached from it by a short steep footpath. These houses were built in 1882, whereas the terrace in which Pevsner lived was built by T Clowser in about 1871. Today, Wildwood Terrace continues as an unpaved road from Pevsner's home towards its intersection with North End. A plaque on a brick wall along this road commemorates that the architect Michael Ventris (1922-1956) lived in the house (which he designed) behind the wall. Ventris, an amateur linguist, is remembered for his deciphering of Linear B, an ancient Aegean script.

North End, which runs eastwards from North End Way, is an old road that appears on maps drawn as early as 1800. It was, and still is, a cul-de-sac. Almost opposite Wildwood Terrace, North End Avenue climbs southwards towards Hampstead. Nowadays, it is a cul-de-sac, but old maps suggest that it was once a route that connected North End with Hampstead. Barely visible through the trees that surround it, there is a large old building in its grounds at the east corner of North End and North End Avenue. A map surveyed in 1912 names this mansion-like dwelling as 'Byron Cottage'. It stands where once, long ago, a farm cottage stood. According to one source, www.british-history.ac.uk, this building was already in existence by 1781. Its inhabitants have included the judge Sir Robert Dallas (1756-1824) and the Quaker philanthropist and anti-slavery activist, Sir Thomas Fowell Buxton (1786-1845). The building was called 'Myrtle' until 1908, when Lady Byron, who was distantly related to the great poet, moved into it that year, and changed its name to 'Byron Cottage'. The building is now called 'Cedar Lodge'.

Further up the Avenue there is a modern house set back from the road. A plaque on its gatepost states: "William Pitt, Earl of Chatham, 1708-1778, Prime Minister, lived in a house on this site". The house where he lived was built on land acquired early in the 18th century by Robert Dingley (died 1742), a goldsmith in the City of London. His son Charles Dingley (see above) inherited this land and added surrounding plots to it. In 1762, Charles owned a house, which was had been named at various times: 'Wildwoods', 'North End', and 'Pitt House'. At the politically ambitious Charles's invitation, William Pitt the Elder moved into this house in 1766. According to GE Mitton in his *The Fascination of Hampstead*, William Pitt, first Earl of Chatham:

"…shut himself up here from all communication with his fellow-Ministers in 1767; he was then a miserable invalid, afflicted with a disorder which in modern times would have been termed "nerves"; he refused to see anyone, even his own attendant, and his food was passed to him through a panel of the door. However, later he returned to public life."

Dingley added a new wing to the house and a gymnasium for the great politician's children. Pitt used the house for several years. In 1787, the Dingley Estate began to be divided. The banker Abraham Robarts (1745-1816) bought Pitt House in 1787, and then sold it in 1807 to the lawyer John Vivian, who was a solicitor to the Board of Excise. The house had various owners during the 19th century including (in 1899) Sir Harold Harmsworth (1868-1940; later 'Viscount

224

Rothermere'). According to an article in *The Camden New Journal* published in May 2008, when the house was put on the market in 1908:

"…it was described by local estate agents Lowe, Goldschmidt & Howland as "the house in which Great Britain lost America" – a historical reference to the fact that if William Pitt had not become something of a recluse there in the 1770s the government would not have imposed its infamous tea tax and the Americas would have been saved."

 In 1910, the politician Valentine Fleming (1882-1917) moved into the house. One of his children was the author and creator of James Bond, Ian Fleming (1908-1964). In his early childhood, Ian lived in Pitt House. Its several owners made numerous modifications to the building. A picture taken of it in 1921 shows that by then it was not an elegant building. Another, taken in the 1940s shows that by then it was in a poor state, uninhabited. It was sold to an investment company in 1948. They demolished it four years later. Only the memorial plaque marks the site where one of Britain's greatest politicians lived. Some stretches of brick wall, which might once have surrounded the house's extensive gardens, survive amongst the trees surrounding the site.

Descending North End Avenue and moving along North End towards the Old Bull and Bush pub, we pass a Victorian house, a 'cottage orné' called Wildwood Lodge. Its centrally placed front door has a row of five small unadorned blank shields above it. Built in the mid-19th century, it was owned by one of Queen Victoria's dentists before 1869. Between this 'Gothick' building and the Old Bull and Bush, there is a terrace of houses that, at first sight, look Georgian in style. Most of them are not old, but the two closest to the pub (numbers 1 and 3: Stowe House) are 18th century. The part of the pub immediately next to these two houses is an old structure, but the rest of the pub is far newer. Made famous in an old music hall song *Down at the Old Bull and Bush* (by Andrew B Sterling and Henry von Tilzer), the Old Bull and Bush began life as a farmhouse that was built around 1645. The pub began in the early 18th century. The artist William Hogarth (1697-1754) visited it regularly. The artists Gainsborough and Reynolds frequented the pub with the actor/director Garrick. The present pub was built in the 1920s and is uninteresting architecturally. When I was a child, there was another pub next door to the Old Bull and Bush. This was the 'Hare and Hounds'. I used to pass it and the two pubs on my way to school in Highgate (between 1965 and 1970). It was already present in the early 19th century. In 1940, during WW2 it was twice destroyed by aerial bombardment. And, according to Christopher Wade, it: "… existed for a time in five linked caravans…" before being rebuilt in 1968. The pub ceased operating in 2000 and has since been demolished. A modern brick apartment block now stands where people used to enjoy a casual pint.

A small cluster of buildings stands across the North End Way on a steep slope surrounded by a wooded part of Hampstead Heath. Surrounded by vegetation at the south-east corner of Sandy Road, there is a house with a black wooden gable on which words from *Proverbs* (Chapter 22, verse 6) are carved in capital letters: "Train up a child in the way he should go, and when he is old he will not depart from it." Beneath them, there is a stone carved with the date 1849 and the letters 'VR'. This was once a village school that was built largely through the support of a cricketer and banker John Gurney Hoare (1810-1875). He was born in Heath House in Hampstead (opposite the former Jack Straws Castle). He was a grandson of Samuel Hoare Junior (1751–1825), the anti-slavery campaigner and a banker, who was a partner in one of the banks that eventually became part of the still extant Lloyd's Bank. John inherited Hill House close to North End from his father, the banker Samuel Hoare (1783–1847). Some of his sisters lived in Stowe House in North End. The Hoare family were Quakers.

One unnamed member of the Hoare family is mentioned by Evelyn Waugh in his memoirs. He wrote about her, when she was living in North End House (where Prime Minister Pitt once lived):

"[she] … devoted her whole life to practical widely ramifying but primarily centred on her own village. benefactions She must have been about sixty when we first knew her, rosy faced, white haired, blunt and cheerful in speech … except when she drove into London, I remember her as always on foot, shod in large, shapeless boots, plainly dressed and followed by two or three Scotch terriers. I rather suppose that my mother was the last neighbour on whom she called formally."

She might have been one of John's daughters, Margaret, who managed the village school that he established.

Opposite the Old Bull and Bush, there used to be (in my childhood) a small shop that sold a variety of groceries, sweets, and newspapers. It and the school mentioned above were there when Evelyn Waugh was a young boy living in North End Road. He wrote of the shop:

227

"… a post office and village shop kept by an irascible man Mr Borely. He was surly with all his customers and positively savage with children … My father refused to have a telephone in his house and it was to Mr Borely that we went on the rare occasions when the doctor was summoned."

Waugh also refers to a dairy run by the Misses Tooley. Their father grazed his cows in a field nearby. I do not recall this existing when I was a child.

This brings us back to the entrance of Golders Hill Park next to Pavlova's former residence, and the end of this exploration of a hamlet with ancient roots, which has largely evaded losing its identity during the years of London's expansion. If it was not for the traffic that races between Hampstead and Golders Green along the often-busy North End Way, one could easily imagine that North End, where both Waugh and Pitt once resided, is a sleepy settlement in the heart of the countryside.

Following North End Road downhill from North End and away from Hampstead, we reach Golders Green, which is not, and never has been, considered part of Hampstead.

POETS AND GOLDERS GREEN

Until about 1907, when the Underground railway was extended from Hampstead to Golders Green, the latter was merely a line of well-spaced houses and gardens on the road between Hampstead and Hendon. This settlement lay mainly west of where Finchley Road (built in about 1827) crosses the current North End Road and its western continuation called Golders Green Road. Today, a clock tower, a war memorial (dedicated in 1923), stands at this intersection. In comparison with Hampstead and its eastern neighbour Highgate, Golders Green has few buildings of architectural merit and little to interest the casual visitor apart from: shopping opportunities; some eateries; St Albans Church (built about 1933 and designed by Giles Gilbert Scott) where the South African theologian and later archbishop Desmond Tutu (1931-2021) was its curate in the early 1960s; a shop designed by Ernő Goldfinger (number 2 Golders Green Road); the former Hippodrome Theatre (built 1913); and several Jewish religious institutions. The first of the area's synagogues to open was in Dunstan Road in 1922. It was designed in a neo-Georgian style by Digby Lewis Soloman (1848-1928). According to Pam Fox in her *The Jewish Community of Golders Green*:

"It was not until the mid-1920s that the Jewish community of Golders Green became firmly rooted in the area. The opening of Golders Green Synagogue in 1922 had made the growth of the Jewish community almost inevitable … Regular advertisements appeared in the Jewish Chronicle specifically encouraging Jewish people to move to Golders Green, 'London's Suburb de Luxe'."

To call Golders Green "de Luxe" is pushing things a bit too far. There was a Chinese restaurant at number 22 North End Road, almost opposite the Hippodrome. In my youth, it was called the Tung Hsing. It opened in the 1960s and was one of the first restaurants in London to serve Pekinese-style food, rather than the then usual Cantonese cuisine. The restaurant was owned by a retired ambassador from Chiang Kai-shek's Nationalist China and his wife, whom I believe was responsible for the very excellent food served. A review in *The Tatler* in November 1965 noted:

"…This restaurant (opposite Golders Green tube station) serves food of a better quality and a greater authenticity than many of its type. The accent is on Pekingese cooking …"

Had you visited Golders Green in the 19th century, you would have arrived at: "… a little outlying cluster of cottages, with an inn, the White Swan, whose garden is in great favour with London holiday makers … from the village there are pleasant walks by lanes and footpaths …"

So, wrote James Thorne in his *Handbook to the Environs of London* in 1876. Of these lanes, Hoop Lane, still exists, and is described in the next chapter. The White Swan was in business until recently but has disappeared since I took a photograph of it in 2017. I do not think that I would recommend Golders Green as a holiday destination anymore. It is not unpleasant, but it is no longer rural and lacks the atmosphere of a resort. The poet and physician Mark Akenside (1721-1770) was a friend of the politician Jeremiah Dyson (1722-1776), who had his house in Golders Green. A frequent visitor to Dyson's place, Akenside wrote, while recovering from an ailment:

> "Thy verdant scenes, O Goulder's Hill,
>
> Once more I seek a languid guest;
>
> With throbbing temples and with burden'd breast

Once more I climb thy steep aerial way,

O faithful cure of oft-returning ill ..."

Another poet, now better known than Akenside, William Wordsworth (1770-1850) wrote:

"I am not unfrequently a visitor on Hampstead Heath, and seldom pass by the entrance of Mr Dyson's villa, on Golder's Hill, close by, without thinking of the pleasures which Akenside often had there."

And during more recent times, the poet Dannie Abse (1923-2014) was based around Golders Green. His collection of poetry, *Poems, Golders Green*, was published in 1962.

In the time before the Underground was built, visitors from London could reach Golders Green either by crossing the range of hills north of Hampstead on a road that follows the path of the present North End Road or, after 1835, when it was completed, by travelling along Finchley Road. The end of Golders Green's existence as a rural outpost of London and its development as a residential suburb began in June 1907, when the Charing Cross, Euston & Hampstead Railway (now part of the Underground's Northern Line) opened the above-ground Golders Green Station.

My family used this station on an almost daily basis. During my childhood, there were two ways of entering it. One way, which still exists, is from the large station forecourt, the local bus and coach station. The other, which was closed at least 35 years ago, was from Finchley Road. An entrance beneath the railway bridge led to a long, covered walkway under an elaborate wooden structure,

231

open to the outside air on most of its two sides. This wooden canopy, which still exists but is not accessible to the public, reminds me of structures I have seen in India. The walkway led to a ticket office, beyond which there was a corridor from which staircases provided access to the outdoor platforms. Our family favoured using the Finchley Road entrance because it was slightly closer to our home in Hampstead Garden Suburb. Bar Linda that faces the bus yard is a friendly little café, which has been in business for over 60 years. Nearby, on Finchley Road, beneath the bridge that carries trains leaving Golders Green station towards the northwest, is an Italian restaurant, Artista. This occupies the site of the long-since closed Bamboo Bar, whose owners, Simone and Lorenzo, later established the still flourishing Spaghetti House group of restaurants. My parents frequented the Bamboo Bar in the late 1950s.

LIFE AND DEATH ON HOOP LANE

Hoop Lane is one of Golders Green's oldest thoroughfares. It was named after a pub in Golders Green, The Hoop, which no longer exists. It runs northeast from Golders Green Road, crosses Finchley Road, and then continues towards the western edge of the Hampstead Garden Suburb, a questionably successful experiment in utopian urban planning that began to be built in 1904. Its planners' ideal was to create an area where different social classes lived side by side. It is now only affordable to the wealthier section of society. Before the Suburb was begun, Hoop Lane followed its present route from Golders Green and ended at a T-junction in open countryside. From this point, in one direction, Temple Fortune Lane ran northwest, and in the other, Wild Hatch ran southeast and ended abruptly, where Hampstead Way meets it today. These byways were almost devoid of buildings in the 1870s. There was one building on Wild Hatch at that date, which appears on a 1900 map, labelled as 'Wild Hatch Cottages'.

Finchley Road was laid out and built in the 1820s and 1830s as a turnpike road (toll-road). It bypassed the road that ran from Camden Town across Hampstead's hilly terrain to Finchley and further north. Before the turnpike was built, traffic had to climb the steep road to Hampstead, and then wind its way down what is now North End Way and North End Road. In the days before Finchley Road was constructed, to reach Finchley from Hampstead it was necessary to proceed as follows. After passing the commonage of Golders Green, the traveller would have taken a right turn into Hoop Lane and then gone along it in a north-easterly direction to its end where it met Temple Fortune Lane. Next, the traveller would have had to go northwest along this lane until he or she reached a triangular open space, which is now the position of modern Temple Fortune. This place's name derives from the fact that it stands on land once owned by the Knights Templars. This spot was the southern end of Ducksetters Lane, which wound its way north-eastwards to Finchley. Thus, prior to the building of Finchley Road, Hoop Lane was part of one of the few ways from London to Finchley. It was a country lane with scarcely any buildings before the late 19th century.

Southwest of Finchley Road, Hoop Lane was devoid of buildings as late as 1897. Near where the road met North End Road (now 'Golders Green Road'), there was a building set in the middle of a large plot called The Oaks. This property. which was marked on a detailed 1912 map, was a large stately home that disappeared by 1920. By 1912, there were plant nursery buildings on Hoop Lane and, also, one building, now the Central Hotel, where Hoop Lane meets Finchley Road on its west side. This is the oldest surviving building on Hoop Lane. There was another early building (now Glentrees estate agent) opposite it on the other side of Finchley Road close to where the Roman Catholic Church of Edward the Confessor stands today. This church's construction began in March 1914, and it was completed by October 1915, despite wartime difficulties such as a zeppelin raid on Golders Green in September 1915.

My earliest memories of Hoop Lane date to when I was three or four years old. At that age, I attended a kindergarten in Hoop Lane. This was in the hall attached to Golders Green's Unitarian Church, which was designed in the 'Byzantine revival' style by the architects Reginald Farrow and Sydney R Turner and opened in 1925. It contains interesting artworks including a mural by Ivon Hitchens (1893-1979). The kindergarten was under the direction of a lady we called 'Miss Schreuer', who lived a few doors away in Hoop Lane. My only lasting memory from my time there was when my father appeared at the school with a white beard and a red outfit, dressed as Father Christmas. One of my fellow pupils was the late Micaela Comberti (1952-2003), who became an accomplished violinist. A few years later, my sister and my cousins attended

Miss Schreuer's. I am not sure what became of Miss Schreuer, but I heard rumours that the end of her life was unhappy. Today, the hall, where her school flourished, is a Montessori kindergarten. When I lived in the area, I often walked past the school and the Unitarian Church. The latter had a panel facing the road, upon which posters with pious messages were posted. One that I will always remember was: "If you think you have seen the light, think again".

At the north-western corner of the point where Hoop Lane meets Finchley Road, there stands the Central Hotel. Undistinguished in appearance, it has been a hotel for over forty years. Directly across Finchley Road on the north-eastern corner of its intersection with Hoop Lane, there stands a corner shop. For at least forty years, it has been the premises of Glentree International, an estate agent. Before that, this corner shop was a dairy shop run by the Express Dairy. Next to it, accessible from Hoop Lane, the company had a depot for re-charging and stocking its electric milk floats. These floats moved almost silently, apart from the clinking of the glass milk, cream, and yoghurt bottles, which they delivered from house to house every morning. Deliveries, such as these and those made by a mobile vegetable seller in a lorry, a Frenchman with strings of onions draped over his bicycle, and a knife grinder (also on a bicycle), made life a little easier for those living in the nearby Hampstead Garden Suburb, which has never had any shops for reasons best known to its principal founder Dame Henrietta Barnett (1851-1936).

Most of Hoop Lane to the east of Finchley Road is dedicated to the deceased. On the northern side of the road, there is a huge Jewish cemetery, an undulating sea of gravestones. On the southern side, stands sprawling Golders Green Crematorium. For almost thirty years, I used to walk between these two necropolises on my way to and from school and then university, both in daylight and after dark. The possible presence of ghosts and other supernatural phenomena associated with the afterlife never bothered me in the slightest. These final resting places were part and parcel of my childhood.

The Golders Green Crematorium was opened in 1902 by Sir Henry Thompson, president of the Cremation Society of England. Before its existence, Londoners had to use the Woking Crematorium that opened in 1885. The buildings of the crematorium are all close to the brick boundary wall that runs along Hoop Lane. Behind them spread attractive and extensive landscaped memorial gardens. According to www.historicengland.org.uk website, the main buildings were designed in the 'Romanesque Lombardic style'. They present a forbidding appearance. Many of the original buildings were designed by teams that included Alfred Yeates (1867-1944) and Ernest George (1839-1922), who was cremated at Hoop Lane. They formed a business partnership in 1892. George's speciality was garden architecture. The gardens and some of the buildings at the crematorium are fine examples of his work. Although the various buildings exhibit a certain architectural homogeneity, they were built over several decades as, gradually, money became available to pay for their construction.

It is well worth asking to visit the inside of the Ernest George Columbarium. This building, which is usually locked, houses urns (containing ashes) and memorials, some placed on masonry shelves in alcoves. Amongst the incinerated remains in this columbarium are those of Sigmund Freud and his wife, as well as Anna Pavlova, the ballet dancer. Many other famous people have been cremated at this crematorium. These include, to name but a very few, Ivor Novello, Bram Stoker, Peter Sellers, Ronnie Scott, Ernő Goldfinger, Kingsley Amis, Enid Blyton, Rudyard Kipling, and Ernest Bevin. Not all the ashes of the cremated are stored or scattered in the Crematorium's grounds. Some are taken away to be disposed of elsewhere, as were, for example, the ashes of Soviet politician and a proposer of the idea of Lenin's tomb in Moscow, Leonid Krasin (1870-1926). His ashes were buried in the Kremlin Wall Necropolis. According to S Kotkin in his *Stalin. Paradoxes of Power*, it was Krasin, who had: "… proposed inclusion of a terrace from which the masses could be addressed…". This was added to the design of Lenin's Mausoleum.

Sadly, I have had to visit the crematorium too often. Friends of my parents and colleagues of my father have been cremated here. These included Professor of Accountancy William Baxter (1906-2006), who was responsible for encouraging my father to come from South Africa to study in the UK in 1938. My father's colleague at the London School of Economics, the philosopher Professor John Watkins, was another person whose funeral I attended in one of the larger of the crematoriums multi-denominational chapels. We attended the final farewell of Dr 'Sushi' Patel, who studied medicine in Bombay with my mother-in-law. She was a Hindu. I remember that the whole congregation filed past her open coffin before she was cremated. Closer to home, my heart was filled with great sadness when I attended the memorial services for three of my

237

uncles. At one of these services, the ceremony for an uncle who lived in Hampstead Garden Suburb was conducted by a Humanist celebrant, who later conducted my aunt's pre-cremation ceremony. At another, that of my uncle who lived in Fleet Road, the Jewish Kaddish was recited, this being the final wish of an uncle who in life showed little overt interest in his Jewish background. Later, when his belongings were being sorted, we discovered to our surprise that his interest in Judaism and its practices was greater than anyone had realised. The saddest funeral that I attended at Golders Green's Crematorium was my mother's. She died young after suffering painfully for two months in the Royal Free Hospital. There were only a very few of us sitting in one of the smaller chapels. There was no ceremony, nothing was said. When my mother's coffin was carried past me along the aisle, I was overwhelmed with emotion as I realised that this was the very last time that I would ever be physically close to her.

My mother was one of many thousands to have been cremated in Golders Green. She was a sculptress. Other artists cremated here included, to mention a few, Boris Anrep, Walter Crane, and Percy Wyndham Lewis. Our family lived in Hampstead Garden Suburb, a stone's throw from St Judes Church, whose architect was Edwin Lutyens, famous for his work in New Delhi. He was cremated at Golders Green's crematorium in 1944. The list of celebrities in all fields who ended up at this place is enormous. However, I knew nothing of this during the many journeys that I made by foot along Hoop Lane during my younger years, when my mind was focussed on the future rather than the past.

Once when I was being shown around the Columbarium by one of the crematorium's officials, I told him that my mother and uncles had been cremated there. To which he smiled, put his hand on my shoulder, and said:

"Well, in that case, I suppose that you will be ending up here one day."

The Jewish Cemetery in Hoop Lane is divided into two sections. One, the western half, contains mostly upright gravestones, and the other, the eastern, mainly horizontal gravestones. The vertical headstones are characteristic of the Ashkenazi tradition, and the horizontal of the Sephardic. A book, *A History in our Time - Rabbis and Teachers Buried at Hoop Lane Cemetery* (published by the Leo Baeck College in 2006), provides an interesting history of the cemetery. It opened for 'business' in about 1896. The juxtaposition of the graves of two types of Jews in the same cemetery is unusual. *The Jewish Yearbook* for the year 5658 (Jewish calendar; 1897 AD) noted of the cemetery:

"… a new cemetery at Golders'-green was also made ready for its melancholy purpose this last year. This cemetery has the curious distinction of being used by both the Orthodox Sephardim and the Reform Congregation of the West London Synagogue of British Jews."

The reason for this juxtaposition was that the two separate Jewish communities had bought neighbouring plots of land. Many years after the purchases, some of the land was sold for house building on Temple Fortune Lane (this happened in 1973, and includes the estate on Sheridan Walk), and another part to build a synagogue, the North Western Reform Synagogue (built in 1936; entered from Alyth Gardens).

The cemetery, which I have seen by peering through its boundary fence but never entered, contains graves of many notable people including that of Dr Leo Baeck (1873-1956), who was born in Germany and became a leader in both Liberal and Progressive Judaism. During WW2, he represented all German Jews and narrowly avoided being murdered at Theresienstadt. More recently, another well-known Ashkenazi Jew, Rabbi Hugo Gryn (1930 -1996), a cleric and a broadcaster, was buried here. Amongst those who are buried in the Sephardi section, one is of particular interest to me. This is the barrister and historian Philip Guedalla (1889-1944), who published many books on historical subjects. He was related to my late mother's family, albeit quite distantly.

Hoop Lane ends at a traffic roundabout east of both the cemetery and the crematorium. Vehicles drive around a small triangular area containing a garden, and then can continue east along Meadway into Hampstead Garden Suburb. Pedestrians can access the small gardens by means of a short staircase, and then walk through them under a wooden pergola entwined with plants. This little garden is called 'Meadway Gate Open Space'. Wild Hatch skirts the eastern boundary of the crematorium grounds. This picturesque cul-de-sac narrows at its south-eastern end to become a footpath, which threads it way between the garden gates of houses on one side of it and the edge of the crematorium gardens on the other. The path ends at Hampstead Way. Crossing this road, one reaches a gravel path that runs beside a stream on the Hampstead Heath Extension. A few feet north of the path on the Heath on the east side of Hampstead Way, there is an elevated clump of wild vegetation. Within this, there are mounds that were used during WW2 as bases for anti-aircraft guns. In my childhood, these mounds were accessible, and the concrete bases were visible. Now, they are fenced-off and hidden by the plants growing around them. Opposite Wild Hatch, and beyond the Meadway Gate Open Space, is the beginning of Temple Fortune Lane. This road has houses on its eastern side and at first none on its western side, where it skirts the eastern boundary of the Jewish cemetery. Between 1954 and 1997, the actor Donald Sinden (1923-2014) lived at number 60 Temple Fortune Lane.

HIGHGATE

This piece, written mostly in 2017, describes a walk through Hampstead's north-eastern neighbour, Highgate, an area rich in history.

Today, a double-decker bus serves route 210, which carries passengers between Golders Green and Highgate. Between 1965 and 1970, when I used that service to get me to Highgate School, the same route was served by a single-decker bus. Buses travel along Spaniards Road, which runs in a straight line through a wooded part of Hampstead Heath. The road is on an embankment, raised above its surroundings, because in the early 19th century large amounts of sand were quarried from the ground on either side of it. The westernmost stretch of Spaniards Road runs beside a brick wall that surrounds the grounds of Heath House. Currently invisible under extensive scaffolding, as it has been for many years, this 18th century building (1762) was bought in 1790 by the Quaker banker and anti-slavery activist Samuel Hoare Junior (1751-1825), who lived there until his death.

About two thirds of the way along Spaniards Road, a lane winds downhill through the trees, south towards the Elms Estate. There have been buildings on this site since the 17th century. Between 1957 and 1981, The Elms, which had been owned by the Woolworth heiress Barbara Hutton (1912-1979), became the home of St Columba's Hospital for the terminally ill. Since 1987, it has been in the hands of private developers.

Spaniards End is a small road that branches off Spaniards Road just before it reaches Spaniards Inn. It leads past a building that used to be called 'The Firs'. This was built in 1734 by a Mr Turner, and later modified. In the 1950s, this house was divided into 3 separate dwellings: The White House, The Chantry, and Casa Maria. The latter was formed from the former billiards room of The Firs. Heath End, a house close to the Spaniards Inn, was home to the Arctic explorer Rear Admiral Sir William Edward Parry (1790-1855) and then from 1889 until 1912, it was the weekend home of the social reformers Canon Samuel Barnett (1844-1913) and his wife Dame Henrietta (1851-1936). It was through their efforts that the Hampstead Garden Suburb came into existence. Heath End and its neighbours, Evergreen and Erskine House, were both built in the 18th century on the plot of an older Erskine House, home to the lawyer Thomas Erskine (1750-1823). The present Erskine House, built mainly for the novelist Sir Hall Caine (1853-1931) in the 1923, incorporates a wing of the former 18th

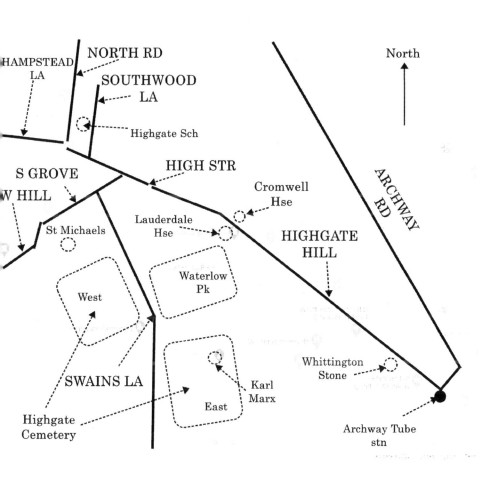

HAMPSTEAD
LA

NORTH RD

SOUTHWOOD
LA

Highgate Sch

North

S GROVE

W HILL

HIGH STR

Cromwell
Hse

ARCHWAY RD

St Michaels

Lauderdale
Hse

HIGHGATE
HILL

Waterlow
Pk

West

Whittington
Stone

SWAINS LA

Karl
Marx

East

Highgate
Cemetery

Archway Tube
stn

243

century Erskine House. These buildings form a cluster next to a pub that was built in the 17th century, The Spaniards Inn. The origin of the pub's name is not known for certain. One suggestion is that the building was once owned by a family connected with the Spanish Embassy. Another is that at some stage, the house was taken by a Spaniard and converted to a house of entertainment.

The Spaniards Inn was the scene of an event during the Gordon Riots in 1780. The causes of the riots were several, but they included anti-Catholic sentiments following the passing of an act of Parliament in 1778, which 'emancipated' the Roman Catholics. At that time, Kenwood House, which is east of the Spaniards Inn was one of the homes of William Murray, 1st Earl of Mansfield (1705-1793), an important lawyer, reformer (his reforms included objections to slavery), and politician. He was Lord Chief Justice when the act was passed. Just prior to the outbreak of rioting, he had treated a Catholic priest leniently in a court of justice. Following this, a group of rioters attacked and burned Mansfield's home in Bloomsbury Square. A correspondent in the *Lady's Magazine* wrote in 1780:
"The furniture, his fine library of books, invaluable manuscripts, containing his lordship's notes on every important law case for near forty years past ... were by the hands of these Goths committed to the flames; Lord and Lady Mansfield with difficulty eluded their rage, by making their escape through a back door ... So great was the vengeance with which they menaced him, that, if report may be credited, they had brought a rope with them to have executed him: and his preservation may be properly termed providential."

Not satisfied with burning down Mansfield's London home and its owner's escape from their clutches, rioters set off towards Kenwood where they planned to destroy his rural retreat. They made their way to the Spaniards Inn, whose publican was then Giles Thomas. This shrewd fellow soon realised the reason for the rabble's arrival and being a man of quick thinking, he opened his house and his cellars to the mob, offering them unlimited refreshment before they continued to undertake their planned work of devastating Kenwood House. As soon as they began enjoying Thomas's generous hospitality, the canny publican sent a messenger to a local barracks to raise a detachment of the Horse Guards. At the same time, he arranged for other rabble-rousers to be supplied with liberal amounts of strong ale from the cellars of nearby Kenwood House. Mr William Wetherell, who was on the spot, encouraged the rioters to adjourn to the Spaniards Inn. By the time that the military arrived, the rioters were in no fit state to either resist the soldiers or to carry out their planned attack on Mansfield's residence, which was a good thing not only for Mansfield but also for posterity because by 1780, the house had already been worked on by the architect Robert Adam (1728-1792), who had made improvements of great artistic value.

The still popular pub marks the eastern end of Spaniards Road and the beginning of Hampstead Lane. Where the two roads meet, the roadway's width is barely wide enough to admit a double-decker bus. This is due to the presence of the former 'Spaniards Gate Toll House', which was built in the 18th century to collect tolls from those passing through the western entrance to the Estates of the Bishops of London, which they owned for almost 1400 years. There was once another tollgate, the High Gate, for the bishops' land at the top of the hill where the Gatehouse pub now stands in Highgate, from which that locality derives its name. Near The Spaniards, there is a 20th century house where the actor Sir Ralph Richardson (1902-1983) lived between 1944 and 1968.

Hampstead Lane skirts the northern boundary of the Kenwood estate, but it has not always done so. The road used to run close to the main entrance of the house along what is now its driveway. A map drawn in 1745 shows this clearly. In the 18th century, the 2nd Earl of Mansfield (1727-1796) employed the landscape gardener Humphry Repton (1752-1818) to improve the landscape of Kenwood House. This work included shifting the route of Hampstead Lane to the north of the house and out of sight of it.

There is a rectangular field where Bishops Avenue, along which many wealthy people reside, meets Hampstead Lane. This is Far Field, owned and used by Highgate School. On a September afternoon in 1965, I took part in a football match on this field designed to assess the soccer abilities of new entrants to the school. The following day, two senior students wearing prefects' uniform (black suit with brown leather shoes), solemnly and regretfully informed me that I was not skilled as a football player and would have to select another sport. This news did not devastate me.

Kenwood House has one of its public entrances and a car park close to The Spaniards Inn. A path flanked by rhododendron bushes (for which Kenwood is well-known) leads from it to the front of Kenwood House. This follows the original route of Hampstead Lane prior to its repositioning by Repton. The path passes a stone sculpture, *Flamme*, carved in 1983 by Eugène Dodeigne (1923-2015), then leads to an open space dominated by the north-facing front façade of Kenwood House with its neo-classical portico.

The first house to stand on the site of the present one was built in brick by John Bill (1576-1630), printer to King James I. He bought the Kenwood Estate (which was known as 'Caen Wood') in 1616. After several changes in ownership, the Estate was bought in about 1747 by a former Prime Minister and King George III's close associate, John Stuart, third Earl of Bute (1713-1792). In 1754, Bute sold the property to the lawyer and law-reformer William Murray (1705-1793), who became the First Earl of Mansfield, and was Lord Chief Justice of the King's Bench from 1756 to 1788. In 1778, he was a supporter of the Roman Catholic Relief Bill that led to the violent protests described above. During the First Earl's stay in the House, he employed the architect Robert Adam (1728-1792) to make improvements. Kenwood House remained the seat of the Mansfield family until the beginning of the 1920s when it was owned by the Sixth Earl of Mansfield. Then, the wealthy soap-maker Sir Arthur Crosfield (1865-1938) helped to save the estate from being developed into a housing area. The brewer Edward Cecil Guinness (1847-1927), the First Earl of Iveagh, first leased Kenwood, and then purchased it. A collector of fine art, he housed his collection of paintings at Kenwood. He bequeathed this and his house to the public, making Kenwood House the home of one of London's great public art collections.

The landscaped grounds surrounding Kenwood House are magnificent. Notable amongst its features, there is a lake with a 'trompe-l'oeil' bridge. This can be seen from the terrace running along the House's graceful neo-classical south-facing rear façade. The lake is one of the sources of the River Fleet, a 'Lost River' which flows towards central London. During my youth, there used to be a hemispherical bandstand large enough to hold a symphony orchestra located on the side of the lake furthest from the House. In Summer, concerts used to be held at Kenwood. The audience sat in the open on deckchairs or on the ground across the lake from the bandstand, listening to classical music that flowed across the lake.

Another thing that I recall from earlier visits to Kenwood has also gone. It was Johnson's Summer House. When I looked for it in 2017, all that remained of it was an octagonal concrete base (hidden amongst bushes) with two benches on it. The rustic hut, in which the great Dr Samuel Johnson (1709-1784) used to sit, was moved to Kenwood from Thrale Place in Streatham, where Johnson lived from 1765. Sadly, the summer house was burnt down after 1984. The concrete base is not far from another of Kenwood's sculptures, the tall limestone, abstract *Monolith Empyrean*, created in 1953 by Barbara Hepworth. The grounds of Kenwood also contain a sculpture by Henry Moore, *Two Piece Reclining Figure No.5*, created in 1963-64. On a long loan from the Tate Gallery, it stands 400 feet south and slightly west of the Hepworth piece.

The House is well-worth entering (no admission charge at present). If I had to select my favourite aspect of the house, I would be torn between the Adam Library and the collection of paintings, the 'Iveagh Bequest'. The library is a masterpiece of interior design by the architect Robert Adam. John Summerson wrote in his *Georgian London*:

"When Lord Mansfield bought Kenwood House, it was a plain brick box. He employed Adam to reface it in stucco and add two low wings: the orangery and the magnificent library."

And, the library is wonderful, especially its intricately decorated barrel-vaulted stuccoed ceiling. Built between 1767 and 1770, it was designed to be both a library and a room in which to receive guests.

The painting collection hanging in the rooms of the ground floor in Kenwood contains masterpieces by artists such as: Frans Hals, Cuyp, Rembrandt, Reynolds, Gainsborough, Turner, Van Dyck, Landseer, and Vermeer. The collection also includes several topographical paintings of historic interest. A painting by John Constable shows a view of Hampstead Heath. Another from the studio of Richard Wilson (1713-1782) provides a view of London from a high point somewhere in Highgate. The spires of the City of London can be seen across the fields that separated 18th century Highgate from London. Another 18th (?) century oil depicts three cows standing in front of three buildings, still in existence and recently restored, which were part of the dairy farm established by Louisa, the second wife of the 2nd Earl of Mansfield. An interesting painting by the Dutchman Claude de Jongh (1605-1663) depicts old London Bridge in

1630. On the first floor, there is also a fine collection of 9 paintings, 'The Suffolk Collection'. These superb portraits were painted by William Larkin (1580s-1619).

The paintings and the library are my favourites within Kenwood House, but there is plenty more to see. An item, which interested me, was the 'Gouty chair' for invalids. Two handles at the ends of its armrests are connected by rods and cogwheels to some wheels on the floor below the chair. The occupant of this chair could rotate the handles, and thereby propel this early form of wheelchair around the room. It was created by the Belgian inventor John-Joseph Merlin (1735-1803). On a recent visit in 2020, I saw that English Heritage, who maintain Kenwood House, have added an exhibition about Dido Elizabeth Belle (1761-1804), who was great-niece of William Murray, The First Earl of Mansfield. Her heritage was not 100% European. Her mother might have been a black African as the historicengland.org.uk website explained:

"Dido was the illegitimate daughter of Lord Mansfield's nephew, Sir John Lindsay, a British Navy captain, and a woman (who, it has been previously suggested, was enslaved) whom Sir John encountered while his ship was in the Caribbean."

She lived at Kenwood for about 30 years. The website mentioned:

"Lord Mansfield was England's most powerful judge. His famous ruling in 1772, over the James Somerset case, was interpreted by many to mean that slavery had no legal basis in England... Many feel that it was likely that his affection for Dido influenced his decisions, but as Lord Chief Justice, he had to balance this with a careful reading of the law, and was reluctant to overturn the whole system which though he, and many others felt was 'odious', had brought many economic advantages to Britain."

Mansfield was also involved in the case of the slave ship *Zong* in 1781, which was held after many slaves had been thrown overboard as part of a fraudulent insurance claim. After fiercely contested legal proceedings, Mansfield found that there had indeed been an attempt to defraud the insurers, one that involved the cold-blooded massacre of over 100 slaves. This trial and the Somerset Case helped sway British opinion in favour of abolition.

Kenwood is not the only grand house on Hampstead Lane. Others, less impressive than Kenwood, included Caen Wood Towers (at various times the home of wealthy men such as Francis Reckitt, Sir Francis Cory-Wright, and Sir Robert Waley Cohen); and Beechwood, which has been home to at least two rulers from the Middle East. These places still exist but have been converted into up-market residences. Bishopswood House at the corner of Bishopswood Road and Hampstead Lane has always intrigued me. When I was at Highgate School in the 1960s, this large Victorian house was easily visible from the road. Then, it was possible to see lights with conical green shades suspended over the game tables inside its enormous billiards room. Now, the much modified and enlarged house is well hidden by hedges. It does not appear on a map surveyed in 1863 but does on one surveyed in 1894.

Bishopswood House is next to a large open space, Senior Field, one of Highgate School's many sports grounds. A Victorian building on the western edge of the field nearest to Hampstead Lane was once the school's swimming pool. When I attended the school between 1965 and 1970, its open-air swimming pool was behind Dyne House (see below) on Southwood Lane. Entering this unheated pool was only bearable when rain was falling. In 1970, an indoor heated pool, financed by regular £10 additions to the pupils' £100 termly tuition fees, opened on the eastern arm of Bishopswood Road. Directly across the field from the former swimming pool, stands the school's dining hall and kitchens. These are next to a small hut that contains the cricket score board. Further east, Hampstead Lane passes the rear of a cricket pavilion, where there is a crest showing a knight's helmet and below it a heraldic animal's head separated by a sword with a twist in its blade. This is part of the crest of Highgate School. The pavilion is across the road from the entrance to Beechwood House (built about 1824), mentioned above. Walking along the eastern part of Bishopwsood Road from Hampstead Lane, one can see yet another of Highate School's playing fields, the Junior Field. At the south end of this, there is a long low brick building, which, in 'my day', contained the changing rooms for day boys. Opposite this on Bishopswood Road, there are the magnificent, recently built edifices housing Highgate's Junior School.

North of these new buildings, there is a large red brick Victorian building bearing the school's crest. This was formerly one of the school's boarding houses, known as 'School House' (built 1880). Now that the school no longer has boarders, this building has been beautifully modernised within and adapted for use as an arts centre called The John Mills Centre in honour of one of the school's recent governors. The Mallinson Sports Centre a little north of this is built around the swimming pool that was constructed when I was at the school. The centre is named in honour of Mr Theodore G Mallinson, a charismatic man who lived until he was 99, one of several teachers who tried to teach me French. Near the sports centre, rows of Eton fives courts are visible. This game is often played in Public Schools (but not exclusively: I have seen public Eton fives courts in North Kensington near to the Westway). It is a bit like squash except that the ball is hit by gloved hands instead of racquets.

The summit of Hampstead Lane, the top of Highgate Hill, is dominated by the Victorian gothic Highgate School building and its neighbouring chapel with its clock-tower and tall centrally located, slender steeple. The large building north of the chapel was known as 'Big School' in 'my day' and was rarely used except when the whole school needed to be gathered in one place. It has been restored recently and has become the school's main library. Big School was built between 1865 and 1867 to the designs of FP Cockerill (1833-1878). The chapel and cloisters that flank this building were added later in the 19th century. North of these buildings, several adjoining edifices of various ages contain classrooms and other parts of the Senior School.

Highgate School was founded as a grammar school by Sir Roger de Cholmeley (c1485-1565) in 1565 near the end of his life. Sir Roger was a great benefactor of Highgate village. A lawyer, a member of Lincoln's Inn, King Henry VII bestowed on him the Manor of Hampstead. Sir Roger lived through six reigns (Henry VII, Henry VIII, Edward VI, Lady Jane Grey, Mary I, and Elizabeth I). One of these, that of Lady Jane, he helped bring about to his short-term detriment. According to James Thorne in his *Handbook to the Environs of London*, Sir Roger, who had been Lord Chief Justice of The King's Bench under Edward VI, was dismissed and imprisoned in the Tower by Queen Mary because of his part in drawing up the King's will so that his sisters (Mary and Elizabeth) were disinherited and barred from acceding to the throne. This 'tampering' of the will allowed Lady Jane to be crowned, albeit only for nine days. After his release from the Tower, he devoted time to setting up his (and my) school in Highgate.

Highgate School never achieved a great reputation in its first few centuries. One of its most celebrated early academic successes was Nicholas Rowe (1674-1718), a noted poet, writer, dramatist, and Poet Laureate (appointed 1715). It was not until the early 19th century when Dr John Bradley Dyne (1809-1898) became headmaster in 1838 (he held this post until 1874) that the school's reputation improved significantly. Even in 1965, when I was ready for secondary school, Highgate did not command a high reputation as compared with, say, Westminster, where my parents hoped that I would apply and attend. I chose Highgate myself, having been introduced to it by a very good friend who was already a pupil there. It turned out to be the right school for me.

In the mid-1960s, Highgate School was like a privately-run comprehensive school. Unlike, for example Westminster, it then catered for boys of all academic abilities, and encouraged whatever they showed flare for, be it woodwork, tennis, music, or, even, academic excellence. I had a friend at Westminster, who was above average in intellectual ability, but because he was unlikely to enter Oxford or Cambridge with an exhibition or a scholarship, he always, I sensed, was made to feel inferior. This never happened in Highgate when I was there. A high scorer in mathematics was made to feel no more superior to someone, who could hardly add two numbers together yet was a brilliant cricketer. I am very grateful that I went to a school where this was the case. With the passing of time and especially after it became coeducational in 2001, the school has enlarged greatly, and now its academic excellence rivals the best of London's schools. I have had the impression when I have visited the school for reunions, that even though I and most of my fellow classmates would have had trouble passing the present entrance exams, the school still maintains a great atmosphere of all-embracing excellence, not only in academic spheres.

The west side of North Road that becomes North Hill, which runs north to join the Great North Road (A1000), is lined with interesting buildings. Prior to the construction of Archway Road, this thoroughfare, which passes Highgate Senior School, was the main road from London to the north of England. Opposite the school, Halfway Cottage, which looks like a mews building or stable, has a block and tackle system hanging from its first floor. It was built in the 1840s and might have been part of a larger estate at the time. A map drawn in 1863 shows that this cottage and its neighbours were next to a large building called 'Grove Lodge', where today there are houses with flats. Eighteenth century Byron House with its early 19th century stucco façade, next door to Halfway, was home of the poet Sir John Betjeman (1906-1984) from 1911 to 1915, when he attended Highgate School. One of his teachers there was the poet TS Eliot

(1886-1965), who was then teaching French and Latin. Next door to Byron House, stands another 18th century building Hampton Lodge. Its neighbour is the older (perhaps 17th century) Byron Cottage, where the poet AE Housman (1859-1936) wrote his poem *A Shropshire Lad*. The above-mentioned houses have other 18th century neighbours.

Further along North Road, we reach a masterpiece of 20th century architecture, the High Point apartment blocks that were constructed between 1933 and 1938 to the plans of the Russian-born Berthold Lubetkin (1901-1990) and his architectural practice 'Tecton', which he established when he arrived in London in 1931. He was influenced by the Soviet Constructivism style – he had already designed the Soviet Pavilion for a trade show in Bordeaux. Highpoint was praised by no less an architect than Le Corbusier (1887-1965), with whom Lubetkin had associated professionally. The classical caryatids supporting the veranda above one of the main entrances make an entertaining contrast to the otherwise modern appearance of this building.

A lane running along the south side of the grounds of High Point leads to an entrance of the Victorian Northfield Hall. A carved stone by its entrance reads "XIV Middlesex. Highgate. Volunteer Rifle Corps. AD MDCCCLIX". The Volunteers adopted the hall as its headquarters in January 1879. It is now used for offices and flats. A little further along the lane, there is a synagogue, Highgate Shul. Across North Hill opposite High Point, and almost next to The Wrestlers Pub (first established in the 16th century, but now housed in a 20th century building), there is a three-storey building with a plain facade, number 92, where the writer Charles Dickens (1812-1870) stayed in 1832. His entire family lived there whilst he was suffering from some financial difficulty. Dickens considered buying a cottage in Highgate but did not. Some members of his family are buried in Highgate Cemetery.

Castle Yard leads from North Hill to Southwood Lane, where, in my schooldays, Highgate School had its 'sanatorium' or health centre in a late Victorian house (number 87). In those days, it was presided by the school doctor, Dr Rankine, who examined us once a year. Part of his examination involved peering inside the fronts of our underpants. The sanatorium contained a few beds to house sick boarders. During WW2 when this building was empty, it was used by Hill Homes, which was founded in 1939 by the wife of the Nobel Prize winning physiologist Professor Archibald V Hill (1886-1977), who taught at University College London. The former sanatorium stands close to a red brick building (number 67) that bears the date 1888 under the insignia of Queen Victoria. This used to be a postal sorting office.

At the corner of Jacksons Lane and Southwood Lane, there is a house on a triangular plot. This is Bank Point, which was built in the Georgian era. From about 1809 to 1815, this was the home of Colonel Joseph P Jackson, after whom Jacksons Lane was named. Southwood Lane continues north, passing a road called The Park (formerly, 'Park House Road'). The Park ran around the grounds of the former 'Park House Penitentiary', which I saw marked on a map surveyed in 1893. On a map surveyed in 1914, its name had changed to 'House of Mercy', and on the current map, the old building has been replaced with the

Hillcrest Estate: three apartment blocks, each with the name of a WW2 British military commander. The Penitentiary, which was demolished, was founded in 1853 for the "reformation of penitent fallen women". In 1900, the Clewer Order of Sisters took it over as 'The House of Mercy'. The old buildings were closed in 1940.

Returning south along Southwood Lane, we pass number 22, Avalon, an 18th century house where the ethnologist Mary Kingsley (1862-1900) lived as a child. This is close to a former chapel, which now houses the Highgate School Museum, something that did not exist when I was a pupil at the school. This early 19th century building was formerly 'The Highgate Tabernacle'. It stands on the site of a former Presbyterian chapel that was founded here in 1622. The Tabernacle faces a row of alms-houses, which stand where in 1658 Sir John Wollaston (1590-1658), Mayor of London in 1643, founded an earlier group of six alms-houses, "…in trust for the use of six poor alms people, men and women of honest life and conversation, inhabitants of Hornsey and Highgate". In 1722, the original buildings, which were in a poor state, were pulled down and replaced by newer ones, paid for by Edward Pauncefort (died 1726, a Member of Parliament between 1698 and 1705, and sometime resident in Highgate). The two-storey central portion of this 18th century building was built as a schoolhouse for "charity girls".

The alms-house abuts the massive wall of a newer brick building with neo-classical pilasters in white stone. This is the Science Block of Highgate School, built in 1928. When I studied at Highgate, the Headmaster's office was on its ground floor. Much of its uppermost floor was occupied by the school's excellent library, which is now in the former 'Big School' (see above). The laboratories for physics and chemistry used to be lined with glass-fronted wooden cabinets containing materials and apparatus. When I went around the school a few years ago, I noticed that these cupboards had been replaced by newer ones with opaque doors. It was seeing and wondering about the nature of the things that I saw in the old cabinets that made me follow the science study route rather than the arts path, abandoning history for physics and geography for chemistry (both at the age of 15).

The Science Block is across Southwood Lane opposite an unsightly construction in brick, glass, and concrete. This is the 'new' Dyne House, which was built in the late 1960s while I was a pupil at Highgate. With a nice auditorium and plenty of music practice rooms, it was built to replace an older Dyne House, and opened in 1967. A subterranean pedestrian subway allows students and staff to cross under the busy Southwood Lane. The violinist Yehudi Menuhin (1916-1999) used to rehearse in Dyne House's auditorium. An old, now disused, weed-filled, open air swimming pool lies down the hillside behind and far beneath Dyne House, next to some unattractive classrooms and an old gymnasium. The school's old printing press, which was run by pupils using old-fashioned type set by hand, used to be housed in a hut on steep the slope halfway between Dyne House and the pool. It was here during lunch breaks that I helped set-up and print the school's calendar each term.

Where Southwood Lane meets Highgate High Street, there is an old burial ground on a triangular plot next to the south wall of Highgate School's Chapel. This cemetery served an earlier, long-since demolished, chapel built beside it. The northwest corner of this graveyard is opposite The Gatehouse pub. Before 1813, when the straight Archway Road was cut through the hillside east of Highgate village, traffic between central London and the Great North Road had to pass through Highgate village, and then through a toll located beside the Gatehouse pub. It was levied by the Bishops of London who owned the land across which the first part of the old Great North Road (the present North Road and North Hill) ran. Thorne wrote that long ago:

"...the tollhouse was a brick building extending across the road from the Gatehouse tavern to the burial ground by the old chapel. The gateway through which the traffic passed had two floors over it...".

The arch was low and very narrow, making it necessary for wagons to be unloaded before they could pass through. In 1769, this structure was removed, and replaced by an ordinary turnpike gate.

The tollgate has disappeared, as has also the 'Highgate Oath', by which visitors to Highgate were required to promise a range of ludicrous and contradictory things mainly relating to women and alcohol. For example, as Karl Baedeker related in his *London and its Environs* (1895), the oath demands that one should never kiss a maid when you could kiss the mistress instead, and never drink a weak beer when a strong one was available, unless the weaker one was preferred. In return, they became a 'Freeman of Highgate'. Taking this oath allowed the holder to have various valueless, ridiculous privileges including being able to kick a pig out of a ditch to take its place to have somewhere to rest. The oath had to be sworn under horns (i.e., antlers), which were kept in each of Highgate's pubs. The oath is mentioned by writers including Lord Byron in verse 70 in the first Canto of his *Childe Harold's Pilgrimage* (published between 1812 and 1818):

> "… And many to the steep of Highgate hie.
>
> Ask ye, Boeotian shades! The reason why?
>
> 'Tis to worship the solemn horn,
>
> Grasp'd in the holy hand of Mystery,
>
> In whose dread name both men and maids are sworn…"

There are still several pubs in Highgate High Street, where the oath might have been taken in years gone by. Many of the buildings lining the High Street are 18th or 19th century. One shop retains an original wooden veranda projecting over the pavement. There used to be more of these when I was at school in Highgate. A coffee shop, a branch of the Nero chain, in deference to its premise's heritage, has erected a modern version of this outside its premises. A shop with a bow window, number 46, currently the premises of 'The Highgate Vet', was, during my school days and for many decades before that, a second-hand book shop run by Fisher and Sperr. When I visited the shop recently, the vet told me that Mr Fisher ran the shop until his death (in the shop) at a very advanced age. He lived there with his sister, whom I never saw during my many visits to the bookshop in my schooldays. This shop is at the top of the steep slope that leads down to Archway. Before descending that hill, let us walk along South Grove.

South Grove skirts Pond Square, which contained a village pond until the 19th century when it was filled in (this had already been done by 1863). Number 10 South Grove, Church House, is a grand brick-built 18th century house facing the square. For a period during the early 19th century, it housed a school for Jewish boys, which was founded by Mr Hyman Hurwitz (1770-1844), a friend of the poet Samuel Taylor Coleridge (1772-1834), who lived in Highgate after April 1816 and was buried there. Mark Bernstein, whose parents lived in Church House for 20 years, told me that it:

"…originally had an ice pit located under the front garden, into which ice from the pond in Pond Square was cut and deposited to keep meat etc. cool, and that later this was reputedly turned into a mikvah [ritual bath]"

Next to it is The Highgate Society, and then the imposing Highgate Literary and Scientific Institution, which was founded in 1839 in a building that had been previously used as a school. Further west stands the imposing Great Hall, which was built in the late 17th century and has some later additions.

After passing a row of several old houses and the modern, award-winning number 16, designed by the Eldridge Smerin practice in 2000, we reach St Michaels Church, a Victorian gothic structure designed by Lewis Vulliamy (1791-1871). It was built in 1831-32 to replace a 'chapel of ease' that had been attached to Highgate School at the top of the village. This probably explains the presence of a weathered stone crest bearing the arms of Highgate School on one side of the arch containing the church's west door. Just inside that door, at the base of the belltower, there is a mark a few feet above the floor, level with the top of the cross on the dome of St Pauls Cathedral). When I was at Highgate School, Church of England services used to be held in the school's chapel every day except on Thursdays. The chapel was only large enough to hold a small number of boys, not the whole school, whereas St Michael's could easily accommodate everyone (including their families during the annual Carol Service). On Thursdays, almost the whole school celebrated morning prayers in St Michaels. Those, who did not, were Jewish boys, who attended the oddly named 'Jewish Circle' in the school, and Roman Catholics, members of the school's 'Roman Catholic Circle', who trooped down Highgate Hill to St Josephs (see below). The school still attends St Michaels once a week. The poet Samuel Taylor Coleridge is buried in the church, his remains having been transferred there in 1961 from the small cemetery already mentioned.

South Grove continues as Highgate West Hill, a steep incline beginning just beyond St Michaels. Witanhurst House stands at its summit. This large neo-Georgian mansion designed by George Hubbard (1859-1936) was built in 1913 for the soap magnate Arthur Crosfield, who helped to save Kenwood, which he could see from his house, as an open space. With its sweeping gardens and wonderful views across Hampstead Heath, this building replaced an earlier one, 'Parkfield', which was first built in the 18th century. Witanhurst, now a private estate, is difficult to see from West Hill, but can be better viewed from a distance from the part of Hampstead Heath just east of Kenwood House.

Unless you have special business, you cannot enter numbers 32-33 West Hill, now the headquarters of a Russian trade mission, formerly the 'Soviet Trade Delegation'. In 1979, its building's windows required new glazing. A former military policeman, Bill Graham, was asked by MI6 to offer to provide double-glazing at a price (subsidised by MI6) which was so good that the Delegation accepted it. While Bill and his team were installing the double-glazing, they installed espionage 'bugs', photographed Soviet documents, and secretly photographed the building. Bill has written about this episode in *Break In*. The main buildings of the Delegation, which are not visible from West Hill, were built in 1957 and in 1973.

Back at the top of West Hill, The Grove, which leads to Hampstead Lane, begins near the Flask pub (first established before 1663, and now housed in an 18th century building). Near the pub, and separating it from The Grove, there is a grassy open space which was, when I visited it in 2017, filled with touching personal memorials to the singer, the late George Michael (1963-2016), who lived in a house on The Grove.

Swains Lane begins at Pond Square, and then descends vertiginously towards the north-east corner of Parliament Hill Fields, to which West Hill also leads. On its west side, the Lane skirts Waterlow Park until it reaches the northern part of the eastern section of Highgate Cemetery, which contains the much-visited grave of Karl Marx. The western section of Highgate Cemetery, which lies on the west side of Swains Lane, is 'punctuated' by occasional private residences next to its eastern edge. One of these, the Eidolon House (number 87), was built in 2014 and designed by Dominic Mckenzie Architects. With its façade covered by mirror glass, it is a spectacular example of contemporary domestic architecture. It is close to John Winter's distinctive house at number 81, constructed in 1967 using oxidised 'Cor-ten' steel.

Highgate Cemetery was opened in 1839 as part of a series of seven new cemeteries around London. These included, for example, those at Brompton, Kensal Green, and Abney Park. The western section of the cemetery is the stuff of dreams and nightmares. When I was at Highgate School, this part of the cemetery was unguarded and unsecured. Anyone could walk in at any time. It is a vast collection of largely disintegrating Victorian funerary monuments and buildings including a spooky Victorian neo-Egyptian circular columbarium (this lies immediately below the terrace upon which St Michael's church stands). In the 1960s, the cemetery was not well-cared for. The funerary objects - graves, sculptures, vaults, and mausolea - were strangled by unrestrained vegetation, including particularly evil-looking weeds whose stems looked like long chains of infants' fingerbones joined end-to-end. Also, many of the graves and tomb chambers (in the columbarium) had been broken open. Dust-covered coffins, some opened, could be seen inside them. Now, several decades since I finished school, the cemetery has become a popular tourist destination. Both sections have been made inaccessible to all those except corpses, bona-fide mourners, and tourists who have purchased admission tickets. The spookier western section, where the scientist Michael Faraday was buried in 1867, may only be

265

visited with an official guide. The tours are worth paying for, and the guides provide interesting information. During the 19th century it was considered very romantic (not ghoulish) for couples to spend time, lingering amongst the graves in the cemetery at twilight on summer evenings.

South of the cemetery, at the corner of Swains Lane and Chester Road, there is a wonderful Victorian gothic fantasy: Holly Village. This is a 'colony' of eight large cottages, profusely decorated with intricate gothic details and arranged around a well-manicured lawn. Although they are private, you can easily slip inside the ornate gatehouse to see them. They were built on the instructions of the wealthy philanthropist Baroness Burdett-Coutts (1814-1906) in 1865 to the designs of Henry Darbishire (1825-1899). The latter was no stranger to philanthropic works, having been the Peabody Trust's architect until 1885. Angela Burdett-Coutts was granddaughter of the banker Thomas Coutts. Her father was the reformist politician Sir Francis Burdett (1770-1844). The Baroness lived at the nearby Holly Lodge Estate, which was sold on her death. The current Oakeshott Avenue, which runs west off Swains Lane and is lined by 20th century half-timbered buildings, stands on part of the former estate.

The former 'Highgate Newtown Clinic' is close to Holly Village on Chester Road. It used to deal with children's ailments, but now it is used for other purposes. Further along the road, stands Highgate Branch Library in a grand brick building with neo-classical features and topped with balustrades. This was built in 1906, designed by William Nesbit, the Borough of St Pancras Engineer. It was the first branch public library to be opened in the Borough of St Pancras.

It was built on land acquired from 'Mr Burdett-Coutts'. A relative of mine, who volunteers at the library, told me that its future is under threat.

Returning to Highgate village, we can begin the descent of Highgate Hill towards Archway Underground station. High up on the wall on Highgate High Street facing South Grove, there is a plaque that says "Feary's Row 1791". The Camden History Society's *Streets of Highgate* revealed that in 1769, Samuel Feary was a shoemaker with a shop across the street from where the row of shops named after him stands. In the 1840s, there was a library, 'Broadbent Library', where now there are shops. A vehicle entrance under number 22 leads to Broadbent Close, which used to be known as 'Broadbent's Yard'. Further south, the ornate doorway of number 42, a late 18th/early 19th century building, above whose front door is displayed the coat of arms of Sir William Ashurst (1647-1720), who lived in Highgate in the late 17th century. He was a Member of Parliament three times and, also, a governor of Highgate School from 1697 onwards. The coat of arms was brought from the c 1700 Ashurst House, which was demolished to build St Michael's Church.

Where Highgate High Street, with its many 18th century buildings, ends and Highgate Hill begins its steep descent, there are two fine very early 18th century (c.1700, according to Nikolaus Pevsner) houses, numbers 128 (Northgate House) and 130 (Ivy House). They may have been built as early as 1660 but have been modified since then. Their neighbour, Cholmeley Lodge, is much more recently built. Constructed in 1934 in the art-deco style with two resplendently curving facades, it was designed by Guy Morgan and Partners. A map surveyed in 1893 shows that there was an older building standing in extensive grounds where the flats stand today; it was also called 'Cholmeley Lodge'. The 1930s flats overlook their neighbour, the main (rather unattractive) Victorian buildings of Channing School for Girls. It was founded in 1885 by the Reverend Roberts Spears and the two sisters, both Unitarians, Miss Matilda and Miss Emily Sharpe. Its Junior School is across the road in a house, which was once the home of Sir Sydney Waterlow (1822-1906), a former Mayor of London. In 1889, he gave his land, now 'Waterlow Park' to London County Council, which opened it as a public recreation area.

Not far below the school, there is a row of houses that date back to the 17th and 18th centuries. The grandest of these with its roof topped by a small tower, is Cromwell House, which, contrary to earlier beliefs, has nothing to do with Oliver Cromwell. It was built by a forgotten architect in 1637-38 for the merchant Sir Richard Sprignell (c1599-1659). He was a trained military band captain and a governor of Highgate School. Pevsner wrote that between 1675 and 1749, the house was owned by the Da Costa family, the first Jewish family to own landed property in England since the expulsion of the Jews in the Middle Ages. Alvaro Da Costa acquired it in 1675. He was joined there by his cousin and brother-in-law Fernando Moses Mendes (1647-1724), who became physician to King Charles II and his wife Catherine of Braganza. Alvaro's daughter-in-law, Catherine Da Costa (1679-1756) was a noted artist, a miniaturist. The family added a wing to the house between 1678 and 1679 and owned three other houses in Highgate. In his *A tour through the whole island of Great Britain* (1714-1737), Daniel Defoe wrote of Highgate, or 'High-gate' as he called it:

"The Jews have particularly fixed upon this town for their country retreats, and some of them are very wealthy; they live there in good figure, and have several trades particularly depending upon them, and especially, butchers of their own to supply them with provisions killed their own way; also, I am told, they have a private synagogue here."

The Da Costas sold the house in 1749. After that, it was used first as a school and then from 1869, as a convalescent home for children from the Great Ormond Street Hospital. Now, it houses the High Commission of Ghana.

Across the road from Cromwell House, there is a small metal plate in the brick wall of Waterlow Park. This records that the cottage in which the poet and wit Andrew Marvell (1621-1678) lived used to be nearby. According to Edward Walford (writing in 1878):

"The house – or cottage, for it was scarcely more – was small, and, like Andrew Marvell himself, very unpretentious."

Built of timber and plaster, it fell into disrepair and was demolished in 1867. Marvell's neighbour is Lauderdale House where John Ireton (1615-1689), Mayor of London in 1658 and the brother of one of Oliver Cromwell's sons-in-law, lived briefly in one of its reincarnations. The present Lauderdale House is an 18th century structure inside Waterlow Park. Built on the site of a 16th century half-timbered house, it contains elements of the original building. In the

1660s, it belonged briefly to the John Maitland, 1st Duke of Lauderdale (1616-1682). Subsequently, it underwent many modifications and had many owners until it reached its present form in the 18th century. The cleric John Wesley (1703-1791) preached here in 1782. Today, it serves as a community arts centre and café. Stairs from its gardens lead down into the grounds of Waterlow Park, which sweep down the slope of Highgate's hill towards the northern edge of the eastern side of Highgate Cemetery.

A conical spire with turquoise tiling adorns the corner of the 19th century Old Crown Inn at the meeting of Highgate Hill and Hornsey Lane. Currently (2021), the pub bears the name Brendan the Navigator. It stands on the site of an older hostelry built in the early part of the 19th century. This used to be a popular day-excursion destination for city-dwellers. Hornsey Lane meets Cromwell Avenue near to the pub. Between 1905 and late 1909, number 65 Cromwell Avenue was a hostel and meeting place for Indian students. Called India House, it was founded by the wealthy barrister Shyamji Krishnavarma (1857-1930) as part of his campaign to liberate India from British Rule. Until it was closed by the police in 1909, it was a hotbed of radical Indian freedom fighters, including Vinayak Damodar Savarkar (1883-1966), the father of Hindutva, a philosophy of Hindu nationalism. I have written about this house and its occupants at length in my book, *Indian Freedom Fighters in London (1905-1910)*.

The pub is opposite the large St Joseph's Roman Catholic church with its distinctive green dome, which is 130 feet higher than the cross at the top of St Pauls Cathedral. It was designed by Albert Vicars (1840-1896). Its interior has some neo-Romanesque features. Known affectionately by Highgate School boys as 'Holy Joe's', this is where the Catholic boys worshipped on Thursdays in the 1960s. The church was consecrated in 1889, a year after its foundation stone had been laid. Next to the church, there is St Joseph's Retreat. This is built on the site earlier occupied by the Black Dog pub, which the Roman Catholic Passionist Order of priests bought by subterfuge to use as a place of worship in the 1860s.

Further down Highgate Hill, there is a former school building with the date 1888. It now houses a 'City Academy'. Almost opposite this, stand the unattractive buildings of Whittington Hospital. The hospital stands close to a former 'Smallpox and Vaccination Hospital', 'St Marys', now part of the Whittington. Across the road from the Whittington, located on a triangular plot formed by the bifurcation of Highgate Hill and Archway Road, there stands a forbidding-looking series of Victorian institutional buildings surmounted by a massive belltower with a spire, which has four mansard windows. This was formerly the 'Holborn Union Infirmary', later named 'Archway Hospital'. Opened in 1879 with accommodation for 625 bedded patients, it later merged with St Marys Hospital across the road and, also, with Highgate Hospital in nearby Dartmouth Park Road. In 1995, it ceased being a hospital, and since 2015, the neglected buildings have been sold to Peabody and another housing developer.

Outside the Whittington, 'The Whittington Stone' stands on the pavement, enclosed in a cast-iron cage. Early engravings of this show that it was once a simple milestone with a convexly curved top. Later, the sculpture of a cat was attached to its top, and then it was surrounded by its protective metal cage. The monument marks the spot where Dick Whittington (c1354-1423), the future Lord Mayor of London and his cat, who had arrived from the country, heard the bells of Bow Church ringing out the famous prophesy of his brilliant future: "Turn again Whittington, thrice Lord Mayor of London!" And here ends this brief survey of Highgate's many attractions.

CODA

This book began by mentioning Hampstead's objection to McDonalds's plans to open an outlet on the High Street and its eventual closure in 2013. Now, eight years on, a branch of McDonalds would no longer stick out like a sore thumb on Hampstead High Street. Many of the independent shops that used to line the thoroughfare and made it a distinctive commercial centre have been replaced by branches of chains that can be found in shopping districts throughout the land. Does the presence of, for example, Waterstones, Boots, Gails Bakery, Bimba y Lola, Planet Organic, Ole & Steen, Zadig & Voltaire, Reiss, Caffe Nero, and Pain Quotidien, and Tesco's on Heath Street, help to preserve the village's rarefied and picturesque nature? I doubt it. Please note that unlike McDonalds and Tesco's, which attract customers from all over the social spectrum, most of the other newer shops that threaten to diminish Hampstead's uniqueness are aimed the people with healthy bank accounts. Plenty of money has become the requirement to live in a part of London that once catered for a community of people with widely diverse income levels and a rich diversity of cultural interests. Fortunately, much remains that is picturesque, and with some imagination and help from this book, you can walk the streets of Hampstead and its environs and gain a good sense of the area's rich heritage.

For several centuries, people have travelled up to Hampstead to escape the bustle of London life. In today's ever-increasingly stressful world, a trip to Hampstead from central London always provides me with a breath of fresh air, both literally and metaphorically. It is not only the refreshing breezes that make visiting Hampstead delightful, but also it is enjoyably exploring its many picturesque corners and pleasant vistas. Although it is a part of London, I always feel that the locality, which is so very different from London's other suburbs, lifts my spirits almost as much as travelling further afield to holiday destinations. Each time I visit this place, rich in both historical and contemporary features, I notice things that I had not registered previously. So, even though I have tried to cover a lot of material, there will be many things I have missed out or have yet to discover for myself. Also, many of the buildings and other places that one can see when in Hampstead can open windows into the past, allowing us to discover aspects of the history of the area as well as that of the whole country. I hope that I have demonstrated this in my book and that you will share my enthusiasm for Hampstead and its environs. It would be satisfying to learn that this volume has encouraged you to make many visits to this area under the wide sky which attracted the eyes of John Constable. It is a locale which attracted the attention of many in times past, and still has a great appeal today. And when you visit Hampstead, why not also see some of its surroundings, which I have described in this book? From Hampstead, there are pleasant walks through open spaces to Highgate and Golders Green, and Primrose Hill can be reached by walking along streets that are not without considerable visual and historic interest. If time is limited, then focus on old Hampstead and you will not be disappointed. What was considered highly satisfactory by the likes of John Constable, John Keats, and George Romney several centuries ago, still provide us great satisfaction today.

SOME BOOKS CONSULTED

ADAMSON J & FOLLAND H *Sir Harry Vane: His Life and Times, 1613-62* (1974)

BARRATT T *The Annals of Hampstead* (1912)

BARTON N *The Lost Rivers of London* (1965)

BOHM D & NORRIE I *Hampstead: London hill town* (1981)

BOLITHO H *Jinnah - Creator of Pakistan* (1954)

BOSWELL J *The Life of Samuel Johnson* (1791)

BURKE C *Lee Miller* (2006)

BURKE D *The Lawn Road Flats* (2014)

CARSWELL J *The saving of Kenwood and the Northern Heights* (2001)

CHERRY B & PEVSNER N *Buildings of England. London 4: North* (1998)

CLAYTON E *Barbara Hepworth. Art & Life* (2021)

DABBY B *Loyal to the Crown: The Extraordinary Life of Sir Roger Cholmeley* (2015)

DEFOE D *A Tour through the whole Island of Great Britain* (1724 – 1726; 1971 edition)

DENFORD S & HAYES D *Streets of Highgate* (2007)

DICK D *St Marys Church Hampstead* (2010)

EMERSON E, HARMAN R, & THOMSON D *Hampstead Memories* (2000)

FIELD O *The Kit-Cat Club* (2008)

FOX P *The Jewish Community of Golders Green* (2016)

GRAHAM B *Break-In* (1987)

HAMBLYN R *The Invention of Clouds* (2001)

HARDCASTLE E *Wine and walnuts; or, After dinner chit-chat* (1823)

HARDING T *Blood on the Page* (2018)

HAYDON B *The autobiography and memoirs of Benjamin Robert Haydon* (1926)

HILL M *Hampstead in Light and Shade* (1938)

HINDE T *Highgate School. A History* (1993)

HOWITT W *The Northern Heights of London* (1869)

HUNT J *Gandhi in London* (1993)

HUNT L *The Town* (1859)

HUNT L *The Autobiography of Leigh Hunt* (1859)

HYAMSON A *A History of the Jews in England* (1928)

LESLIE C *Memoirs of the Life of John Constable RA* (1911 edition)

LLOYD J *History, Topography, and Antiquities of Highgate* (1888)

MACLEAN C *Circles and Squares* (2020)

MITTON G *Hampstead and Marylebone* (1902)

POPLE K *Stanley Spencer. A Biography* (1991)

POTTER G *Hampstead Wells* (1904)

READ H *The Philosophy of Modern Art* (1964)

SHEINIS Z *Maxim Litvinov* (1990)

STERN M & ROSTENBERG L *Old Books, Rare Friends: Two Literary Sleuths and Their Shared Passion* (1998)

STOW J *Survey of London* (1603)

SUMMERSON J *Georgian London* (1988)

THORNE J *Handbook to the Environs of London* (1876)

WADE C *For the poor of Hampstead, forever...* (1998)

WADE C *The Streets of Hampstead* (1984)

WALFORD E *Old and New London: volume 5* (1878)

WAUGH E *A Little Learning* (1964)

WEDGWOOD C *The Trial of Charles I* (1964)

WHITE C *Sweet Hampstead and its Associations* (1900)

WILLIAMS-ELLIS C *Architect Errant* (1971)

ACKNOWLEDGEMENTS

The following people have provided me with ideas and information for which I am grateful:

Peter Urbach, Micky Watkins, Jane Rindl, Keith Fawkes, Mark Bernstein, Peter Bunyard, the Highgate Vet, Denis Herbstein, Gary McDonald, Liz Elliott, Jim Roberts, and Murari Kaushik.

Any errors or inaccuracies that might have crept into the text are entirely my fault and I hope that no one will feel offended by them.

Special gratitude is reserved for my wife Lopa, who has accompanied me on many visits to Hampstead and around, providing wonderful companionship as well as plenty of inspiration. and often pointing out things that have proved very interesting

INDEX OF SOME OF THE PEOPLE IN
THE BOOK

List of pages on which the person(s) is (are) discussed at length.
There may well be many other mentions of the people in the list
elsewhere in the book.

A

Abbotts	family			67
Abse,	Dannie			231
Adam,	Robert			249
Ader,	Inge			162
Ainger,	Thomas			151
Akenside,	Mark			230
Ambedkar,	Bhimrao	Ramji		209
Arber, Agnes	and	Edward	Alexander	203

B

Baeck,	Leo			240
Baillie,	Joanna			91
Barbauld,	Anna			176
Barnett,	Henrietta			242
Barratt,	Thomas			126
Baxter,	William			237
Beecham,	Thomas			126
Bell,	George	William		206
Belle,	Dido	Elizabeth		250
Besant,	Walter			177
Betjeman,	John			255
Blackmore,	Richard			43
Blake,	William			201
Bliss,	Arthur			128
Blomfield,	William			197
Bomberg,	David			200
Bowler,	Clifford	and	Norman	194
Breuer,	Marcel			103
Brodie,	Benjamin			59
Bunyard,	Anneliese	and	Peter	162
Burgh,	Allotson			51
Butler,	John	Dixon		147
Byron,	Lord			62, 261

C

| Carline, | Hilda | and | Richard | 97 |

Chappelow,	Allen		99
Charles,	Elizabeth	Rundle	186
Cholmeley,	Roger		199, 253
Christie,	Agatha		106
Coates,	Wells		103
Cole,	Henry		29
Comberti,	Micaela		234
Connell,	Amyas and	colleagues	181
Constable,	John		55, 91
Coren,	Giles		168
Coutts,	family		266
Crichton-Miller,	Hugh		158
Crosfield,	Arthur		247

D

da	Costa,	family	268
Dale,	Henry		87
de Bertodano	y Wilson,	family	179
de	Gaulle,	Chrles	76
de	László,	Philip	157
Dickens,	Charles		256
Dingley,	Charles		214
du	Maurier,	family	177
du	Pré,	Jacqueline	146
Duffield,	John		57
Dyne,	John	Bradley	254

E

Eliot,	George	148
Ellis,	Ruth	131
Engels,	Friedrich	204
Erskine,	Thomas	242

F

Faraday,	Michael	121, 265
Feldman,	Marty	128
Fenn,	Charles	107
Fenton,	PI	91
Field,	Horace	145
Fields,	Gracie	179
Fisher,	Ronald	213
Fleming.	Ian	225
Foot,	Michael	145
Fowles,	John	35
Freud,	Clement	168
Freud,	Sigmund	159
Fry,	Maxwell	180
Fuseli,	Henry	84

G

Gandhi,	Mohandas	K	28
Gardnor,	Thomas		50
George,	Boy		128
George,	Ernest		236
Gertler,	Mark		100

Gilbert Scott, Adrian 81
Goalen, Gerard 161
Godfrey, Edmund Berry 203
Goldfinger, Ernő 107
Gotto, Sarah and Edward 154
Graham, Bill 264
Greenaway, Kate 183
Greene, Grahame 82–83
Gropius, Walter 104
Guedalla, Philip 240

H

Harmsworth, Alfred 67
Hazlitt, William 72
Heartfield, John 98
Henrion, Daphne 136
Henson, Jim 98
Hepburn, Patrick 124
Hepworth, Barbara 102
Hoare, family 227
Hogarth, William 226
Hopkins, Michael 98
Housman, AE 256
Hunt, Leigh 70
Hurwitz, Hyman 262
Huxley, Julian 136
Hyndman, Henry 55

J

Jacobs, Michael 204
Jinnah, Muhammad Ali 191
Joad, CEM 177
Johnson, Samuel 183
Joseph, Delissa 196

K

Kean, Charles and Edmunf 75
Keats, John 72
Khan, Liaquat Ali 192
Klugman, James 168
Klyshko, Nikolai 111
Krasin, Leonid 237

L

Lakatos, Imre 117
Lamb, Henry 96
Laski, Marghanita 121
Lawrence, DH 67
Lawyers, senior 120
Lever, William 213
Lewis, John 120
Linnell, John 222
Litvinov, Maxim and Ivy 111
Lovell, Maria 75
Lubetkin, Berthold 108, 256

Lutyens, Edwin 238

M

MacDonald, Ramsay 114
Mackenzie, Compton 66
Magarshack, Christopher and David 55
Magrath, Edward 121
Maisky, Ivan 89
Mallinson, Theodore G 253
Mansfield, Katherine 128
Marvell, Andrew 269
Marx, Karl 26
Masaryk, Thomas G 190
Matthews, family 177
Menuhin, Yehudi 259
Miller, Lee 97
Moholy-Nagy, Laszlo 104
Mondrian, Piet 102
Moore, Henry 102, 105
Morel, Jean-Jacques 77
Morganwg, Iolo 202
Murray, William 1st Earl of Mansfield 244

N

Nessler, Walter 95
Nevinson, Christopher 146
Nicholson, Ben 102
Nollekens, Mary and Joseph 61
Norman, Francis (bookseller) 35
Norrie, Ian 33

O

Orton, Joe 133
Orwell, George 132

P

Park, Thomas and John James 175
Pavlova, Anna 218
Penrose, Roland 97
Permayer, Louis 37
Pevsner. Nikolaus 222
Pitt, William, Earl of Chatham 224
Plath, Sylvia 207
Platt, Thomas Pell 189
Pritchard, Jack and Molly 102

R

Reynolds, Alfred 117
Reynolds, Joshua 85
Richardson, Samuel 46
Rizal, Jose 208
Robeson, Paul 114
Romney, George 84, 86
Rothenstein, William 64
Rowe, thomas 254
Russell, Charles 113

S

Salisbury,	Francis	Owen	187
Savarkar,	Vinayak	Damodar	270
Schwabe,	Randolph		178
Sellers,	Peter		186
Sharp,	Cecil		160
Shaw,	George	Bernard	222
Shelley,	Percy	Bysshe	72–73
Sheridan,	Richard	B	130
Sickert,	Walter		102
Siddons,	Sarah		121
Sinden,	Donald		241
Snow,	John		151
Spence,	Basil		164
Spencer	Wells,	Thomas	215
Spencer,	Stanley		96
Spender,	Stephen		168
spies,	Soviet		105
Spilsbury,	Bernard		183
Stanhope,	Katherine		170
Stopes,	Marie		55
Strange,	William	Heath	135
Suzman,	Janet		131

T

Tagore,	Rabindranath		64
Talleyrand,	Charles	Maurice	78
Teulon,	Samuel		136
Tutu,	Desmond		229

U

Unwin,	Raymond	222

V

Vane,	Sir	Harry	137
Ventris,	Michael		223
Vincent,	John		148
Vizard,	PE		124
Von	Hugel,	Friedrich	82

W

Wallace,	Edgar		70
Walpole,	Robert		42
Waterhouse,	Alfred		137
Waterlow,	Sydney		268
Waugh,	Arthur	and	Evelyn	219
Wedderburn,	Alexander		143
Wells,	HG		175
Whittington,	Dick		272
Williams-Ellis,	Bertram	Clough	88
Wilson,	Charlotte		222
Wimperis,	John	T	157
Wordsworth,	William		231
Wrottesley,	Francis		167

Y

	Yeates,	Alfred	236
Z			
	Zuckerman,	Solly	89

Printed in Great Britain
by Amazon

31636857R00159